SPITFIRE!

Courage & Sacrifice

Dilip Sarkar MBE

Victory Books

Dedication

For all who built, maintained & operated the Spitfire during WW2

Other books by Dilip Sarkar: -

SPITFIRE SQUADRON: *19 Squadron at War 1939-41*
THE INVISIBLE THREAD: *A Spitfire's Tale*
THROUGH PERIL TO THE STARS: *RAF fighter pilots failed to return 1939-45*
ANGRIFF WESTLAND: *Three Battle of Britain Air Raids*
A FEW OF THE MANY: *Air War 1939-45, A Kaleidoscope of Memories*
BADER'STANGMERE SPITFIRES: *1941, The Untold Story*
BADER'S DUXFORD FIGHTERS: *The Big Wing Controversy*
MISSING IN ACTION: *Resting in Peace?*
GUARDS VC: *Blitzkrieg 1940*
BATTLE OF BRITAIN: *The Photographic Kaleidoscopes Vols I - IV*
FIGHTER PILOT: *The Photographic Kaleidoscope*
SIR DOUGLAS BADER: *An Inspiration in Photographs*
JOHNNIE JOHNSON: *Spitfire Top Gun, Parts 1 & 2*
BATTLE OF BRITAIN: *Last Look Back*
Dilip also contributed a chapter on historical accuracy to the late Robert Rudhall's
best-selling BATTLE OF BRITAIN: *The Movie* (being re-printed 2006).

Most of Dilip's books have been out of print since shortly after their release dates. **Victory Books** will be re-printing the majority of these works so that, for the first time, all will be concurrently available from May 2006 onwards. To receive early notification of our publications and signed limited editions, join the Victory Books privileged customer mailing list.

SPITFIRE! Courage & Sacrifice
© Dilip Sarkar MBE, 2006
ISBN: 0-9550431-6-6

First published 2006 by Victory Books, PO Box 573, Worcester WR5 3WU
Tel: 07921 503105. Fax: 01905 767735. Web: www.victorybooks.co.uk

Design & layout by Victory Books, printed and bound in the UK.

Contents

Acknowledgements

Firstly I must thank all of the casualties' relatives, friends and comrades in arms, too numerous to mention individually, who have assisted and supported my research over many years.

Secondly I would like to thank all of my many fellow enthusiast friends worldwide, particularly Dr Gordon Mitchell, Dr Bernard-Marie Dupont, Andrew Long, Mark Postlethwaite, Ken Potts, Antony Whitehead, Don Caldwell, John Foreman, Don Wiltshire & Jesse Knight.

The excellent painting, Legend, used on the cover of this book is by aviation artist Mark Postlethwaite G.Av.A and is available as a fine art print from the artist, via Victory Books.

My family and all at Victory Books make my life all I ever wanted it to be, and all involved have my love and sincere gratitude.

Bibliography

The sources for this book were both numerous and extensive, including access to unpublished papers and records owned by both the relatives of casualties and myself, innumerable files at the Public Records Office, & masses of personal correspondence and interview notes. Certain published sources, however, are standard references: -

RJ Mitchell: Schooldays To Spitfire, Dr Gordon Mitchell, Tempus Publishing, 2002.
Spitfire: The History, EB Morgan & E Shacklady, Key Publishing, 1987.
Spitfire Story, Dr Alfred Price, Jane's, 1982.
Battle of Britain: Then & Now, Mk V, Edited by W Ramsey, After the Battle, 1989.
Men of the Battle of Britain: Ken Wynn, Gliddon Books, 1989.
Battle Over Britain: Francis K Mason, Aston Publications, 1990.
The Blitz: Then & Now, Vols I-III, Edited by W Ramsey, After the Battle, 1989 & 90.
RAF Fighter Command Losses of WW2, Vols I - III, Norman Franks, Midland Publishing, 1998, 2000 & 2002.
The JG 26 War Diary, Vols I & II, Don Caldwell, Grub Street, 1996 & 1998.

Foreword

This is another of Dilip Sarkar's excellent and very readable books in which the words flow along easily, making it a pleasure to read. This by no means applies to all reading matter, but thankfully I have been told that my book about my father, R.J. Mitchell, is also a pleasure to read!

My father was heard to say on a number of occasions that "A Spitfire without a pilot is just a lump of metal", which was meant to show the high regard and respect he had for the pilots whose job it was to fly his 'lump of metal'. I think that this book mirrors those sentiments, in that the first part is devoted to describing the Spitfire accurate detail, this being followed by in-depth descriptions of 11 individuals who had the task of flying the 'lump of metal' into battle.

I was pleased to see that Dilip went out of his way to emphasise what a truly great flying machine the Spitfire is, and also to make it absolutely clear how superior it was to the Hurricane. I have preached this, hardly surprisingly, for many years, but it is comforting to see it repeated by an author of Dilip's standing.

Dilip quotes the research carried out by John Alcorn, and I am able to add a few words to this. Alcorn's work was published in *The Aeroplane*, and I recently asked the Editor, Michael Oakey, whether he had received any significant criticisms of this work in the years since it was published; the answer was no, and Michael considered that Alcorn's statistics remain the definitive study, a conclusion with which I totally agree.

Dilip is to be congratulated on the quality of his photographs. It is to be noted, incidentally, that I own the copyright to a number of photographs included in this book, and the fact that I gave Dilip permission to use them is a clear indication of my approval of it. I never cease to be amazed how today a poor photograph can be turned into a first class one; my photograph of my father standing by the prototype Spitfire on March 8th, 1938, three days after its first flight, was taken with a cheap box camera and the resulting snapshot was really pretty poor. Now, after the experts have got at it, it is a very acceptable reproduction.

A question I am sometimes asked is whether my father actually flew the Spitfire himself, and people are rather surprised when I say he did not, their impression being that flying it himself would be essential. He did, of course, have to rely entirely on his

Test Pilots to tell him everything about his creations in the air. He did obtain his Pilot's Licence a year or so before he died, but this enabled him to fly aircraft such as the Gipsy Moth, not the Spitfire. I guess this helped him to understand some of the problems encountered by his Test Pilots. The high regard my father had for his pilots, which I mentioned earlier, is mirrored in the fact that throughout his career, no pilot of any of his many creations lost their life due to some fault in the aircraft.

This book again cleverly shows that Dilip has the personality and ability to approach individuals of whatever stature, and get them, in a friendly way, to give him exactly what he needs. It would also, I think, not be an exaggeration to describe him as a detective, an ability arising, no doubt, from his many years in the British police service and during which he was actually a detective constable. The way, recorded in these pages, that he was able to sort out the complications concerning the reasons Douglas Bader had to bale of of his Spitfire over France in 1941, is an excellent example of Dilip's detective abilities.

In his conclusion, Dilip clearly states the reason for the failure so far of my father being awarded a posthumous honour for his creation of the Spitfire. I have worked hard for this, but the answer from both Buckingham Palace and the Cabinet Office was 'Yes, your father certainly deserves such an award, but none of our high honours have ever been awarded posthumously and, so far as we are concerned, never will be"! The person who has the power to create a new posthumous award is the Prime Minister, but he has never given any indication that he might do so in spite of the letter I received from 10 Downing Street in January 2000: 'The Prime Minister fully understands your wish to see your father's services to aircraft design recognised with a posthumous high honour'.

However, at the time of writing this foreword (January 2006), I am endeavouring to achieve for my father a very different type of honour, but one that I would consider at least as great, if not greater, than a conventional knighthood. As everyone knows, the Spitfire made its first flight on March 5th, 1936, from Eastleigh Airport and in the following months all its intensive flight testing was carried out there, often watched by my father personally. During the whole of the 1939-45 war, Eastleigh Airport was used for the flight testing of the production Spitfires from Supermarine, and all of the new Marks as they were developed. Eastleigh Airport is now a very busy one, with the name changed to 'Southampton International Airport Ltd'.

Clearly it can rightly be said that the Spitfire was born and bred at this particular airport, and that there is an extremely close association between the airport, the Spitfire and R.J. Mitchell. This I am using for the basis of my request that the owners of the airport (BAA) change the name to 'R.J. Mitchell International (Southampton) Ltd'. Fortunately a number of influential people support this proposal, but now I must patiently await a decision.

Finally I would like to conclude by reproducing a couple of quotes from Dilip's book which I particularly liked, and by so doing they will appear twice!

"Everybody who has flown a Spitfire thinks it is the most marvellous aircraft ever built."

"If you were a fighter pilot, you were a cocky-so-and-so, but if you were a *Spitfire* pilot then you were cockier still, a definite cut above the rest!"

Dr Gordon Mitchell, Lower Slaughter, 2006.
www.rjmitchell_spitfire.co.uk.

Dr Gordon Mitchell signing a copy of his excellent book, 'RJ Mitchell: Schooldays to Spitfire', for Dilip Sarkar on the occasion of their first meeting, 08.08.88.

Chapter One

Spitfire!

Spitfire: the very word is evocative, the perfect description of a fighter aircraft. The shape and sound of the Spitfire is perfect too, particularly those marques powered by the equally legendary Rolls-Royce Merlin engine. Look at a Spitfire today and its sleek elliptical shape would not be out of place on the computer screen of a modern designer, 70 years after it was actually created without the benefits of a computer. No, the genius Reginald Joseph Mitchell designed the Spitfire at a comparatively simple drawing board. That Mitchell's Spitfire, ever the air show star, should still excite, and the deeds of those who went to war in her continue to inspire, can only be a special tribute to everyone connected with this wonderful aircraft.

So what was it about the Spitfire that made it so *great*? What is it about a vintage aircraft that continues to fascinate us nearly a century on? What is it about the Merlin's roar that makes brings a tear to the eye, a lump in the throat? To understand this phenomenon we need to travel back in time, to a desperately dark period in world history.

The genius RJ Mitchell with his prototype Spitfire.
Dr G Mitchell

After the Great War (1914 – 1918), the war supposedly to end all wars, Britain and France determined to destroy forever Germany's military might. At the Versailles Peace Treaty in 1919, Germany, historically a militarily minded and jingoistic power, was made to accept full War Guilt and agree to pay the victorious nations a massive sum in reparation, but, amongst other restrictions, was prohibited from having an army greater than 100,000 volunteers, no air force, no submarines, and only naval ships of a certain tonnage. A democratic government was imposed upon the Germans, this being seen as nothing more than a puppet of the victorious powers and therefore unpopular with the people. The Allies believed that their objective had been achieved, but in reality unstable political and disastrous economic conditions had been created for fascism, extreme right wing politics based upon nationalistic and racist ideology, to thrive. Nevertheless, France still felt it necessary to construct and hide behind the much vaunted, but actually incomplete and ultimately useless, defensive Maginot Line, and Britain thought only of administering and maintaining its Empire. America, which had entered the Great War late, but none-the-less suffered significant casualties, turned its back on events in Europe, steadfastly pursuing a policy of Isolationism. The Allies, confident that Germany's capacity to wage war had once and for all been dealt a fatal blow, busied themselves with disarmament.

Economic collapse, devastated national pride and political unrest, not surprisingly, led to the German nation, and ex-servicemen in particular, feeling bitter and angry. The country became a political vacuum, with numerous right wing and paramilitary factions all vying for control. Eventually, in 1933, the violently anti-Semitic National Socialists, or 'Nazis', were democratically elected to power; Adolf Hitler was now Chancellor. The democratic process in Germany, however, was subsequently completely eroded and Hitler became the *Führer*, the leader whose ideas and orders had to be carried out without question by the masses. Hitler immediately set about rectifying what he and his followers saw as the injustice of Versailles, and secretly re-built the army, air force and navy with a view to ultimately once more waging war and achieving a new world order dominated by Nazi Germany. So it was that German designers produced modern tanks, aircraft, ships and submarines, whilst the generals devised a new and decisive tactic on the battlefield: *Blitzkrieg*, or 'Lightning War'.

The Great War had largely been a stagnant affair, with enemies facing each other across 'No Man's Land' from trenches; after the Great War military thinking did not change in Britain and France. Whilst the Allies disarmed and grew weaker, Nazi Germany flourished. Hitler's new weapons were put to the test during the Spanish Civil War during the mid-1930s, when the German *Kondor* Legion fought for the fascist General Franco. Indeed, when ultimately unleashed against Poland and the west, *Blitzkrieg*, essentially tanks and mechanised infantry moving forward at speed, supported by flying artillery, would shock and paralyse all defenders.

It is impossible to appreciate today why the governments of Britain and France buried their heads in the sand and ignored the numerous warnings regarding Hitler's military intentions. Certainly in many quarters there was a degree of sympathy for the Germans, who had suffered in various ways as a result of Versailles, and many saw Hitler as merely righting wrongs. In England there was precious little interest in military research and development in every respect. Those who warned against this foolishness were seen as 'Hawks', whilst the 'Doves' remained both in the majority and unmoved.

In terms of aircraft development, Britain and France held the belief that 'the bomber will always get through'. There was little or no interest in fighter development. Indeed, in 1921, Marshal of the RAF Sir Hugh Trenchard said: -

It is not necessary for an air force, in order to defeat the enemy nation, to defeat its armed forces first. Air power can dispense with that immediate step, can press over the enemy navies and armies, and penetrate the air defences and attack direct the centre of production, transportation and communication from which the enemy war effort is maintained. It is on the destruction of the enemy industries and, above all, in the lowering of morale of enemy nationals caused by bombing that the ultimate victory lies... The aeroplane is the most offensive weapon that has ever been invented. It is a shockingly bad weapon for defence.

In fact, Trenchard thought so little of defensive aeroplanes that he considered it 'only necessary to have some defence to keep up the morale of your own people'.

The misconception regarding the value of bombing was articulated by no less a statesman than Stanley Baldwin in 1932: -

I think it is well for the man in the street to realise that there is no power on earth that will save him from being bombed. Whatever people may tell him, the bomber will always get through. The only defence is offence, which means that you have to kill more women and children than the enemy if you want to save yourselves. I just mention that so that people may realise what is waiting for them when the next war comes.

Fortunately not everyone in a position of influence shared this view. On September 1st, 1930, Air Vice-Marshal Hugh Dowding, a veteran Great War fighter pilot, was appointed Air Member for Supply & Research (later Research & Development). 'Stuffy' Dowding did not share the belief that 'the bomber will always get through' or indeed that spending on the bomber force was necessarily the priority. On the contrary, he considered that although the fighter force should not be expanded at the bomber's expense, a powerful bomber force would be useless unless the fighter force was strong enough to ensure that the commander did not lose a decisive battle before the bomber force commander had time to fight one. Trenchard, Dowding believed, had 'forgotten that security of base is an essential prerequisite'. It would prove fortunate indeed for Britain that Dowding held this view and, moreover, was prepared to fight anyone who opposed his efforts to prepare a sound defence for these islands.

At the time of Dowding's appointment the RAF's fighter squadrons remained equipped with biplanes. Constructed largely of wood and fabric, and lightly armed with just two machine-guns, their performance remained comparable to those primitive machines that had fought in the Great War. Great progress in aviation design was actually being made, in fact, but in the civilian, not military, sector.

In 1912, Jacques Schneider, of the French armaments family, had instituted the Schneider Trophy, to be awarded to the victor of an international seaplane race. The experience gained by aircraft designers during the course of this competition, which was a matter of fierce national pride, was later put to good use in the creation of modern warplanes. The leading British Schneider Trophy designer was Reginald Joseph Mitchell.

RJ Mitchell's trophy winning racer, the S6.

Although Dowding had been against government funding of Mitchell's Supermarine built S.6B 1931 winning entrant, he did appreciate that Mitchell's designs held enormous promise for fighter aircraft. In 1930, in fact, the Air Ministry had issued the specification for a modern day and night fighter, capable of being flown by the average squadron pilot, to replace the RAF's existing and obsolete biplanes. The requirement was for higher speed and an enclosed cockpit in conjunction with eight-gun armament. It was in line with this specification that the Rolls-Royce engined Hawker and Supermarine fighter projects progressed, leading to Specifications F.36/34 and F.37/34 being drafted around the designs that would respectively become the Hurricane and Spitfire respectively.

The racing seaplanes that Mitchell had designed as Schneider Trophy entrants were monoplanes, and much like flying bullets, so sleek and fast were they. Mitchell had first designed a proto-type fighter under the Air Ministry Specification F7/30, but the result was an ugly gull-winged monoplane that he knew was not up to Germany's challenge. Mitchell returned to the drawing board and created the Spitfire.

In 1933, at the age of 38, Mitchell had actually been diagnosed with rectal cancer, requiring surgery. After the operation he was told that there was every chance of the cancer returning, and with it the inevitability of an untimely death. Who would have blamed Mitchell if he had retired to spend more time with his wife and son? Thankfully our hero did not; had he done, there would have been no Spitfire, the iconic and charismatic fighter that contributed so much to final victory.

The Spitfire was a revolutionary design, whereas Sydney Camm's Hawker Hurricane was not. Spitfire production called for new skills and techniques, and was a complex process. The fuselage was of three sections, a tubular case for the engine, a monocoque centre section and a detachable tail section. The wing's main spar comprised girders of different lengths, the thickest part being at the wing root where most strength was needed. The wing leading edges were covered in heavy gauge aluminium, the trailing edges in a lighter covering. Such construction provided an unparalleled combination of strength and lightness. The Spitfire was powered by Sir Henry Royce's Merlin engine, Royce having provided engines for Mitchell's Schneider Trophy entrants. Once more it would prove to be a winning combination.

On March 5th, 1936, a small group of men gathered at Eastleigh airfield, near the Supermarine works, which was on the banks of the River Itchen at Woolston, near Southampton. The occasion was an event which could be considered as one of the most important flights since the Wright brothers flew at Kittyhawk: the first test flight of the prototype Spitfire, K5054. Vickers' Chief Test Pilot, 'Mutt' Summers, made a short but successful flight, after which he told excited onlookers that he did not want any of the aircraft's controls altered in any way. Spitfire legend interprets this as meaning that the aircraft was perfect from the off, but such a statement is quite ridiculous even for an aircraft as outstanding as Mitchell's Spitfire. What Summers really meant, of course, was that he did not want any of the controls interfered with before his next flight. Nevertheless, the Spitfire legend was born.

After the Spitfire's first flight, March 5th, 1936; L-R: Mutt Summers, Major Payn, RJ Mitchell, S Scott-Hall & Jeffrey Quill.
Dr G Mitchell

It is worthy of note, however, that Camm's Hurricane first flew in November 1935, and was immediately ordered by the Air Ministry. Although a monoplane the Hurricane relied upon tried and tested design and production, meaning that it was not difficult to produce; in fact it would reach the squadrons in January 1938, eight months before the Spitfire. A month before the Air Ministry ordered the Hurricane, however, the Germans had also ordered a new monoplane fighter: the *Messerschmitt* 109. Ominously the 109 was 30 mph faster than the Hurricane.

The prototype Spitfire, K5054.

Shortly after the Spitfire's maiden flight it was demonstrated to a group of Air Ministry officials at Martlesham Heath. Suitably impressed the Air Ministry ordered 300 Spitfires, but this was against an order for 600 Hurricanes. Why did the Air Ministry order twice as many of an inferior design, an aircraft already slower than its German counterpart? The answer no doubt lay in the problems arising from the Spitfire's complicated construction, which was time consuming at this early stage. It is perhaps, however, fortunate that so many Hurricanes were ordered at this juncture, because at least RAF Fighter Command would find itself equipped with monoplanes, as opposed to its existing biplanes, when called upon in Britain's greatest hour of need, even if the majority were not the superior Spitfire.

With the Spitfire in production, Mitchell finally succumbed to cancer, aged 42, on June 11th, 1937, over two years before WW2 broke out and three years before the Battle of Britain. The Spitfire's creator therefore died without ever knowing of the immeasurable contribution made by his fighter during the global conflagration of 1939-45. Moreover, due to an oversight in the current system it has not been possible to confer any posthumous honour in respect of this massive achievement. Reginald Joseph Mitchell therefore remains amongst Britain's most worthy but unsung heroes.

On January 1st, 1938, No 111 (F) Squadron at RAF Northolt took delivery of the first Hurricanes. On August 4th, Supermarine Test Pilot Jeffrey Quill delivered the first production Spitfire to No 19 (F) Squadron at RAF Duxford. Those lucky squadrons chosen to re-equip with the new, modern, monoplanes enthusiastically busied

themselves with learning to fly the Hurricane and Spitfire. Slowly, over the next year, virtually all Fighter Command's squadrons would exchange their Gladiator and Gauntlet biplanes for the fast monoplanes, which was just as well: had the squadrons had to go to war in biplanes then the pilots' courage would not have been found wanting; but the fact is that the 109 would have swept the Gladiators and Gauntlets from the skies with little ado.

The obsolete Gloster Gauntlet fighter, with which Fighter Command could so easily have gone to war in 1939.

Just a month after 19 Squadron received its first Spitfire, Europe was on the brink of war. By this time Hitler had re-occupied the Rhineland, and unified Germany and Austria, both prohibited by Versailles. The extent of Germany's re-armament and contempt for the provisions of 1919 were no longer hidden but flaunted in demonstrations of national military pride. Still many sympathised with Germany and believed that Hitler's demands for the restoration of former German territories were reasonable. The British Prime Minister, Neville Chamberlain, believed that Hitler could be appeased if his essentially just demands were agreed, and that this would lay the foundations of a lasting peace. In September 1938, Hitler demanded that the German-speaking Sudetenland of Czechoslovakia be incorporated into the Third Reich. Hitler actually expected, and was prepared for, a confrontation over the issue, but Britain and France betrayed the Czechs and failed to make a stand. Although Chamberlain returned to Heston Airport clutching his famous piece of paper, bearing his signature alongside Hitler's proclaiming 'Peace for our time', all the policy of appeasement did was actually encourage Hitler to more brinkmanship. Confident that the leaders of Britain and France were too weak to oppose him, in March 1939 Hitler occupied the remainder of Czechoslovakia, land to which Germany had absolutely no claim whatsoever and a clear indication that Hitler's territorial ambitions were far more sinister than the doves had hoped and prayed for. It was now a time for hawks.

In the Far East too another territorially ambitious and jingoistic nation, Japan, looked to expand its territories. In 1936, Japan was condemned by the League of Nations for invading Manchuria; Japan simply resigned its membership and instead became a party to the anti-communist pact with Germany and Italy. On August 23rd, 1939, the Soviets signed a Non-Aggression Pact with Hitler, a secret clause of which divided up a conquered Poland between the Russia and Germany. Six months earlier, in the wake of having sold out Czechoslovakia to Hitler, Britain and France both pledged themselves to the defence of Poland, which, in fact, neither was geographically situated to actually do. On September 1st, 1939, German troops invaded Poland, unleashing *Blitzkrieg* and against which the Poles, with their obsolete aircraft and mounted cavalry, were powerless. Britain and France delivered Hitler an ultimatum: withdraw from Poland or face the consequences. Needless to say Hitler ignored this. On Sunday, September 3rd, 1939, Britain and France declared war on Nazi Germany. The storm had broken at last.

As Britain and France were unable to offer Poland actual military assistance, the two powers prepared and braced themselves for war in the west. The British Expeditionary Force, comprising largely of territorials and reservists, was despatched to France, there to await events. The King of the Belgians, however, was determined to remain neutral and refused, therefore, to allow British troops to fortify his country's border with Germany. The British and French therefore dug in along the Franco-German border and awaited events. Poland fell in three weeks and the world held its breath, awaiting Hitler's next move which, everyone knew, would be an attack in the west.

Naturally Spitfire production increased throughout the rest of 1939, as the nation braced itself. The original Mk I Spitfires were powered by the Merlin II engine and fitted with a two bladed propeller made of mahogany. Improvements were rapidly made by way of the Merlin III engine and fitting of a metal de Havilland twin speed propeller. This meant that, as opposed to the fixed pitch propeller, the pilot had two settings: coarse and fine pitch, the pitch being akin to changing gear in a car. In June 1940, however, this device was replaced by the de Havilland Constant Speed Unit, enabling the pilot to change the propeller's 'bite' throughout a large selection of settings to suit different flying conditions and needs. Needless to say, the 109 was already fitted with such a device.

At this time, Spitfires were still produced at Supermarine's Woolston factory. In May 1940 a young school leaver by the name of Terry White joined the workforce there as a 'handy lad'. In 1988, Terry remembered those days for me when he was 'utterly bewildered by the noise and, it appeared to me, confusion of what was a very, very busy factory'. That month saw Hitler's long awaited offensive against the west begin.

Supermarine factory at Woolston.

Early Spitfires at Woolston.

In April 1940, Germany successfully invaded Denmark. On May 10th, 1940, Hitler's *Wehrmacht* crashed into Belgium, Holland, Luxembourg and France. Two days later Leige fell and the *panzers* crossed the Meuse at Dinant and Sedan; the following day the Dutch surrendered. The BEF immediately pivoted forward some 60 miles into Belgium, across unprepared ground, to meet the Germans at what was believed to be the main thrust, i.e. into northern France via Holland and Belgium as in the Great War. In fact German armour was actually undertaking the supposedly impossible and was negotiating the Ardennes forest, much further to the south. Once through, *Panzergruppe* von Kliest was able to bypass the Maginot Line defences and punch upwards, the *panzers* racing for the coast. So quickly did Erwin Rommel's 7th *Panzer* advance that it was soon nicknamed the 'Ghost Division'. By May 20th the Germans had, incredibly, reached Laon, Cambrai, Arras, Amiens and even Abbeville. Soon Lord Gort, the British Commander-in-Chief, had no option but to retire upon Dunkirk, from which French port the BEF was evacuated; the British soldiers were shocked and exhausted, their heavy weapons and vehicles left strewn across the battlefields of France. On June 3rd Dunkirk fell, and the evacuation concluded with over 300,000 British, French and Belgian soldiers having been rescued. Many stayed behind, though, either buried in foreign fields or as prisoners of war.

During the Battle of France, the Commander-in-Chief of RAF Fighter Command, none other than the far sighted Air Chief Marshal Sir Hugh Dowding, had committed only Hurricane squadrons to the fray. He was, thankfully, obsessed with the defence of base, and therefore preserved his Spitfire squadrons for the assault on Britain itself. The Spitfire squadrons, however, were used in the air operation covering the evacuation, known as DYNAMO, and engaged the Me 109 for the first time over the French coast. Losses were suffered and the RAF's fighter tactics were found wanting; Wing Commander George Unwin was a Flight Sergeant with 19 Squadron at the time and remarks that: -

The tacticians who wrote the book believed that in the event of war it would be fighter versus bomber only. What they could not foresee was Hitler's modern ground tactics that would take his armies to the Channel ports in an unprecedented period of time, thus providing bases for his fighters and putting England within their limited range. Over Dunkirk we found that our tight formations were all very well for the Hendon Air Pageant but useless in combat.

At home the need for fighters, to make good losses of 25% suffered in France and over Dunkirk, was urgent. The anvils toiled night and day to forge more swords, and the period was exhausting for all involved.

Once built, the Spitfires emerged from the paint shop resplendent in green and brown camouflaged upper surfaces and half white, half black undersides. The national colours were over sprayed as red, white and blue roundels and flashes, the propeller and spinner black, the blades having bright yellow tips. Out on the airfield, new Spitfires awaited their test flights, successful completion of which meant that the fighter was ready to be taken on charge by the RAF. The standard test flight was formulated at Eastleigh by test pilots Jeffrey Quill and George Pickering after production of the first Mk Is. Other than alterations to cater for changes in Spitfire design, the formula remained unchanged throughout the 10 years of Spitfire production. The test was thorough indeed, and there was no doubt that if a machine passed 30 minutes at the hands of an expert test pilot it was definitely ready for operational service. The courage, hard work and dedication of the test pilots must neither go unrecognised: to them went the task of making the first flight in every Spitfire, so if anything was unsafe it would be the test pilot who found out; the consequences could be fatal, and all too often were. In 1988, the now late Jeffrey Quill told me that: -

It usually took a few short flights of not more than five minutes duration each at the start of a production test to clear the engine and propeller settings. This would be followed by a flight of at least 20 minutes to check performance at full throttle settings. For simplicity we usually entered in our log books a total of 30 minutes per aircraft under the general heading of 'Production Test'. No doubt we did ourselves out of a lot of logged airborne time as a result of this clerical laziness, but one's mind was not focused on posterity in 1940!

Jeffrey Quill at Duxford in 1988.

As Jeffrey suggests, it was survival, which focussed the nation's minds in 1940.

Before WW2, newly qualified pilots fresh from Flying Training School received operational training with their actual fighter squadron. After the outbreak of war, the squadrons were too busy for training, and so by April 1940 there were three Operational Training Units (OTU) providing the Basic Fighter Course of two weeks duration. Students were first tested by an instructor in a two-seater Harvard training aircraft before going solo on the Spitfire. Over the next few days, the young pilots would fly a variety of exercises to gain experience on and confidence in the Spitfire. On average students received 10 flying hours on Spitfires during the Basic Fighter Course, which has led to a myth; it is widely believed that these precious 10 hours were the *only* flying hours logged by these pilots, which is absolutely not so. Most pilots had accumulated some 200 hours (dual and solo) throughout their training, so the 10 hours on Spitfires were additional to that figure and just experience on type. Having said that, being able to fly and fight in a Spitfire were two very different things, so it is fair to say that the 10 hours received at OTU were inadequate. If pilots were lucky they would be posted to squadrons away from the combat zone, which were in a position to provide extra training; if not, they went straight into combat and, as we shall see, often did not even see what hit them.

In those far off days it must have been the dream of most young men to fly Spitfires, to be a fighter pilot, one affectation of which was wearing the top tunic button undone. But it was not just pilots to whom the Spitfire appealed; Bob Morris: -

I joined the RAF before the war started and was more interested in the technical rather than the flying side. I studied aeronautical engineering at the RAF Technical School, Halton. In May 1940 I passed out as an Airman 1st Class, looked at the list pinned on the board and discovered that I had been posted to 66 Squadron at Coltishall in 12 Group. I knew not where Coltishall was, or what aircraft 66 Squadron had.

As it happened, Coltishall was in Norfolk, and my first glimpse of 66 Squadron was from the bus which travelled along the airfield for a short distance; what an absolute thrill to see *Spitfires*! Here was a young man's dream!

Bob Morris in 1940.

Pilot Officer Hubert 'Dizzy' Allen was a pilot with 'Clickety-Click', and had joined 66 Squadron at Duxford the month before Bob Morris arrived: -

I didn't know where Duxford was and nor was I aware of what aircraft 66 Squadron had – they could have had Hurricanes, which did not appeal to me in any way. On the other hand they might be Spitfires, which appealed to me *very* much. I had seen the Spitfire in flight, had seen many photographs of it, to me it was the very pink of perfection (and after due experience proved to me that it was indeed perfection). When I arrived at Duxford's hangars I could see nothing but Spitfires littering the airfield – not a Hurricane in sight. Wherever Heaven is, St Peter opened the doors when I arrived at Duxford!

In May 1940, Pilot Officer David Crook, an Auxiliary Air Force pilot, completed his Service Flying Training and joined 609 'West Riding' Squadron at Turnhouse in Scotland. An indication of the uncertainty of the times is provided by this simple statistic: of the 15 pilots who trained together with Crook, just a few months later five had been awarded the Distinguished Flying Cross, but eight, alas, were dead. In his superb first-hand account *Spitfire Pilot*, published in 1942, Crook wrote: -

The next day I did my first trip in a Spitfire. I had waited for this moment for nearly two years, and when it came it was just as exciting as I always expected.

Having mastered the cockpit drill, I got in and taxied out on the aerodrome, sat there for one moment to check that everything was OK, and then opened up with a great smooth roar, the Spitfire leapt forward like a bullet and tore madly across the aerodrome, and before I had realized quite what had happened I was in the air. I felt though the machine was completely out of control and running away with me. However, I collected my scattered wits, raised the undercarriage, and put the airscrew into coarse pitch, and then looked round for the aerodrome, which to my astonishment I saw was already miles behind.

After a few minutes cruising round I realized that this fearsome beast was perhaps not quite as formidable as I had thought in that breathless minute, so I decided to try a landing. This came off reasonably satisfactorily, and I took off again, feeling much surer of myself. So I climbed up to a good height and played in the clouds in this superb new toy and did a few gentle dives to 400 mph, which gave me a tremendous thrill. Altogether I was almost light-headed with exhilaration when I landed at the end of an hour's flight, and I felt that I could ask nothing more of life.

Actually, once you have done a few hours flying in a Spitfire and become accustomed to the great power and speed, then it is an extraordinarily easy machine to fly and is absolutely marvellous for aerobatics. Practically everybody who has flown a Spitfire thinks it is the most marvellous aircraft ever built, and I am no exception to the general rule. I grew to like it more than any other aircraft I had flown. It is so small and compact and neat, yet possessed of devastating fire power.

The Fall of France in June 1940 saw Europe dominated by Hitler, only Britain now stood alone but free. RAF Fighter Command braced itself for the onslaught to come; indeed, as the Prime Minister, Winston Churchill, said 'What General Weygand called the Battle of France is over. The Battle of Britain is about to begin'.

For the Germans, the proposed invasion of England was an unexpected bonus, made possible through Hitler's unprecedented advance to the Channel coast, which, as Wing Commander Unwin has said, put London within the Me 109's range. Like the Spitfire and Hurricane, however, the 109 was designed as a defensive fighter and not as a long-range offensive aircraft. Quite simply it had not the fuel capacity for operations over England, 20 minutes over London was the maximum a pilot could expect at combat settings. Although the 109s were in a position to undertake sweeps and bomber escort missions, fuel calculations were critical and, I daresay, distracting. The 109 did, however, have three technical advantages over the RAF fighters. Firstly, armament comprised not only two 7.9 mm machine-guns but also two hard-hitting 20 mm cannon (as opposed to the eight .303 machine-guns of the Hurricane and Spitfire). Secondly, the 109's Daimler-Benz engine was fuel injected, meaning that it was not starved of fuel during a dive, unlike the gravity affected float carburettors of the British fighters. Fuel injection ensured that the 109 could escape in a dive, and this became the Germans' standard evasive tactic. Thirdly, the 109's canopy was completely jettisoned by the pilot in the event of needing to abandon the aircraft; both Hurricane and Spitfire had canopies which slid back along rails, which could be damaged in combat and jammed. Recent research suggests that there was a much higher incidence of survival amongst 109 pilots forced to bail out when compared to Spitfire and Hurricane pilots. The other technical differences between the Spitfire and 109 were really inconsequential: the Spitfire was a little faster below 15,000 feet but slightly slower above 20,000; the Spitfire could always turn tighter than the 109, but the 109 was superior in both climb and dive.

Hawker Hurricanes.

Before the war, when Air Member for Research & Development, Dowding had far-sightedly supported research into Radio Direction Finding, or radar, and had integrated this wizardry into his System of Air Defence. Radar masts around the British coast were able to detect formations of approaching German aircraft, this information being immediately passed to the Sector Stations so that fighters could be scrambled in good time to meet the threat. Another advantage enjoyed by the RAF pilots was that they would be fighting over home territory, meaning that a parachute descent would end in safe, friendly hands, or if over the Channel close enough to the shore to facilitate rescue.

As can be seen, both sides had certain advantages and disadvantages with which to contend, but the greatest advantage the Germans possessed was in the department of air fighting tactics and combat experience. Many of the enemy fighter leaders had been blooded in Spain some years before, and the fighter force had, in any case, seen very recent action both in Poland and the west. During the Spanish Civil War the Germans had realised that tight formations of fighter aircraft were unsuitable for actual combat. It was found far better to have fighters strung out far enough apart so that collision was not an issue, thus enabling the pilot to concentrate upon searching the sky for the enemy. The optimum number of fighters per section was found to be four, which would split into two pairs, each of leader and wingman, when battle was joined. The Germans called their formation the *Schwarm*. The RAF tacticians, however, insisted that squadrons flew in tight 'vics' of three aircraft apiece. This was because, again as George Unwin has said, it was never envisaged that a situation would arise in which single-engined enemy fighters would be active over England. The RAF's tactics were consequently formulated with queues of fighters taking it in turns to attack slow moving bombers, which would obligingly fly on straight and level without applying violent evasive action. A 'vic' of three fighters could, therefore, bring 24 machine-guns to bear, as opposed to the eight of a single-machine. In practice it proved suicidal to fly the 'vic', as pilots concentrated more on formation flying than seeking the enemy. During the Battle of Britain, Fighter Command was literally going to have to learn its bloody trade on the job.

This is not the place for a detailed description of the Battle of Britain, but it is necessary to understand the basic overview so that the deeds and sacrifices related in subsequent chapters of this book can be fully appreciated. Suffice to say that the Germans, so far undefeated on the battlefield, were sublimely confident, as *Reichsmarschall* Hermann Göring boasted 'My Luftwaffe is invincible… And so now we turn to England. How long will this one last – two, three weeks?' Dowding, however, saw the situation much differently: 'My strength has now been reduced to the equivalent of 36 squadrons… we should be able to carry on the war single-handedly for some time, if not indefinitely'.

The Battle of Britain was a contest for aerial superiority over England, essential for Hitler's proposed invasion. The German intention, therefore, was to destroy RAF Fighter Command. Amongst the German fighter pilots was *Leutnant* Max-Hellmuth Ostermann of JG 54: -

At once I flung my machine around and went down after them. Now I was about 200 yards behind the Tommy. Steady does it, wait; the range is much too far. I crept nearer slowly until I was only 100 metres away and the Spitfire's wings filled my reflector gunsight. Suddenly the Tommy opened fire and the 109 in front of him went into a dive. I too had pressed the firing button after having taken careful aim, being in a gentle turn as I did so. The Spitfire caught fire at once and, streaming a long grey plume of smoke, dived down vertically into the sea.

In July 1940, when the Battle of Britain began, Fighter Command had 30 squadrons of Hurricanes but only 19 of the superior Spitfire. Not surprisingly, as there were more of them, the Hurricane force suffered by far the greater casualties, but it is widely accepted that in the process the Hurricane executed more damage to the enemy than all other defences combined. Indeed, by the battle's end, the top scoring Fighter Command squadron was officially a Hurricane unit. Recent research by an American, John Alcorn, contests this, however, and has revised our perceptions completely. Cross-referencing RAF combat claims with *actual* German losses, John Alcorn discovered that the *Spitfire* really had the lion's share of kills, and that the top scoring fighter squadrons during the Battle of Britain were, in fact, Spitfire squadrons. Moreover, the first three out of the leading five fighter squadrons were Spitfire. Statistically, according to Alcorn, Spitfires and Hurricanes shot down 1,185 aircraft during the Battle of Britain, of which 55.4% were accredited to Hurricanes, Spitfires 44.6%. Of the Hurricane's kills, 66.2% were bombers, whilst these slower targets made up 46.7% of Spitfire victories. Clearly, therefore, the Spitfire was superior against German fighters (53.3%) than the Hurricane (43.8%). The average number of enemy aircraft destroyed by each Hurricane squadron was 21.9%, whilst the Spitfire exceeded this figure with 27.8%. The conclusion drawn from John Alcorn's research is that contrary to popular myth and legend, the Hurricane was not more successful than the Spitfire during the Battle of Britain, even though Camm's fighter considerably outnumbered Mitchell's Spitfire. This will no doubt be a bitter pill for Hurricane aficionados, but appears to be fact all the same. Legend also has it that the Hurricane was a far more rugged machine than the Spitfire, but an analysis of the quantity of both types that returned to base in a badly damaged state is actually fairly equal.

Pilot Officer Eric Burgoyne of 19 Squadron shows the cannon shell damaged tail of his Spitfire, P9391, September 5th, 1940.

The Hurricane's problem was speed, or rather a lack of it (Hurricane: 311 mph, Spitfire: 355 mph). Tony Pickering was an 18-year old Hurricane pilot during the Battle of Britain and remembers: -

I came across a lone Ju 88 somewhere over Kent, heading back to sea. I thought it no problem to catch up with the Hun, press the button and that would be it. I slotted in behind and ran flat out to catch him. Suddenly he just pulled away from me, just left me standing, had at least an extra 50 mph on me, and that was the last I saw of him. The Hurricane just wasn't fast enough, we even used to bend throttle levers in combat trying to squeeze a bit more boost out of the Merlin. A Spitfire would have caught that Ju 88.

Me 109Es of III/JG 26 await another escort sortie at their base in the Pas-de-Calais, summer 1940.

On some occasions, however, the Spitfire and Hurricane ideally complemented each other, the Spitfires duelling with the 109s whilst the Hurricanes attacked the slower bombers.

By September 30th, 1940, the *Luftwaffe* was unable to sustain such heavy losses to its bomber force and the He 111 was withdrawn from daylight service. From then on the Germans attacked with the faster Ju 88, in *gruppe* strength, against targets connected with the aircraft industry. So late in the day, however, such targets could have no effect on the battle's outcome, the bombing of London having completely failed to bring the British people down. On the contrary, London carried on working and functioning, and won the free world's admiration. By the end of October the Germans were forced to bomb at night, although by day the fighter forces of both sides continued to clash over southern England. As the season came to a close it was clear that the *Luftwaffe* had failed to win aerial supremacy and the invasion was indefinitely postponed. The Germans had suffered a reversal for the first time, and RAF Fighter Command had proved Hitler not to be the invincible warlord he appeared. By having held out in 1940, Dowding had achieved his objective of keeping the base safe, a base from which, with American help, the liberation of Nazi occupied Europe would one day be launched. Had Britain fallen, such an endeavour would have been impossible. Over 2,000 Allied airmen took part in the Battle of Britain, 544 of them gave their lives. German fighter pilot Ottomar Kruse remarks that: -

Had the Germans a fighter in 1940 with twice the range of the 109, and likewise a four-engined strategic bomber, the outcome of the Battle of Britain might have been very different. In contrast to the B-17s and other American heavy bombers which I attacked during the defence of Germany later in the war, I consider the He 111s, Do 17s and Ju 88s operating over England in 1940 to have been sitting ducks.

The fact of the matter, however, is that RAF Fighter Command could have won the Battle of Britain had all its squadrons been equipped with the Spitfire. It could not have prevailed had all those units flown Hurricanes, and this was the informed opinion of no less a personality than the late Air Commodore Alan Deere DSO OBE DFC, himself a Battle of Britain Spitfire 'ace'. Indeed, *Leutnant* Heinz Knocke of 1/JG 52, wrote: -

The Supermarine Spitfire, because of its manoeuvrability and technical performance, has given the German formations plenty of trouble. "*Achtung* Spitfire!" German pilots have learned to pay particular attention when they hear this warning shouted in their earphones. We consider shooting down a Spitfire to be an outstanding achievement, which it most certainly is.

Achtung! Schpitfeur!

Group Captain Peter Townsend (a Hurricane pilot in the Battle of Britain): -

The 109 pilots held our Hurricanes in contempt. The *Luftwaffe* airmen often mistook Hurricanes for Spitfires. There was the crew of the Heinkel which landed 'in the sea' on Wick airfield and swore that a Spitfire had downed them, when it was in fact a Hurricane. During the Battle of France, Theo Osterkamp seemed to see Spitfires everywhere, but there were no Spitfires in France, only Hurricanes. Even General Kesselring said 'Only the Spitfires bothered us'. The Luftwaffe, it seemed, suffered from 'Spitfire Snobbery'.

Flight Lieutenant Ken Wilkinson: -

If you were a fighter pilot you were a cocky so-and-so, but if you were a *Spitfire* pilot then you were cockier still, a definite cut above the rest.

The Battle of Britain is officially deemed to have ended on October 31st, 1940, having lasted for 16 weeks of high summer. Wing Commander Frank Brinsden: -

Not many of us at squadron level realized at the time that we were engaged in a full scale battle, nor how important the outcome would be if lost.

Wing Commander George Unwin: -

At the time I felt nothing out of the ordinary. I had been trained for the job and luckily had a lot of experience. I was always most disappointed if the squadron got into a scrap when I was off duty, and this applied to all of the pilots I knew. It was only after the event that I began to realise how serious defeat would have been – but then, without being big headed, we never ever considered being beaten, that was impossible in our eyes and was our simple outlook. As we lost aircraft and pilots, replacements were always forthcoming. Of course the new pilots lacked experience, but so did the German replacements and it was clear by the end of 1940 that these pilots had not the stomach for a scrap with a Spitfire.

Group Captain Peter Townsend: -

Our battle was a small one, but on its outcome depended the fate of the western world. At the time, however, no such thoughts bothered us, although obviously we knew that we had to win. More than that, we were somehow certain that we could not lose. I think it had something to do with England. Miles up in the sky, we fighter pilots could see more of England than other defender's had ever seen before. Beneath us stretched our beloved country, with its green hills and valleys, lush pastures and villages clustering round some ancient church. Yes, it was a help to have England there below. She was behind us, too. When, at the end of the day, we touched down and slipped out for a beer at the local, people were warm and wonderfully encouraging. They were for us, the fighter boys, who had once been the bad boys, who supposedly drank too much and drove too fast. Now people realised that, on the job, we were professionals. They rooted for us as if we were the home team, and we knew that we had to win, if only for them.

After the Battle of Britain it was clear that in fighter-to-fighter combat the Hurricane was inferior to the Spitfire, and by the end of 1940, therefore, all of 11 Group's squadrons were exclusively Spitfire-equipped. Wartime demands soon indicated that the small Supermarine factory at Woolston was unable to produce Spitfires in the quantity now required. The new site chosen for a 'shadow factory,' was at Castle Bromwich, near Birmingham, where it was intended to apply the mass production techniques of the motor industry to building Spitfires. Lord Nuffield himself, pioneer of the inexpensive and mass produced automobile, was chosen to oversee the project.

Hurricanes of 87 Squadron on patrol in 1940.

The Castle Bromwich Aircraft Factory (CBAF) produced the first Spitfire Mk IIs in June 1940, and these started reaching the squadrons in July. Unlike the Spitfire Mk I, all production Mk IIs incorporated an engine-driven hydraulic system for undercarriage operation, and constant-speed propellers. The Mk II also enjoyed the benefits of the Rolls-Royce Merlin XII engine, increasing the Spitfire's ceiling by 2,000 feet. This new engine also ran on 100, as opposed to 85, octane petrol, and was fitted with a Coffman cartridge starter. Naturally there were teething problems at CBAF, as at first the motor industry production line technique lacked the flexibility to keep up with the ever changing list of modifications required by the RAF. With great determination on behalf of all involved, these various problems were overcome and production of the Mk II steadily increased: 23 in July 1940, 37 in August and 56 in September. 611

Squadron was the first to be fully equipped with the Mk II, which saw action towards the end of the Battle of Britain. The dedication of the CBAF workforce during the years of Spitfire production is now legendary, and it is no small measure of commitment that 57.9% of the 20,334 Spitfires ultimately built were made in Birmingham.

An extremely rare and unofficial personal snap belonging to a CBAF worker.

Spitfire production in full swing at CBAF.

During the autumn of 1940, there were changes to the command structure of Fighter Command (see *Bader's Duxford Fighters: The Big Wing Controversy*, also by Dilip Sarkar). Sholto Douglas replaced Dowding as Commander-in-Chief, and the ambitious Leigh-Mallory took Park's place as commander of 11 Group. Douglas and Leigh-Mallory were keen to drive forward an offensive strategy, to 'reach out' and take the war across the Channel to France. On December 20th, 1940, two 66 Squadron Spitfires strafed the coastal airfield at Le Touquet. On January 9th, 1941, five RAF fighter squadrons swept the skies above north-east France. Sensibly the Germans did not react, so the following day 11 RAF fighter squadrons escorted six 114 Squadron Blenheims to Fôret de Guines. The operation was known as 'Circus No 1', the idea being that the Germans could not ignore the presence of bombers so would have to scramble fighters, which would be met by numerically superior force of (at that time mainly but not yet exclusively) Spitfires. As a portent of things to come during the so-called 'Non-Stop Offensive' of 1941, the RAF lost two fighters, the Germans none.

Improvements were constantly being made to the Spitfire. The advantages of the 109's 20 mm cannon were evident early on, and Fighter Command rapidly made efforts to give the Spitfire such a weapon. During the Battle of Britain, the experimental Spitfire Mk IB saw service in small numbers with 92 Squadron, and 19 Squadron was entirely equipped with the cannon-armed fighters. The Mk IBs, in fact, were armed only with two 20 mm Hispano Suiza cannons, all .303 machine-guns being removed. The Spitfire's wing, however, was too thin to mount the cannon upright, as intended by the manufacturer, but side-mounting led to numerous stoppages. In combat, when the cannons, his only weapon, jammed, the Mk IB pilot had no option but to break off the engagement. So frustrating, and not to mention downright dangerous, did this become, that Dowding himself personally flew to see 19 Squadron's pilots at Fowlmere on September 3rd, 1940. Having listened to his pilots' complaints, the Commander-in-Chief immediately arranged for the troublesome Mk IBs to be replaced by the machine-gun armed Mk IA. Nevertheless, the problem had to be resolved, as 20 mm armament was essential. Ultimately the answer was found in adding blisters to the upper and under surfaces of the Spitfire's wing, which made it possible to mount the cannon upright. Moreover, the 'B' wing was designed, which permitted the use of two 20 mm cannons and four .303 Browning machine-guns. The Mk IIA, introduced in small numbers towards the end of the Battle of Britain, were all machine-gun armed, but the Mk IIBs had the 'B' wing. By early 1941, therefore, Fighter Command's front line fighter squadrons were equipped with a mixture of Mk IIAs and B. The cannons, however, weighed 96 lbs each, and the Merlin XII of the Spitfire Mk II was not powerful enough to cope with this. So it was that the Merlin 45 was developed, which powered the Spitfire Mk V. This new Spitfire weighed 6,622 lbs, had a top speed of 359 mph at

25,000 feet, an altitude it could reach in 8½ minutes, and could attain 35,000 feet in 15 minutes. Biggin Hill's 92 Squadron received the first Mk Vs, which began reaching Fighter Command's remaining squadrons, in numbers, during May 1941.

A visiting Spitfire Mk VB at RAF Shobdon, Herefordshire, in 1942.

Flight Lieutenant Ron Rayner, of 41 Squadron, recalled flying Spitfires on operations across the Channel when a sergeant pilot, in 1941: -

I suppose it was a bit noisy, but with the flying helmet strapped down tight, the ears were almost sealed by the ear pieces' rubber rings, which helped. Anyway, after a combat started, from then on until back at Merston the R/T was chatting away constantly. Of course these Spitfires had no cockpit heating at all, and so we had to take steps to protect against the cold. My mother knitted me some woollen stockings which I used to pull up over my legs at high altitude. Flying a Spitfire was also a very physical business, especially when in formation which required constant jiggling about of the control column. Regarding range, this depended on use of the throttle, and of course combat used up more petrol; when attacked you would automatically go into a steep climbing turn, pushing the throttle forward for maximum boost as you did so. Crossing the water with one engine was always a concern, so of course we monitered our fuel gauges very carefully. After an operational flight I suppose we were tired, but we were young and fit and just glad not to be in the infantry!

Warrant Officer David Denchfield was also a sergeant pilot flying Spitfires in 1941: -

Until the day I was shot down over France and captured (February 5th, 1941), I thought the war an exciting affair which I would not have missed for all the tea in China. The war had released me from a hum-drum office job and realised my ambition to fly His Majesty's Spitfire and I got paid to do it! We seldom thought or spoke of any downside, although we knew that our occupation held little long term future, but we were young and unimaginative and thought 'it won't happen to me'.

Squadron Leader Jack Stokoe, 54 Squadron: -

The offensive operations of 1941 were just as vital as the Battle of Britain, and certainly more nerve-wracking as we were operating at range, over enemy territory.

In a reversal of the Battle of Britain scenario, in 1941 it was the Spitfire pilots who now had to cross the Channel and fight over enemy occupied territory. Air Sea Rescue remained embryonic, and downed pilots were often, if they were lucky, rescued by passing vessels. Jack Stokoe: -

On April 20th, 1941, we were patrolling off Clacton, about 10-20 miles out over the North Sea, having been vectored there by Control due to a report of 'bandits' in the area. Suddenly we were in a combat situation and I was firing at an enemy aircraft. Then – a blank! I was still airborne but minus my Spitfire, which had disappeared entirely, probably as the result of one or more direct hits from cannon shells behind the armour plated seat. I had not opened my hood or disconnected my oxygen supply or intercom, or unstrapped the seat harness, but I seemed not surprised or unduly worried that I was apparently flying with no visible means of support. Nor did I have any sensation of falling! My helmet was missing, as were my gloves and a flying boot. When I got round to looking, my parachute seemed rather the worse for wear, however I pulled the ripcord, the chute opened and I landed in a very cold and somewhat wild sea.

Jack inflated his dinghy, which then burst. Managing to maintain a small amount of air in a pocket, the hapless pilot desperately clung onto this buoyancy. Soon suffering from the effects of the cold water, Jack was relieved to see a ship, from which ropes were thrown. Grabbing one, the exhausted pilot was hauled aboard and subsequently returned to shore and admitted to Harwich Hospital. On May 6th, 1941, Jack Stokoe was back in action.

Bob Morton was a sergeant pilot with 616 Squadron, at Westhampnett, in the Tangmere Sector, and makes some interesting observations regarding the fighting in 1941: -

Although we maintained strict radio silence on the way across the Channel, the enemy fighters generally got wind of our approach and were waiting near their ceiling by the time we crossed the French coast. This meant that they could gain a greater speed than us through a long dive, overhaul us rapidly from behind, get in one long burst and break away. To avoid this, one Spitfire pilot in each section had to fly with his chin on his shoulder, watching his tail. Naturally this did not make for good formation flying.

By now we had copied the Germans and were flying sections of four aircraft, known as the 'Finger Four'. Although in action each section split into two pairs, after a time almost every pilot found himself alone. At this point the 109s, having broken up the Spitfire formation, would re-climb, ready to attack loners.

In these scraps we were disadvantaged in several ways, not least regarding combat claims. To claim and aircraft destroyed, a pilot had to see the aircraft concerned strike the ground, the enemy pilot bale out, or the aircraft burst into flames. The first was almost impossible, as most of our fighting was down above 10,000 feet, and no-one would be fool enough to keep his eyes on an aircraft he had shot at, or follow it down. The second took time to occur, and in any case other enemy aircraft would probably be shooting at the Spitfire pilot because the Germans always worked in pairs. As for the third, although in the film *Battle of Britain*, every German machine hit exploded, I never saw such a thing happen. Finally, if we were shot down over Enemy Occupied Territory, unless you were very lucky and received help from civilians, you would see out the war incarcerated in a German prison camp.

The new chiefs of Fighter Command were convinced that the more fighters were put in the air the better results would be, but this was based upon what, recent research has shown (see *Bader's Duxford Fighters: The Big Wing Controversy*), was a flawed theory. During the Battle of Britain, contrary to Dowding's system, which revolved around fighters intercepting the enemy in squadron strength and as individual units, five of Leigh-Mallory's 12 Group squadrons, operating from Duxford and under the aerial leadership of Acting Squadron Leader Douglas Bader, flew as a massed formation. The 'Big Wing's' combat claims were high and accepted with little cross-reference, much higher, in fact, than those by neighbouring 11 Group, which was adhering to the System. On this basis tactical thinking changed, but we now know that the 'Big Wings' combat claims were actually hugely inflated. This was because with so many fighters in action simultaneously, several pilots could attack the same enemy aircraft independently but oblivious to the fact that, in that split second, other RAF fighter pilots were attacking the same target. The result was that one enemy aircraft destroyed could ultimately be credited to a number of pilots, therefore becoming not a single aircraft destroying but sometimes, on the score sheet, several more. The Big Wing's combat claims have since been proved to be highly exaggerated, meaning that, in fact, it was 11 Group, after all, which destroyed more enemy machines and in so doing confirmed the excellence of Dowding's thinking. In 1941, however, the Big Wing theory was believed to hold true by Sholto Douglas and Leigh-Mallory, and they therefore planned operations over France by fighters in wing strength, the intention being to engage and destroy smaller formations of enemy fighters in an ongoing war of attrition.

The changeover to operations in wing strength, of up to three squadrons (36 fighters), led to the creation of a new appointment: 'Wing Leader'. Each Sector Station boasted a wing, so each sector was appointed its own Wing Commander (Flying). Air Vice-Marshal Johnnie Johnson, who should need no introduction as the RAF's official top scoring fighter pilot of WW2: -

The Wing Leader's job was every fighter pilots' dream, as the Wing Commander (Flying) was responsible for his wing's performance in the air. The logistics were left to the Station Commander, usually a Group Captain, and the wing's three squadron commanders.

Wing Commander Johnnie Johnson: Wing Leader and Spitfire pilot par excellence.

On December 7th, 1940, Leigh-Mallory drew up a list of potential Wing Leaders. Amongst them were 'Sailor' Malan, who ultimately went to Biggin Hill, Harry Broadhurst got Hornchurch, Victor Beamish North Weald, Johnnie Peel Kenley, and the indomitable Douglas Bader, went to lead Tangmere's Spitfires. On March 18th, 1941, Sergeant (now sir) Alan Smith was sitting at readiness in 616 Squadron's dispersal at Westhampnett, in the Tangmere Sector: -

I heard the roar of a Spitfire as it dived low, climbed, did a half-roll and lowered its undercarriage whilst inverted, rolled out, side-slipped and made a perfect landing. Out of the cockpit climbed none other than Wing Commander Douglas Bader, who walked with his distinctive gait over to us at dispersal. Our new Wing Commander (Flying) introduced himself and announced that he would be leading the Tangmere Wing at the head of our 616 Squadron. He seemed to already know Flying Officer Hugh 'Cocky' Dundas and Pilot Officer Johnnie Johnson, and said "You'll be Red 3, Cocky, and you Johnnie will be Red 4". Looking around he caught my eye and said "Who are you?"
"Sergeant Smith, sir!" I replied.
"Right. You will fly as my Red 2 and God help you if you don't watch my tail!"
I couldn't believe my ears; it was like God asking me to keep an eye on heaven for him! Flying with Douglas, Cocky and Johnnie was to become the greatest experience of my life, and I considered myself quite the most fortunate sergeant pilot in the RAF!

During that 'season', it was Flying Officer Dundas who persuaded Wing Commander Bader to copy the German *Schwarm* formation. This was duly imitated and became the 'Finger Four', soon adopted as Standard Operating Procedure throughout Fighter Command. Although this undoubtedly saved the lives of countless RAF fighter pilots the cross-Channel operations were proving costly, particularly in respect of experienced leaders. There were no targets of strategic importance in Northern France, and the mixed bomber and fighter operations were merely the only means of continuing the fight against the enemy during the day; leaders such as Finucane, Lock, Tuck and even Bader himself, as we shall see, all ended up either dead or incarcerated and were a poor exchange for the results achieved. On August 14th, 1941, Flight Lieutenant (later sir) Archie Winskill was shot down near Calais: -

It was the first sweep flown by the Tangmere Wing since Wing Commander Bader was lost on August 9th. I baled out and was fortunate to receive help from the French, which ultimately enabled me to escape over the Pyrenees and return home via Spain. Whilst hiding on a farm in the Pas-de-Calais, I was visited by a British agent, Sidney Bowen, from an escape organisation based in Marseille; he asked me why more Spitfires were crashing in France than 109s. I had no answer for him.

After the German invasion of Russia on June 22nd, 1941, the politicians, anxious to relieve the pressure on Soviet Russia, put Fighter Command under pressure to increase the tempo of its operations over France. At that time, the Germans had two fighter groups on the *Kanalfront*, namely JG 26 & JG 2, but it was never necessary for the strength of these units to be supplemented by Eastern Front fighters. In fact, Fighter Command was losing the day-fighter war by a loss ratio of 2:1 in the enemy's favour. Johnnie Johnson: -

The Germans had a slight edge over us in those early years. The 109E was superior to the Spitfire Mk IA and B, because of 20 mm cannon and fuel injection. I also thought that the Me 109F was slightly superior in performance to the Spitfire Mk V. Of course then the FW 190 appeared and saw everyone off.

The FW 190 had first appeared in small numbers during September 1941, the new shape in the sky causing great confusion amongst RAF Intelligence Officers who were bemused by Spitfire pilots' reports of a squat, snub-nosed, radial engine German fighter which out performed them in every respect. At first the possibility of it being a new and awesome enemy fighter was dismissed, and the puzzling fighters were written off as being Curtis Hawks, some of which had been captured by the Germans. The RAF pilots knew that this was not so, however, as the Hawk is considerably inferior to the Spitfire in every respect. Eventually intelligence from the continent confirmed that this was indeed a potent new enemy fighter.

The FW 190 was powered by a 1,700 hp BMW 801D-2 14 cylinder radial engine which gave a maximum speed of 312 mph at 15,000 feet; with a one-minute override boost it could exceed 400 mph! The 190's operational ceiling was 35,000 feet, and it could reach 26,000 feet in 12 minutes. Furthermore, it was extremely manoeuvrable. By comparison, the Spitfire Mk VB, with which Fighter Command's squadrons were most commonly equipped at this time, could achieve 371 mph at 20,000 feet, but could not operate much above 25,000 feet, by which height the speed dropped to 359 mph and too 15 minutes to reach. The German pilots were impressed with their new mounts rate of roll and acceleration, but, significantly, the 190 was unable to out-turn a Spitfire Mk V. For the first time, Spitfire pilots began losing confidence in their machine, and morale sank.

The 190 threat caused so much consternation, in fact, that plans were hatched to capture an airworthy example for evaluation. A commando raid was to cross the Channel and steal a 190, which would be flown back to England by Jeffrey Quill. Fortunately this hazardous undertaking became unnecessary when on June 22nd, 1942, *Oberleutnant* Armin Faber (of *Stab* III/JG 2) became so disorientated after combat with the Exeter Wing off Start Point that he mistook the Bristol for the English Channel and mistakenly landed at RAF Pembrey in South Wales. The quick thinking Duty Pilot, Sergeant Jeffries, rapidly stuck a flare pistol under Faber's nose, until which point the German was blissfully unaware of his catastrophic mistake. Faber's 190 was quickly evaluated and compared to the Spitfire Mk V. The essential information gained was rapidly fed into the Spitfire development programme and eventually the Spitfire Mk IX emerged, putting the Spitfire back on top.

Johnnie Johnson: -

When I commanded 610 Squadron we had Spitfire Mk Vs and were cut to pieces by the FW 190. On one particular occasion we went over to Cherbourg but got chased out, and on the way home I lost four chaps. We could see the 190s coming in, and we were breaking round and that sort of thing, but those bloody things were far superior and of course you couldn't spend all day turning in mid-Channel, you have to make a dash for it sometime. So the Spitfire Mk IX gave us the chance of getting stuck into the bastards again. The IX was a very good combination of engine and air frame. In my opinion the Mk IX was the best ever Spitfire. When we got the Mk IX we had the upper hand back, which did for the 190s! We could turn inside him and hack him down, which we did. Those cannon shells were as thick as your wrist and when you sent them crashing through his armour plate the 190 pilot didn't like it one bit!

Oberleutnant *Armin Faber's FW 190 at RAF Pembrey.*

Interestingly, by this time the Spitfire pilots' war had changed again. Hitler was now fighting on two fronts, which in the long term would prove a fatal mistake. Then, on December 7th, 1941, in what was a completely criminal and undeclared act of war, the Japanese attacked the American fleet at Pearl Harbour. The Americans immediately declared war on Japan, and when Germany declared war on the United States, 'Uncle Sam' found itself not pursuing Isolationism but shoulder-to-shoulder with Britain in the fight for democracy. The 'Yanks' lost no time in sending Brigadier General Ira Eaker and his staff to England where they prepared for the arrival of American Eighth Air Force combat units. Eaker wholeheartedly believed in the use of aerial strategic bombardment as a war winning use of air power, but believed that best results would be achieved by daylight attacks. From bitter experience the RAF thought otherwise, and bombed the Third Reich by night. Eaker was determined to stick to his guns, however. Although the Americans initially suffered heavy losses, with no shortage of men or materials Eaker pressed on with his 'Round-the-Clock Bombing'. On April 17th, 1942, General Eaker flew in the lead B-17 attacking the railway marshalling yards of Rouen-Sotteville, which was a success. During these early raids, whilst the Americans felt their way and gained experience, the bombers' depth of penetration was confined to the range of escorting fighters, which meant targets close to the French coast. This new requirement for fighters to have offensive range changed everything, in terms of both new fighters being designed and Spitfire development.

As we have seen, the genius RJ Mitchell created the Spitfire as a defensive fighter, to win such a battle as indeed visited Britain during the summer of 1940. A defensive fighter needs but short range, as the enemy is bringing the war to his territory. Successfully escorting long-range strategic bombers in a defensive fighter is therefore, virtually impossible. Johnnie Johnson: -

That efforts were not quickly made to significantly and properly increase the range of our Spitfires was a disgrace, and that was down to the Chief of the Air Staff, Portal, who wrongly believed that to do so would impede the Spitfire's performance as a defensive fighter. Had we more appropriate and increased range in 1943, we could have prevented many American bomber losses. I well remember those sad days in 1943 when the Americans got chewed up at Schweinfurt and Regensburg. We escorted them as far as we could but then had to turn around to get home and re-fuel. Then we were off again to meet them on their way back. In the meantime the German fighters had set about them like packs of dogs, and their once proud formations came home battered, bleeding, and with many gaps.

Various means were explored with a view to increasing the Spitfire's range, all of which involved the fitting of auxiliary fuel tanks which, in the main, could be jettisoned when empty or in the event of a 'bounce'. The airframe itself could not accept permanent additional fuel tanks, the fuselage already being cramped and the wings too thin. 'Drop tanks' were, therefore, the only answer, but as the Americans flew deeper and deeper into enemy territory, the Spitfire pilots were continually frustrated at having to leave their charges just when the *Jagdfleiger* pounced. It is, however, to the credit of this defensive fighter that it was possible to extend the range at all, indicating the versatility of Mitchell's flexible but robust design.

The answer to the problem of range, however, was at hand in the shape of the North American P-51. The 'Mustang' had first flown in October 1940, and did so due to a British requirement for an offensive fighter. The original Allison engine provided only mediocre performance, and the Mustang was found particularly wanting at high altitude. Consequently the first Mustangs received by the RAF in April 1942 could only be assigned to army co-operation roles. The British soon replaced the inadequate American Allison engine with the mighty Merlin, and the results were awesome. Comparison trials indicated that the Mustang had parted company with mediocrity and was now superior to all comers in every respect. The P-51A had a range of 2,200 miles, the P-51B 2,301 miles. Both figures are staggering when compared to the Mk IX's range, which, even with a 30 gallon drop tank, was around 980 miles. By early 1944, Mustangs were with the bombers all the way to Germany and back; in August that year a Mustang even flew over Berlin. So it was that Mustang became the long-range offensive fighter that the Allies had needed so badly from 1942 onwards.

Squadron Leader TH Drinkwater DFC in his 122 Wing Mustang, 1944.

Johnnie adds a final informed comment on the subject of range and offence: -

The problem was that throughout WW2, Fighter Command was not really aggressive enough, never really fought as a proper offensive force. We became a tactical air force, which was of short range and therefore within the Spitfire's capability. In any case we only had one wing of Mustangs, 122 Wing, the Americans had all the Mustangs and that bloody great Thunderbolt!

Reference to the tactical air force is opportune for our purposes. The Mustang relieved the Spitfire of long-range bomber escort missions, but the Spitfire's contribution was far from over.

The control of the Mediterranean was also bitterly contested during the first half of the war, this struggle beginning when Italy entered the war on the Axis side in June 1940. Geographically the key to that theatre was the tiny island of Malta, which was on the supply route to North Africa where British and German forces were engaged, and the Italians lost no time in trying to neutralise British resistance. For three weeks the island's defence was undertaken by three antiquated Gladiator biplanes, known as 'Faith', 'Hope' and 'Charity'; at the end of June 1940 four Hurricanes arrived and throughout the following month these seven fighters resisted the best efforts of some 200 enemy aircraft based in Sicily. So furiously did the defenders fight that eventually the Italians, like the Germans over England, were forced to operate only at night. More Hurricanes arrived but by March 1942 the Italians had been joined by superior *Luftwaffe* units and the contest was at its height. That month 15 Spitfires flew off the aircraft carrier HMS Eagle, landing at Takali. Within three days the Spitfires had destroyed their first enemy aircraft, but the very fact that Spitfires were on the island incensed the enemy: time after time Takali was bombed, and by April 2nd not one complete section of Spitfires was operational. Indeed, the defenders thought themselves lucky if they could field six fighters at any one time, two for airfield defence and four to intercept. Incredibly, sometimes the RAF pilots had no ammunition, it being in such short supply, but the Germans could never be sure, so always treated the Spitfires with respect.

Johny Plagis, just one Malta hero .

On April 15th, 1942, Malta was awarded the George Cross, and five days later 47 more Spitfires reach the besieged island. Following intense attacks, a day later only 18 Spitfires were serviceable; two days later none were airworthy. For some unknown reason, however, the *Luftwaffe* then made another classic tactical blunder, as it had at a crucial moment in the Battle of Britain, and eased off the pressure. This enabled 64 Spitfires, flying off USS *Wasp* and HMS *Eagle*, to get through to Malta, and a clever system was devised to rapidly turn the aircraft around to prevent them being caught on the ground: six Spitfires were up again within just six minutes of landing! It is perhaps worthy of note that the Air Officer in command of Malta was none other than Air Vice-Marshal Sir

Keith Park, commander of 11 Group during the Battle of Britain, and the 'Boss' Controller was Group Captain AB 'Woody' Woodhall of Duxford and Tangmere fame.

A Spitfire pilot famously described the action over Malta as making the 'Battle of Britain seem like child's play', but still the island held out. By October 23rd, 1942, Rommel had been defeated in the desert, and soon, after the Americans landed, the Allies were rolling up North Africa from both directions. The defence of Malta has rightly become legendary, but Spitfire operations from the island are important for another reason: it was from Malta that Spitfire fighter-bombers first flew, two 500 lb bombs being carried beneath their wings, attacking enemy airfields in Sicily. As we have seen RJ Mitchell designed the Spitfire as a defensive fighter, but early in the war it had to perform as an offensive escort fighter; now came another unexpected task which reflected the airframe's great strength and flexibility. Spitfires too had flown in the Desert Air Force during the North African campaign, and many of these units now gathered on Malta ready for the push into Europe via Sicily. From Malta the Spitfire wings swept over Sicily in an attempt to bring German fighters to battle, in much the same way as was happening over northern France. Flight Lieutenant Ron Rayner was on Malta with 43 Squadron: -

Flight Lieutenant Ron Rayner DFC.

On July 10th, 1943, the Allied invasion of Sicily, Operation HUSKY, commenced, and on that day we actually landed our Spitfires at Comiso. I remember it well as I parked my Spitfire in a dispersal area adjacent to a runway – my aircraft was next to a *Stuka* with Italian markings which had tipped over on its back with the two dead crew members still hanging upside down from their straps!

In Sicily we started the slog up the western coast, and flew patrols of Augusta and Catania, eventually landing at the latter. From there we began escorting American daylight bombers attacking targets in Italy itself. We were escorting Mitchells and Bostons, and in addition to this escort work we were attacking the retreating Germans ourselves. As they tried to escape up the coast to Messina, we strafed them in what looked like the equivalent vessel to our tank landing craft. We were then transferred to an airstrip which had been made for us on the northern side of Sicily, and continued patrolling Messina and Augusta. Eventually we arrived at Falcone, another strip prepared for us by army engineers.

It was in Sicily that we received our Spitfire Mk IXs, rushed through to combat the FW 190 threat that had caused serious problems for Fighter Command in England. The IXs were marvellous, absolutely incredible. I remember that on my first flight in a Mk IX, an air test, I went up to 35,000 feet, just for the joy of experiencing what it was like to operate at high altitude. It was definitely a different aircraft altogether at high altitude compared to the Mk V, it really was quite something. We only received a certain quantity of Mk IXs at first, so we flew a mixture of Vs and IXs. In fact the IXs were not even painted with an individual aircraft letter, they were just given a number. My personal aircraft at that time remained a Mk V, and I always flew FT-J.

The arrival of the Spitfire Mk IX was a major milestone in Spitfire history. Air Vice-Marshal Johnnie Johnson: -

The Mk IX was more powerful that the V, the Merlin 61 perfectly matched the airframe, there being no undue torque or bad flying characteristics like there was later with Griffon engined Spitfires. In my opinion the IX was the best Spitfire, we had the upper hand back then, which did for the 190s.

Squadron Leader Dan Browne: -

Although I was an American, I joined Johnnie's Canadian Wing at Kenley in 1943. I was delighted to find that we had Spitfire Mk IXs, which had a two-stage, two-speed engine. When you got up to about 19,000 feet the second stage kicked in, at which point it was your air and no longer the Germans' air.

Ron Rayner's Mk IX with flak damage in Italy.

Flight Lieutenant Ron Rayner: -

On September 8th, 1943, we were assembled and told that the invasion of Italy was to commence the next day. Our role was to support the army, which was landing on a beach in the bay of Salerno. On September 9th, therefore, our patrol area was Salerno, about 170 miles across the sea from our base at Falcone. We patrolled the beaches, milling about with German aircraft attacking the ground forces, and whilst the navy shelled German positions inland. This went on until September 15th, by which time the army had secured the beach-head, and a landing strip, called 'Roger', had been pushed up parallel to the beach at Salerno. We were then able to land at Salerno itself, but not without danger as not only were the Germans still shelling us but the trajectory of our own artillery also went across our new airfield!

A Seafire landing on a carrier, a snapshot from Basil King's album.

Also operating over Salerno were Seafires, the carrier version of Mitchell's Spitfire. Indeed, as early as 1936, the designer had considered a naval version of his fighter but, as we know, he died in 1937. No further interest was shown in a sea-going Spitfire until 1941 when the Admiralty decided there was an urgent need for such an aircraft to operate from carriers in the Fleet Air Defence role. Subsequently a number of elderly Spitfires were transferred from the RAF to the Fleet Air Arm, for trials and training, and from the data arising these aircraft were converted to Seafires. The modifications necessary for the Spitfire to operate from a carrier at sea included the fitting of an arrester hook, four spools for catapult launches and a strengthened airframe to cope with the extra strains imposed by such rapid acceleration and deceleration. Later, folding wings were also introduced to facilitate the storage of more aircraft below deck. Sub-Lieutenant Basil King flew Seafires and remembers the difficulties of deck landings: -

For some reason I was not given the opportunity to try a simulated deck landing on dry land at RNAS Yeovilton, but instead went straight to 808 Squadron on HMS *Battler*. The CO was not at all pleased. How I came to envy RAF pilots who could put down on dry land! We had to approach the narrow deck of the carrier, which left no room for error. Because of the Seafire's approach angle our view of the deck was virtually nil – we could only see about two feet of it and the Batsman, who used coloured bats, one in each hand, and gave the pilot signals to tell you whether you were coming in OK. Fortunately I landed safely on most occasions.

Ron Rayner continues: -

We continuously patrolled the battlefront, making sure that the army was not troubled too much by the *Luftwaffe*. Eventually the Germans got the message that we were not going to be pushed out of our beach-head and so the pressure started to ease off, as the army pushed inland and north towards the town of Salerno and then on to Naples. On September 19th we swept over the enemy airfield at Foggia, just to show the Germans that we were in control.

The fighting in Italy for what were just small hills was intense. I once walked over one with the Squadron Padre and found it littered with bodies. Truckloads of bodies were also driven past our landing strips as the battlefields were cleared. For us it was a time of living in tents, often in deep mud, very uncomfortable to say the least. We were largely engaged in ground attack against the German army, strafing columns of their motor transport and armour. This entailed flying very low, so low that once I returned to base trailing a length of telegraph wire from my wingtip; the airfield cleared rapidly!

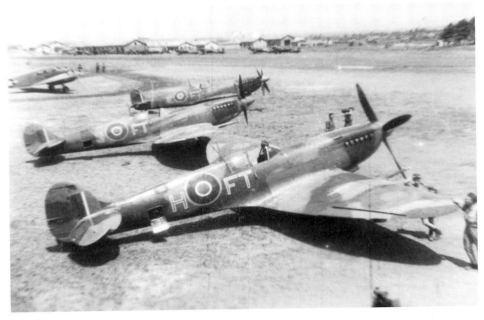

Ron Rayner's Spitfire Mk IX, FT-J, at Catania, Sicily.

The experience of all three services during the invasions of Sicily and Italy provided crucial experience for the later Allied liberation of enemy occupied France. Having recognised that there was an impending change of role for RAF fighter pilots, in that come the invasion they would be required to provide tactical support to the advancing British and Canadian armies, it was necessary to re-organise the existing service structure. Consequently the 2nd Tactical Air Force was created in June 1943, the concept being to provide a composite force of fighters, bombers, fighter-bombers and army co-operation aircraft which was independent of existing commands. This new air force would exist exclusively for deployment in support of the Allied Expeditionary Force which would undertake the proposed invasion.

The Italian campaign also provided experience, as Ron Rayner related, of whole airfields living under canvas and keeping on the move to support the ground forces. So it was that in August 1943, many Spitfire squadrons of 2nd TAF left their comfortable Sector Stations to begin operating under canvas. Canadian Wing Commander Bob Middlemiss was flying with Johnnie Johnson's Kenley Wing at the time: -

We had to leave the luxuries of batmen, soft beds, hot showers, good food, nice bar and lounge, and a short ride by electric train to the bright lights and excitement of London night life. We traded all this for tents, canvas beds, canvas wash basins, cold water for shaving, damp, cool nights and the general lack of amenities that we had become accustomed to. The 'Mess Hall' was a large tent, for example, where we ate off tin plates and sat at great wooden tables. The idea was to prepare and train us for the eventual landing in France and the mobile aerial and ground warfare that an eastward Allied advance would dictate. These primitive living conditions were not exactly what we had bargained for, however!

The Kenley Wing became known as '127 Wing', that numerical designation being the airfield at Lashenden where the Canadians now lived under canvas. The Spitfire's wings, however, were not strong enough to carry a couple of 500 lb bombs and auxiliary fuel tanks, so a compromise was reached with just one external fuel tank fitted between the inboard wheel wells and beneath the pilot's cockpit. Rather than bombs, however, most pilots would have preferred to see extra fuel, thus enabling penetrations deep into enemy territory and the welcome prospect of some decent air fighting. It was not to be, though, as times were changing. The *Luftwaffe* in the west was fighting the American heavy bombers by day, the RAF by night, so gone were the days of opposing fighters clashing on sweeps. Gone too would be the days of 'Big Wings'; Johnnie Johnson: -

Big wings of 36 Spitfires were OK for pre-planned offensive operations, but we knew that this would have to change once the invasion started. The time factor would not allow for such a large number of aircraft to take off and form up, and if the Germans struck at low level there would be no warning whatsoever. Also, we knew that after the invasion our main task would be flying in support of our advancing armies, which meant a fundamental change as our role would be that of a fighter-bomber, rather than a bomber escort or offensive fighter. It meant that we would have to respond quickly to calls for help from the army, and the only way to do this would be to operate smaller formations at a tactical level, such as a flight or squadron, as opposed to an entire wing.

When bombing you had to put the Spitfire into a steep dive, aim it at the target and release the bombs as you pulled out. Allowances had to be made for wind strengths etc because the bomb had not the same flying characteristics as a Spitfire. As there was no dedicated sight for this kind of work it was a case of developing our own technique of how to time the bomb release so that the target was hit. In Sicily and Italy it had been discovered that bridges were easier to hit with dive-bombers rather than light or medium bombers.

2nd TAF's fighter-bombers prowled over northern France, seeking out targets of opportunity. Naturally enemy airfields were always a popular choice, but on April 21st, 1944, Wing Commander Johnnie Johnson and his Canadians nearly bit off more than they could chew: -

The tactical bombers were operating in the Paris area so I led a section of Spitfires back down to the deck to sweep the numerous airfields scattered around the French capital. After 20 minutes at low level I was lost, although I knew we were a few miles south of Paris. I put away the map and concentrated on flying the various courses I had worked out before leaving base. About another five minutes of this leg and then a turn to the west to avoid getting too close to Paris. Our horizon was limited to about three miles over level country but was considerably reduced as we dipped into a valley.

We crossed a complicated mass of railway lines which indicated that we were close to Paris. We sped across a wide river and ahead of us was a heavily wooded slope, only a few feet above the topmost branches, and found ourselves looking straight across a large grass airfield with several large hangars on the far side.

The German gunners were ready and waiting. Shot and shell came at us from all angles, for some of the gun positions were on the hangar roofs and they fired *down* at us! I had never before seen the like of this barrage. It would have been folly to turn back and make for the shelter of the wooded slope, for the turn would have exposed the vulnerable bellies of our Spitfires. Enemy aircraft were parked here and there, but our only thought was to get clear of this inferno. There was no time for radio orders, it was every man for himself, and each pilot knew that he would only get clear by staying at the very lowest height.

It seemed that our exits were sealed with a concentrated criss-cross pattern of fire from 100 guns. My only hope of a getaway lay in the small gap between two hangars. I pointed the Spitfire at this gap, hurtled through it and caught a glimpse of the multiple barrels of a light flak gun swinging on to me from one of the parapets. Beyond lay a long, straight road with tall poplars either side, and I belted the Spitfire down the road with the trees forming some kind of screen. Tracer was still bursting over the cockpit, but with luck I would soon be out of range. I held down the Spitfire so she was only a few feet above the cobbled roadway. Half a dozen cyclists were making their way up the road, towards the airfield. They flung themselves from their bicycles in all directions. If you're a Frenchman, I thought, I am sorry, but I've had a bigger fright than you!

I pulled up above the light flak and called up the other pilots. Miraculously they had all come through the barrage, and when the last one answered I pulled up the Spitfire into a climbing roll with the sheer joy of being alive.

Johnnie and his pilots landed at Tangmere, and were enjoying a cigarette and cup of NAAFI tea when General Eisenhower himself appeared, on an official visit with Air Chief Marshal Leigh-Mallory, commander of the new 2nd TAF, and Air Vice-Marshal Harry Broadhurst, commanding No 83 Group. Seeing that Johnnie had just landed from an operational flight, Broadhurst introduced the Supreme Allied Commander to the Spitfire pilots; Johnnie: -

Eisenhower said to me 'Did you have any luck over there?'
I thought quickly, for we had not actually fired a shot and what words could accurately describe our desperate encounter with the flak?
'No sir', I answered, 'Our trip was uneventful.'

At last the invasion came on June 6th, 1944. a vast Allied armada crossing the Channel in secret and landing American, British and Canadian troops on the Normandy beaches near Cherbourg. Flight Lieutenant Bob Beardsley DFC, described to the press what he had seen from the cockpit of his Spitfire: -

The sky over the target was absolutely packed with aircraft. Fighters and bombers seemed to fill the air, wingtip to wingtip. From above we fighter pilots could see the bombs go down. The whole target area was a mass of flames. It was both an impressive and terrifying sight, and I for one was glad not to be a German soldier.

A Norwegian Spitfire wing leader added that: -

Looking down on the target area was like looking down into hell.

Flying Officer Kazek Budzik, a Pole, had flown Spitfires operationally since 1941. On D-Day he flew with 317 Squadron: -

We must have been amongst the first fighter aircraft over the beach-head as dawn was just breaking on our arrival. The invasion armada was enormous. Most of the landing craft were still in the sea, heading towards the beaches, it really was quite a spectacle. There was flak everywhere, though, mostly from the Allied fleet, and that was quite frightening. Watching the start of Europe's liberation was a fantastic experience, particularly the naval bombardment. You could see the guns fire and the shells hitting the coastline, getting further inland the more our troops advanced. It was amazing.

In spite of this massive bombardment from both air and sea, D-Day was far from one sided and American casualties were exceptionally heavy on 'Omaha' beach. By nightfall the Allies remained on the continent and were moving inland; Johnnie: -

In August 1943 the *Luftwaffe* had reacted swiftly and ferociously to the Canadian and British landing at Dieppe. That was an isolated landing but this time the stakes were infinitely higher. We expected the German fighters to respond in numbers on D-Day, but they did not, so, awesome though the sight of our invasion fleet was, from our perspective as fighter pilots the landings were an anti-climax.

The German chain of command was in confusion, so reaction to the landings was slow. The Allies flew a staggering 14,000 sorties on D-Day, with a loss ratio of 1.1%; the *Luftwaffe* flew but 319 sorties and suffered 6.9% casualties.

Once the Allied armies began moving inland, the 2nd TAF fighter-bombers were constantly above the battlefield, dive bombing and strafing the enemy wherever he could be found. *Sturmann* Karl Heinz Decker was an 18-year old grenadier in the 12th SS *Hitlerjugend Panzer* Division: 'The Mustangs and Spitfires fired at everything that moved, and Typhoons poured rockets down on us. It became only safe for us to move by night.'

On D-Day plus 3, Johnnie Johnson's 144 Wing actually landed and re-fuelled in Normandy:-

We received news that an airstrip, 'B3', had been created at St Croix-sur-Mer by our engineers, just inland of the beach-head, and 144 Wing was given the honour of being the first Spitfires to land in France. I sent Squadron Leader Dal Russell and three other 442 Squadron Spitfires to go across from our base at Ford and ensure that all was well at St Croix. It was, and so I took the whole Wing across to B-3 to re-fuel and re-arm before sweeping further south. The chance of operating from Normandy itself was welcome indeed, because we knew that there were concentrations of enemy aircraft based south of the River Loire, which was hitherto beyond our limited range.

We first made a low pass over St Croix, familiarising ourselves with the location, and then made a tight circuit to avoid barrage balloons protecting the beach-head. It was a strange experience, landing in what had been enemy territory and from which we had experienced all manner of hostile shot and shell. We touched down and RAF Servicing Commandos attended to our Spitfires. As we pilots gathered together the Airfield Commander came over and told us not to stray too far because of minefields and snipers. The Airfield Control system had been established in an adjacent orchard where we were soon approached by a delegation from St Croix. The villagers brought with them gifts of fruit, flowers and wine. Whilst we and the French rejoiced, dead German soldiers lay all around.

How fitting it was that Spitfires should be the first Allied aircraft to land in Normandy.

By August 19th, Field Marshal Montgomery considered the Battle for Normandy to be over. By that time the American 1st Army had advanced along the Contentin peninsula and broken through the bocage country, the British and Canadians had broken out into the open countryside beyond Caen, and the Germans were trapped as if by a giant pincer. After the enemy counter-attack failed at Mortain, the Germans had no option but to retreat across the Dives, 80,000 men struggling to reach the River Seine via the 'Falaise Gap'. The battlefield was completely dominated by rocket-firing Typhoons and other fighter-bombers. Time and time again the Spitfires took off to pound the enemy in the 'Corridor of Death'. The aircraft flew in pairs to facilitate a rapid turnaround. As all pilots involved knew the area well, there was no need for lengthy briefings, this also increasing the number of sorties possible. Pilots were flying up to six or seven trips a day to the killing ground. The 127 Wing diary indicates just how busy things were: -

It was the busiest day in the history of the Wing. Approximately 290 operational hours were flown by our aircraft. About 30,000 rounds of 20 mm ammunition was expended on the Hun. Nearly 500 enemy vehicles were destroyed or damaged by our squadrons.

This was a terrible crescendo to the bloody Battle for Normandy, complete proof of the total tactical aerial superiority enjoyed over the battlefield by the Allies. On that last day, Flying Officer Peter Taylor of 65 Squadron wrote in his log book: 'Forcing on with big strafe. Sifta Section dive-bombed. Not so dusty but too many Spitfires.' Of another sortie later that same day, the young Scot complained bitterly that the area was 'getting clapped. Too many Tiffies and too few trucks.' Aircraft from both 2nd TAF and the American 9th Air Force continued attacking until it was too dark to aim their bombs and guns. The withdrawal became a rout, and Allied pilots maintain that the stench of death even permeated their cockpits a thousand feet above the 'Shambles'. The destruction wrought upon the retreating enemy was enormous: 12,369 tanks, guns and vehicles were lost in a defeat every bit as catastrophic as El Alamein and Stalingrad. The gap was sealed by the Polish Armoured Division linking up with the US 90th Division at Chambois, by which time total German losses numbered some

A 2nd TAF Spitfire of 222 Squadron that dared to argue with the 'front end of a 190!'. From the album of Squadron Leader R Beardsley DFC.

300,000 men. Although the victory was both definite and decisive, it was not actually complete because before the gap was closed 20,000 German troops escaped.

After Normandy life continued in much the same vein for the Spitfire pilots of 2nd TAF, flying in support of the armies advancing through Belgium and Holland into Germany itself. There were fighter-to-fighter engagements but these were increasingly rare given that the *Luftwaffe* was by now an overstretched and all but spent force. There was still danger, however, mainly from light flak which harried the Allied fighter-bombers wherever they appeared. Kazek Budzik was a flight commander in 308 Squadron when he was shot down by flak near the Breda-Dortrecht bridge in Holland on October 29th, 1944: -

It was a low-level strafing attack and I was leading a section of four Spitfires. I think that the target was a flak position. I went in first, got hit, turned back and crash landed safely. There were another four Polish Spitfires doing a similar job nearby and their leader was also shot down; Flight Lieutenant Krzemanski was killed whereas for some unknown reason I survived.

Two days later Budzik was back in action but was again shot down by flak during a dive-bombing attack against a train on the Zwolle-Mardewijk line. Again luck was on Kazek's side and he survived a wheels up forced landing near Gorinchem. Just a few days later he was, needless to say, back in action over the Arnhem area.

Flight Lieutenant Budzik just before he was shot down on October 29th, 1944.

Another precious CBAF snapshot: a Mk XIV with what appears to be a squadron leader's oblong shaped pennant and a kangaroo motif.

Another menace combated by Spitfires during 1944 were the pilot-less V-1 robot bombs, known as 'Doodlebugs', at first launched on England from 'No Ball' sites in the Pas-de-Calais. By now there were yet more new Spitfires on the scene, the Mk XII and XIV, powered not by a Merlin but a Griffon engine, and these machines out performed even the popular Mk IX. In their Griffon Spitfires, pilots chased and destroyed many V-1s, some even drawing level with the flying bombs and using their wingtips to tip the Doodlebug over, upsetting its sensitive gyroscope, and causing the bomb to crash harmlessly. As the Allies advanced, the V-1 launch sites were moved east, first to Belgium and then to Holland. Hitler's next secret weapon was the V-2 rocket, which also caused havoc but was a threat beyond the capability of any fighter aircraft.

German technology was ever impressive, and over Germany Allied fighter pilots were astonished by a new and incredibly fast shape in the sky: the Me 262 jet fighter. On October 5th, 1944, the first Me 262 to be destroyed was shot down by Spitfires of 401 Squadron, an incredible achievement. Flying Officer Tony Minchin flew Mustangs with 122 Squadron, and remembers seeing an Me 262 take off from Paderborn: 'He must have seen us for he opened the tap and just left us standing, even though we were doing over 500 m.p.h. in the dive!' Although Hitler completely mismanaged this potent resource, the appearance of such a fighter heralded the Spitfire's swansong. The days of piston engine fighters were drawing to a close, the jet engine providing far greater performance in every respect.

Still the war in Europe went on, and on New Year's Day 1945 the *Luftwaffe* mounted its last offensive: Operation BODENPLATTE, a surprise attack on Allied airfields in Holland. Although successful to a degree, the *Luftwaffe* was unable to deliver any kind of decisive hammer blow by that time, the operation really was a last gasp show of strength. The Allied war machine ground ever eastwards, whilst the Russians advanced west. Flight Lieutenant Ron Rayner: -

By March 1945 we were still attacking German army positions in support of our advancing armies. One day that month we were ordered off to drop what had been described as 'fire bombs' on some German positions that were proving particularly difficult to shift. These bombs had been made up in drop tank shells. Off we went and dropped them accordingly, watching rivulets of fire running into the German trenches. On reflection I believe that this flammable substance was Napalm, and I have often wondered whether this was actually the first ever use of it.

On May 8th, 1945, Germany signed an unconditional surrender. Hitler was dead, his empire destroyed; the war in Europe was finally over. In the Far East, however, the Japanese menace had yet to be beaten. The RAF air component serving in that theatre is often referred to as the 'Forgotten Air Force', with just cause. It was Hurricanes, though, that arrived in theatre first, and held the fort admirably until the arrival of Spitfires and American P-47 Thunderbolts in 1944. Spitfires had, however, reached Australia in 1943, and the Port Darwin Wing Leader, Clive 'Killer' Caldwell, frequently led his pilots into action against the enemy Mitsubushi Zero, with success. The Zero was a light and high manoeuvrable fighter but unable to withstand a beating from Caldwell's Mk Vs which had 20 mm cannon. Seafires too operated in the Far East, and by July 1945 the carriers of Task Force 37 were in the Pacific just 130 miles from Tokyo. One offensive sweep was flown before the order came to cease all aerial activity due to a special operation: the B-29 Superfortresses 'Boxcar' and 'Enola Gay' were poised to drop atom bombs on Hiroshima and Nagasaki. The result stunned the world, and on August 15th, 1945, the Allies celebrated victory against the Japanese. The Second World War was over at last.

Nevertheless, the Spitfire's fighting days were not yet over. In 1948 came the Malayan Emergency, two Spitfires destroying a terrorist base that July. The Spitfire force in Malaya, flying FR.18s, flew a total of 1,800 operational sorties during the campaign. Although no Spitfires fought in the Korean War, Seafire F.47s did. Most incredibly, Spitfire fought Spitfire over the Middle East. The Egyptian Air Force operated LF Mk IXs, which attacked Tel Aviv on May15th, 1948, the day on which Israel was born. RAF Spitfires were based in Israel, to provide support to the new state, and Nos 32 and 208 Squadron were strafed by the Egyptians at Ramat David. The next time the Egyptian Mk IXs appeared, three were shot down by RAF Spitfires. Perhaps even more amazing is the fact that Spitfires operated alongside FW 190s in the Turkish Air Force, and with Me 109s in Israel! Spitfires flew operationally over the Middle East until 1953, when Syria replaced its F.22s with jets.

The following year was the Seafire's last in operational service, although the RAF continued to use PR.19s for non-operational work. Those aircraft gathered data for the Temperature & Humidity Testing Flight, based at Woodvale near Manchester, making the very last Spitfire service flight in June 1957, by which time military aviation was completely dominated by the jet.

Proud memories: Ray Johnson, an armourer with 152 Squadron both during the Battle of Britain and in the Far East, with a BBMF Spitfire painted to represent a machine of the 'Forgotten Air Force'.

It is interesting that the Spitfire was eventually developed through 24 different marques, which included a complete engine change. Although designed purely as a short range defensive fighter, the Spitfire had performed its intended roll admirably but had also been pressed into service as an offensive escort fighter, fighter-bomber and photographic reconnaissance aircraft, all evidence of the incredible potential and flexibility of RJ Mitchell's inspired design. Would this have happened had Mitchell lived? It has often been said that he was more an innovator than developer, so it is suspected that instead of continually upgrading the Spitfire RJ Mitchell would have created new designs, purpose built for the job in hand. Certainly this is what the Hurricane's designer, Sydney Camm, did; although the Hurricane was developed, and also carried bombs, rockets and cannons, it was nothing like the process applied to the Spitfire. Instead Camm applied himself to the creation of new aircraft, such as the Typhoon and Tempest. The Spitfire, however, like no other icon, became the absolute symbol of defiance and freedom during the Second World War, and has earned its place in both history and legend.

The Spitfire, though, let us not forget, is a machine. It was designed, developed, built, maintained and flown by human beings. The deeds of flesh and blood, therefore, made the Spitfire what it is, and all too often those involved made the ultimate sacrifice or suffered deprivation as prisoners of war. Whilst the story of Mitchell's Spitfire has been told many times, by as many different authors, the personal stories of individuals, especially those who died or were not famous, are in danger of being lost to living memory. The following accounts, therefore, represent an effort to keep that memory alive, although the number of pilots featured in this book does not even represent the tip of this particular iceberg. There remains a massive amount of work to be done, to record and preserve as much of this moving and poignant history before it is too late.

The Spitfire story and the deeds of those involved are so incredibly inspirational that they must never be forgotten.

Chapter Two

Pilot Officer Jack Pugh

John Connolly 'Jack' Pugh was born the middle of three boys on June 19th, 1919, in Hong Kong, where his mother, a Queen's Army Schoolmistress, had joined her husband who was a teacher in the Army Education Corps. The family returned to England in 1920, youngest son Robert being born the following year. In 1924, Mrs Pugh was posted to India and accompanied overseas by her three sons, Tom, Jack and 'Bob', not returning to their home town of Farnborough until until 1927. The Pughs were then educated at the town's Silesian College, along with Patrick and Tony Woods-Scawen, both of whom would later become successful fighter pilots only to die within 24 hours of each other during the Battle of Britain. In 1934, Jack and Bob Pugh joined their mother on her latest posting, Cairo, but Tom remained at Silesians, completing his education before being commissioned into the RAF in 1936. The elder Pugh became a pilot and inspired both of his younger brothers to follow in his footsteps, Jack and Bob both being commissioned into the regular service and accepted for pilot training in August 1939.

Jack Pugh gained his civilian pilot's licence at Yatesbury, and began his service flying training in November. Whilst Jack was earmarked to become a fighter pilot, Pilot Officer Bob Pugh went straight to 502 Squadron at Aldergrove, flying twin engine Avro Ansons on dull convoy protection patrols.

At the outbreak of the Second World War, there were differing opinions at high level regarding the training of fighter pilots. Under the existing system, pilots who had completed their elementary and advanced service flying training were converted to the type of aircraft they would fly operationally actually by their squadron. The Air Ministry proposed to change everything by ensuring that new pilots were already trained to operational standard before arrival at their first squadron. The Air Officer Commanding-in-Chief of RAF Fighter Command, Air Chief Marshal Sir Hugh Dowding, however, felt that equipping such new training schools was a waste of operational aircraft. The Air Ministry won the argument, and arrangements were soon made for the creation of three 'Group Pools' to provide 300 replacement pilots per annum for the 36 fighter squadrons. Nevertheless, Dowding insisted that training be ongoing at squadron level, and impressed upon commanders the very great need for this.

In March 1940, both 11 and 12 Group Pools were renamed Operational Training Units (OTU), becoming Nos 5 and 6 respectively and, in June 1940, placed under the control of 10 Group. The Air Ministry's action was prompted by a spate of flying accidents, allegedly due to inadequate training, but Dowding still disagreed and believed the new OTUs to be an unaffordable luxury at such a time of crisis. In May 1940, the urgent need for fighter pilots suddenly became an even greater priority as Hurricane squadrons began taking casualties in France. The pilots who arrived on the continent fresh from training units were criticised greatly by the squadrons, which was hardly surprising: during their 'operational training', these youngsters were recording just 10 hours flying on Hurricanes and Spitfires, but given no high altitude or fighter attack experience. Heavily engaged in what was an extremely negative and fluid military situation, the squadrons were, understandably, just too busy to provide any further training whatsoever at this time. In any case, the training units were only achieving a maximum output of 80 pilots per month; the actual monthly requirement for casualty replacements alone was 200, and 300 if raising squadron establishments was taken into account. The provision of suitably trained replacement pilots was, therefore, a complicated matter with no easy solution.

There is a common misconception that aircraft allocated to OTUs were well-worn and obsolete machines, tired airframes prone to unexpected malfunction accounting for the deaths of many inexperienced pilots. This was often the case, but Supermarine Mk IA P9517 was an exception. This aircraft was built at Woolston, near Southampton, and given its 30 minute production test flight, from Eastleigh, by company test pilot Jeffrey Quill on April 26th, 1940. Three days later the Spitfire was taken on charge by No 24 Maintenance Unit (MU) at Ternhill, from where it was allocated to No 5 OTU at Aston Down on May 11th, one day after Hitler attacked the west.

Pilot Officer Jack Pugh arrived at Aston Down in mid-May 1940, and after passing a dual test in a Harvard soon soloed on that type before flying a Spitfire. Three other student pilots reported for instruction the same day, two of whom were killed and the third wounded a few weeks later in the Battle of Britain.

On May 21st, 1940, Pilot Officer Jack Pugh took off from Aston Down in Spitfire P9517, on a cross-country navigation exercise. Over the small Herefordshire town of Leominster, however, the Spitfire's engine inexplicably failed, bursting into flame. Standing Orders dictated that providing the fire was contained in the engine compartment, which in this case it was, the pilot should make a forced landing in an appropriate field. Losing height, Jack searched for a suitable meadow, which had to be some 800 yards long and 60 yards wide. Such a feature the young pilot found about four miles south-west of Leominster, at Alton Cross in the parish of Dilwyn, a small village a mile north-west of the chosen site. By now the Spitfire, trailing thick black smoke, was attracting attention from those on the ground: local schoolboys Lionel Weaver and Dennis Fletcher were beside themselves with excitement as they watched the stricken fighter pass overhead!

The smoke and oil pouring from the engine, however, was seriously reducing the pilot's forward visibility. Soon P9517 was on finals, fuel supply already shut off and in a glide as Jack Pugh pumped down the undercarriage. Air Ministry Pilot's Notes for the Spitfire Mk IA recommend an ideal indicated air speed of 90 m.p.h. for such a 'non-power assisted' landing, but, at the last moment of Pilot Officer Pugh's approach, tragedy struck. Suddenly, ahead of him and through the thick smoke, Jack made out the shape of a man working a horse. Instinctively the pilot hauled back on his control column, desperately trying to gain height and avoid a collision. Rising a few feet, and missing the man, farmer Leonard Deakin who was ploughing the field, the Spitfire then stalled. Mr Deakin's daughter, Kathleen, remembers the scene vividly: -

When the pilot tried to miss Dad and passed over him, the Spitfire was so low that Dad's shirt was covered in the black oil that was leaking from the plane, which was also trailing black smoke. Immediately after the pilot swerved to miss Dad, the Spitfire crashed in the next field, between some trees. Dad, Mum and myself were at the scene and I can picture it to this day, seeing the pilot there and the plane burning. The flames were so fierce that we couldn't get anywhere near him. He saved my father's life, but in so doing lost his own. Never a day went by that Dad didn't say something about the pilot's bravery, and that if he had not been working in that particular field that day then the young man would still be alive.

Leonard Deakin.

The tree hit by Spitfire P9517.

Pilot Officer Pugh's incinerated remains were eventually recovered and kept overnight in a wooden hut near the village church at Dilwyn. The 20-year old pilot was subsequently buried at St Mary's RC Church at Woodchester, near Stroud in Gloucestershire. The grave, a privately provided example and not a Commonwealth War Graves Commission headstone, was inscribed 'In Loving Memory of My Son: JC Pugh, Pilot Officer RAF. Killed on Active Service 21.5.40.'

At a time when examples of bravery were commonplace, Pilot Officer Pugh received no recognition for his courage that fateful day, and as memories became dimmed by the passing of years, his grave became overgrown and forgotten.

Jack's elder brother, Tom, became the RAF's first Hawker Typhoon Wing Leader, decorated with the DFC, but was killed on August 2nd, 1943, when his bombs exploded before release during an attack on Dieppe harbour. The 25-year old Wing Commander was never found, and is remembered on the Runnymede Memorial to missing Commonwealth airmen.

Bob Pugh flew Wellingtons in the Middle East before being posted back to England as a flying instructor following Tom's death. In March 1945 he was awarded the Air Force Cross for his work in training, subsequently enjoying a successful and varied flying career before retiring from the RAF in 1968. He then trained the Royal Saudi Air Force to fly jet fighters at Riyadh and Dhahran, names that would become familiar to RAF Tornado GR1 crews during the Gulf War of 1991. In 1981, aged 60, Bob qualified as a microlight pilot. He has also flown gliders, made a parachute jump, 'had a go at a hovercraft', and flown in a hot air balloon! Indeed, his total flying time is an impressive 6,667 hours on 65 types.

In 1988, having traced Squadron Leader Bob Pugh still living in Farnborough, the former Malvern Spitfire Team, in partnership with Dilwyn Parish Council, erected a memorial to Pilot Officer Jack Pugh on the village green. The tribute was unveiled by Bob, and the local flying club provided a fly past in a 'missing man' formation. As ever with such events there was a huge turnout and the dedication service was extremely moving.

Squadron Leader & Mrs Pugh unveil the memorial at Dilwyn in 1988.

Later that day I took the Pugh family to Jack's crash site, where Bob recalled that he and Tom had both attended their brother's funeral: -

We were told that Jack was doing well on his fighter course and that he had made an excellent effort in setting up what would have been a perfect forced landing under difficult conditions. Seeing the crash site now for myself, it is clear from a professional point of view that my brother chose an excellent location for a forced landing.

The trees still bear silent witness to the tragedy, several damaged and missing boughs being visible. All we could find of P9517 was an ingot of molten aluminium, poignant indeed given that the family were previously unaware that there had been a fire.

The last word, however, goes to eyewitness Lionel Weaver, who described Pilot Officer Jack Pugh's bravery as 'remarkable'; further comment would be superfluous.

Scene of the Pugh tragedy. The trees still bear scars today.

Chapter Three

Pilot Officer Laurie Whitbread

Herbert Laurence Whitbread was born on August 21st, 1914, in the picturesque market town of Ludlow, which sits astride the River Teme in Shropshire. Overlooked by Ludlow Castle, where Prince Arthur died on April 2nd, 1502, in times past the town was an important English garrison in the Marches. In time, Ludlowvian 'Laurie' Whitbread would find himself defending England, not against Welsh barons but Germans, and from the cockpit of a Spitfire.

Laurie lived with his parents and sister at 4 Linney View, Ludlow, and attended the local primary and grammar schools. At the latter he was a popular pupil and, like other young fighter pilots featured in this book, excelled at sport. In 1933 he became House Captain of Wright's, a master, George Merchant, later describing Laurie in a house photograph as 'sprawling in his majesty, flanked by his henchmen and surrounded by his minions'. At Ludlow Grammar School Whitbread's name became synonymous with boxing and rugby, and our hero also represented Shropshire at hockey. His best friend was fellow pupil Charlie Knight, who was the son of Rev. & Mrs Lacey Hulbert of St Mary's. Charlie's younger sister, Margaret, remembers Laurie as a 'second brother', and humorously recalls him dressing up in her father's cassock and walking around the town!

After leaving school, young Laurie became an apprentice at Fisher & Ludlow in Birmingham, manufacturing sheet steel for the automotive industry. Ken Brown, another Ludlovian, worked with Laurie but was not surprised when his friend left the firm in 1939 to become a fighter pilot.

On January 12th, 1939, Laurie sat for interview at the Air Ministry and subsequently received a Short Service Commission. Having volunteered for aircrew, by March Pilot Officer Whitbread was undertaking his *ab initio* flying training at Desford, where he recorded the following notes in his diary: -

March 9th: Flying lots in afternoon – instructor to myself from 1.30 – 4.30. Managed OK.
                     Stalling, gliding, turning and taxying.
March 11th: Looking forward to first solo.
April 25th: RAF Test after 45 hours solo, passed OK.

Having won his 'wings', Laurie moved on to the Service Flying Training School (SFTS) at Kinloss, in Scotland. There he flew twins, as indicated by his diary: -

May 19th: Airspeed Oxford. Splendid instructor.

May 25th: Went solo on Oxford OK, rough wind.
June 9th: Solo, 40 minutes, N6289.
June 19th: Definitely difficult to land with a closed throttle. Two bad landings.
June 22nd: Someone's going to get hurt before long. Oxford aircraft not being maintained in very
                     good condition. Petrol gauge and undercarriage lights all wrong. Not good
                     enough.
July 3rd: Night flying. Suicide, but made perfect first landing, solo not so hot.

Two months later Britain and France declared war on Nazi Germany following Hitler's refusal to withdraw his troops from Poland, which he had invaded on September 1st. The world was now at war for the second time that century.

On November 26th, 1939, Pilot Officer Whitbread's service flying training was considered complete and he was posted to 222 'Natal' Squadron, a new unit based at Duxford. 222 Squadron was commanded by Squadron Leader HW 'Tubby' Mermegen, a Cranwell graduate who had led the Inverted Flying Formation at the 1937 Hendon Air Pageant, and performed solo aerobatics for His Majesty the King. In 1992 I had the privilege of interviewing the now late Air Commodore Mermegen, who remembered those heady days: -

I formed 222 as a 12 Group night-fighter unit equipped with Bristol Blenheim twin-engined aircraft. As I was previously an A1 qualified staff flying instructor at the Central Flying School (CFS), to convert pilots to this type I was supplied with a dual Blenheim.

Whitbread was one of the earliest postings to the new squadron, straight from flying training school. I can remember him as a pleasant, well-mannered, quiet individual. A shortish, stocky, cheerful character whom I instantly liked – a good mixer.

*Air Commodore
'Tubby' Mermagen
pictured in
Germany, 1945.*

My flying log book records that on December 12th, 1939, at 1200 hours, I took him up in the dual Blenheim, L6712, for a test/conversion to Blenheim Mk Is. The flight lasted 25 minutes and I must have been suitable impressed since, so far as my log book shows, Whitbread had no further instruction and went solo immediately afterwards. I understand that he trained on twin engined Oxfords, but even so he displayed a good standard of flying. The Squadron subsequently conducted a very large number of flying hours and we were soon operational, with no accidents.

Throughout December 1939, 222 Squadron flew monotonous convoy protection patrols over the North Sea, all without incident. As the winter progressed so flying weather deteriorated, there being no flying whatsoever during the first nine days of February 1940, due to heavy snow. On Wednesday 14th, Laurie wrote in his diary: 'Narrowest escape to date, nearly spun in whilst night flying'.

222 Squadron shared Duxford with the Spitfire equipped 19 and 66 Squadrons, which, from the cockpits of their comparatively uninspiring Blenheims, Mermagen's pilots must have viewed with envy. 222 Squadron, however, was suddenly ordered to convert to Spitfires, five of which arrived on March 9th. Air Commodore Mermagen: -

To our delight the AOC, Air Vice-Marshal Leigh-Mallory, decided to re-equip us with Spitfires. The already enthusiastic pilots faced this conversion from twins to singles with great excitement. To help me with the conversion of all pilots, I was supplied with a Miles Master dual training aircraft, N7570. My log book records that at 1600 hours on March 18th I took Pilot Officer Whitbread up for 40 minutes conversion-to-type flying. I did the same the following day for another 30 minutes and he must have then satisfied me completely because he went solo on a Spitfire with no further instruction immediately afterwards.

There followed an intensive flying training programme for 222 Squadron, including much formation flying. Laurie's diary: -

March 20th: Spitfire solo.
March 24th: Spitfire. Try guns at Sutton Bridge.
April 6th: Practising attacks.
April 10th: Buy Wolseley Hornet, 1932, not bad!
April 14th: Squadron formation of 12 aircraft. Height climb 26,000 feet.
April 15th: First accident, nose in Spitfire but CO exonerates me from blame.

On April 17th, 222 Squadron became fully operational on Spitfires. 19 Squadron moved from Duxford to Horsham St Faith, so 222 took over their recently vacated dispersals at the aerodrome's eastern end. Squadron Leader Mermagen continued to train his pilots hard, introducing night flying into the programme; Laurie's diary: -

April 21st: Pilot Officer Vigors almost writes both of us off overtaking at 60 mph and missed by
                 five!
April 28th: Formation flying.
May 1st: Formation flying. Bad weather.
May 3rd: Night flying.
May 9th: Squadron shabbles. AOC very pleased. 12 minutes for refuelling and reloading the
                 entire squadron, a record!

On Friday, May 10th, 1940, the 'Phoney War' came to an abrupt end when Hitler's forces, with surprise, speed and ferocity, swept into Holland, Belgium, Luxembourg and France. The Defiant equipped 264 Squadron, based at Martelsham Heath in the Debden Sector, was ordered to move to Duxford and anticipate operating from forward basis in support of the Dutch. To make room, 222 Squadron was sent north, to Digby in Lincolnshire. Laurie wrote in his diary: 'At 12 mid-day we are told to go to Digby at 9 p.m.! What a scramble packing. Arrived safely.' Two days later he wrote: 'More formation flying. Oh, to be abroad!'

222 Squadron moved from Digby to Kirton-in-Lindsey, also in Lincolnshire, on May 23rd. By that time it was clear that the situation on the continent was catastrophic. Before the German invasion, the Belgian King, in a misguided attempt to maintain his country's neutrality, refused to allow British troops into his country, even for reconnaissance. Consequently the British Expeditionary Force (BEF), commanded by Lord Gort, dug in on the Franco-Belgian border; when the shooting started the Belgians called for help immediately, meaning that Gort's men had to pivot forward 60 miles, moving from a prepared to an unprepared defensive line, and across unfamiliar ground without stashes of fuel or ammunition. When German airborne troops landed in Belgium and Holland, it was assumed that the *Schwerpunkt*, or main point of effort, would come from that direction, as in the Great War. In fact, *Panzergruppe* von Kliest was cleverly negotiating the supposedly impassable Ardennes, thus outflanking the much-vaunted French Maginot Line and punching an armoured fist into the Allies' soft under belly. The *panzers* raced towards the coast, and Gort had no option but to fall back, from one river defence line to the next, in order to escape envelopment. Eventually it was agreed to evacuate the BEF from Dunkirk. Incredibly, however, Hitler stopped his tanks at the Aa Canal, for reasons never satisfactorily explained; had the *panzers* kept rolling then the 338,226 Allied troops evacuated could all have been lost. Fortunately the German armour stayed its hand, and the evacuation has gone down in history as little short of a miracle. Calm seas assisted the Royal Navy and gallant civilian craft known as the 'Little Ships', their sailors being the undisputed heroes of this desperate hour.

During the Battle of France, Air Chief Marshal Dowding had far-sightedly only deployed Hurricanes to the continent, maintaining his smaller Spitfire force for home defence. The Hurricane squadrons had taken such a pounding in France, however, that there was now no option but to commit the Spitfire squadrons to battle across the Channel in an effort to provide the evacuation with aerial support. These squadrons found themselves sent south, operating from forward bases such as Manston and Hawkinge, and tried to prevent German aircraft attacking either ships or soldiers on the ground. Most of the air battles arising were either fought above cloud or behind German lines, unseen, therefore, by watchers on the ground. Some German aircraft did get through and mercilessly attacked the columns of soldiers on the sand, giving the impression to many that the RAF had let them down – badly, although in reality this was not the case. Fighter Command's squadrons flew a total of 4,822 operational hours during Operation DYNAMO, destroyed 258 enemy aircraft and damaged 119, offset against their own losses of 87 machines.

On May 29th, 222 Squadron flew south to Hornchurch in Essex, remaining there for two days. Air Commodore Mermagen: -

At 6.30 a.m. that day I led the Squadron, in fact a wing of several squadrons, on its first patrol over the Dunkirk beaches. The sortie lasted two hours and 45 minutes, a long flight for a Spitfire. The Squadron carried out several further sorties, ending on June 3rd when the wretched evacuation appeared completed – no life could be seen either on the beaches or in the country behind. I lost four pilots killed and one missing during that period. Pilot Officer Whitbread must have taken part in most if not all of these sorties. I know that I had already recognised him as a good, reliable and sound Spitfire pilot.

Indeed, the record shows that Pilot Officer Whitbread did fly on the majority of 222 Squadron's sorties from Hornchurch, in Spitfires P9318, P9360 and P9378. Laurie was a member of 'B' Flight, but 'A' Flight had a very colourful Flight Commander: Flight Lieutenant Douglas Bader, who had lost both legs in a flying accident during 1931. In spite of having mastered 'tin' legs and passing a flying test, King's Regulations did not allow for disabled pilots and so the young Cranwell graduate subsequently left the service. At the time of Munich in 1938, however, Bader offered his services to the Air Ministry and was told that if war broke out he would be given another flying test. After war was declared in September 1939, Bader attended the CFS at Upavon in Wiltshire where he was tested in a dual control, American built, Harvard training aircraft. All American aircraft of the period have foot controlled brakes, whilst British machines had a hand operated lever on the control column. The Harvard's brakes were therefore foot controlled, which the legless Bader could not actually operate; at the appropriate juncture during the flying test, therefore, his instructor, none other than a Cranwell contemporary, Rupert 'Lucky' Leigh, dabbed the brakes himself so

Bader passed the test. Initially, in February 1940, Flying Officer Bader was posted to fly Spitfires with 19 Squadron at Duxford, which was commanded by his old Cranwell and aerobatic chum Geoffrey Stephenson, but Bader found being his friend's subordinate so difficult that the following month he used 'Old Boy' connections again to obtain a posting as a flight commander to 222 Squadron; the Commanding Officer, 'Tubby' Mermagen, was, needless to say, another Cranwell contemporary. It is also noteworthy that Bader's meteoric promotion to Acting Flight Lieutenant and flight commander was in spite of having bent a couple of Spitfires in careless accidents. Over Dunkirk, however, the Spitfire pilots would meet the Me 109 for the first time, one of which Douglas Bader destroyed on June 1st.

Flight Lieutenant Douglas Bader (centre) with pilots of 92 & 222 Squadrons at Hornchurch during the Dunkirk fighting.

It was now that the years of practising set-piece Fighter Command attacks against slow moving bombers that took little or no evasive action would be exposed as useless. Fighter-to-fighter combat was not envisaged by British tacticians between the wars, and the tight and inflexible vic of three aircraft would now be found wanting. Flight Lieutenant Reg Johnson (who sadly passed away during my research for this story) remembered this of that period: -

I was posted to 222 Squadron in April 1940 at RAF Duxford. I arrived there only to be told that the Squadron had moved to Digby. I arrived there to learn that 222 had moved to Kirton, such was the level of administration in 1940. On joining the Squadron no-one was unkind to me but I was the first RAF Volunteer Reserve pilot (recognisable by my badges) to join this regular Squadron. After about a week I was shown the 'knobs and things' by Sergeant JI Johnson, an ex-Halton apprentice, and sent solo. After successfully landing my engine failed and I was collected in a green MG sports car by Flight Lieutenant Douglas Bader.

I was a member of 'B' Flight and soon learned that 222 Squadron was addicted to tight formation flying, for which I had no training whatsoever. A study of the pre-war career of our CO, Sqyadron Leader Mermagen, might explain this addiction, particularly in flying so tight that our wings overlapped. From Kirton he led us off in squadron formation; three behind three we even looped in formation. We even rolled as a squadron on one occasion. Mermagen was an exceptional pilot but such training was to prove unsuitable for the Battle of Britain that lay ahead, although at the time, of course, he was not to have the benefit of hindsight.

When I joined 222 Squadron in April 1940, Pilot Officer Whitbread was already an established member. During the following weeks and months he proved himself to be a pleasant and friendly young man. We spent many hours together in conversation at Dispersal, and I have a photograph of him beside 'my' Spitfire at dawn readiness, about 4 a.m. on a June morning. We each took each other's picture, despite the light at that early hour being poor as we were forbidden cameras so had to take our snaps in secret.

Sergeant Reg Johnson and Spitfire, snapped at Kirton by Pilot Officer Whitbread.

Pilot Officer Whitbread and Spitfire, snapped less well by Sergeant Johnson!

Pilot Officer Whitbread was also a very good hockey player and spent long periods with his hockey stick dribbling around the aircraft and running around bouncing a ball on his stick. We also spent many hours together flying in squadron training, often wing tip to wing tip. He was much more skilled at tight formation flying than I was at that time.

In our Squadron there was definitely an RAF social barrier between officer and NCO pilots. Pilot Officer Whitbread, whom I never knew as 'Laurie' but always 'Sir', overcame this with his natural charm and was at ease with all ranks. He never lost face because of it and we were firm friends. We enjoyed a number of squadron flying adventures together at Kirton and would later suffer a number together during the Battle of Britain.

Squadron Leader Iain Hutchinson was also a sergeant pilot with 222 Squadron: -

In general I remember Pilot Officer Whitbread as an unassuming, approachable person, without affectation. You will understand that during the time we served together in 222 Squadron I was a sergeant pilot whilst Laurie Whitbread was commissioned. Therefore there was only a very limited opportunity for an association between each group. Nevertheless there was less 'side' in Laurie's relationships than there was with other officers. I should emphasise, however, that within the constraints imposed by differences in rank there was still an excellent spirit in the Squadron.

The only incident in which I was involved with Pilot Officer Whitbread occurred on August 10th, 1940. An intruder was detected by the forward radar station and he and I were scrambled to intercept. We taxied out at speed, Laurie leading and me following. I was swinging the nose of my Spitfire from side to side, according to the relevant rules, to ensure that I could see ahead as the nose blocked out a large sector of forward view. When I swung the nose right I suddenly saw the tail of Laurie's machine ahead of me, stopped! Despite heavy braking and evasive action I was unable to clear his aircraft and my wing demolished his tail.

I also recall that one night a raider attacked the Scunthorpe steel works and Laurie was sent up to intercept. Unfortunately the fighter controllers were apparently unable to get their act together and we watched frustrated as we heard the bomber droning on a western approach to its target whilst Laurie was vectored in the opposite direction.

After the danger and excitement of Dunkirk, the flying at Kirton that August must have been dull, especially with 11 Group's squadrons being so heavily engaged over southern England. By that time, Squadron Leader Mermagen had been sent to temporarily command 266 Squadron at Wittering before being promoted and posted to command RAF Station Speke. His successor as CO of 222 Squadron was Squadron Leader John Hill, to whom it would fall to lead the Squadron during its turn in the combat zone.

On August 29th, an uncharacteristically quiet morning permitted Fighter Command to rotate and rest several squadrons. Amongst the latter was 264, a Defiant unit decimated whilst flying from Hornchurch and whose place in the line was taken by 222 Squadron. The following day, Hill's Spitfires were scrambled to patrol Gravesend. 'B' Flight soon contacted 10 Me 109s north-west of Dover. No general combat ensued but Sergeant Hutchinson was shot at from behind and forced landed a mile from the airfield. Reg Johnson: -

In the first 48 hours that 222 Squadron was at Hornchurch we lost 18 aircraft and a number of pilots. We proceeded to go into action in tight formation and our losses were heavy. Eventually we evolved a weaving 'Tail End Charlie' section, Green Section, which weaved about above, below and to the Squadron's rear (still in tight formation). It helped. I was made a permanent member of Green Section, with Pilot Officer Whitbread and one other, and we were given the job to do.

According to the 222 Squadron diary, on August 30th, 1940, 'the Squadron was very positively engaged in operations and flew three patrols during the day. Sergeant JI Johnson was killed. Flight Lieutenant Matheson and Flying Officer Edridge were wounded.' During the three separate actions fought that day, 222 Squadron lost six Spitfires destroyed and three damaged. In response, Flight Lieutenant Robinson had probably destroyed an Me 109, Pilot Vigors a 110 destroyed, Pilot Officers Davis and Cutts an He 111, and Squadron Leader Hill an Me 109 damaged.

August 31st saw Fighter Command suffer the heaviest losses of any day during the Battle of Britain. During the day's first patrol by 222 Squadron, Pilot Officer Whitbread flew Spitfire L1010 and patrolled base uneventfully at 25,000 feet. Laurie flew the same Spitfire on the next sortie, which was flown from the forward field at Rochford: 222 Squadron was vectored to intercept bombers and their fighter escort 26,000 feet over Gravesend. 222 Squadron attacked the 109s, Pilot Officer Vigors claiming one destroyed and another as a probable. Later, Pilot Officer Whitbread and 10 other 222 Squadron Spitfires patrolled Canterbury at 20,000 feet. Over Maidstone 24 Me 109s protecting a formation of He 111s were Tally Ho'd, the ensuing combat concluding very much in the Spitfires' favour: several of the enemy were shot down, against the loss of two Spitfires, the pilots of which were safe. Pilot Officer Whitbread reported his combat, which took place at 1.30 p.m., 16,000 feet over Sittingbourne: -

I manoeuvred until the Me 109 appeared in my sights, the enemy aircraft climbing slowly away not having seen me. I fired at about 400 yards and rapidly closed to within 50 yards, when I could see the bullets entering the fuselage from tail to cockpit. The 109 half rolled onto its back and remained at that attitude, flying quite slowly with a little white smoke issuing from it. It eventually nosed down slowly when I was obliged to lose sight of it having noticed an aircraft approaching my tail which turned out to be a Spitfire.

This enemy machine was possibly one of 1/JG 77, which crashed between Walderslade and Boxley; the pilot, *Unteroffizier* Keck, baled out and was captured.

The next few days followed an identical pattern, with numerous scrambles and interceptions being made by 222 Squadron. On September 7th, the Germans bombed London round the clock, and by 4.30 p.m. all 21 Fighter Command squadrons based with 71 miles of London were airborne. Pilot Officer Whitbread later wrote the following of his combat, which took place at 27,000 feet over the capital: -

We engaged an enemy formation of Me 109s. I became separated from the rest of the Squadron so climbed back to my original altitude and flew round looking for a target. I found one in a formation of 25-30 Do 215s which appeared to have no fighter escort. Keeping in the sun I dived down on the last aircraft which was straggling behind some 100 yards at the rear of the formation and flying at 20,000 feet. I carried out a quarter attack from the port side (formation was flying westwards along south bank of the Thames at Dartford). I opened fire at 300 yards, range closing rapidly. The starboard engine set on fire and I broke away, the return fire from the three rear gunners and my closing range making this advisable.

By the end of that day, 306 civilians had been killed and 1,337 Londoners injured. The reader should note that this was long before RAF Bomber Command and the American 8th Air Force pounded German cities, and we must not forget that the Germans had also reduced the defenceless town of Guernica to rubble during the Spanish Civil War. Current German condemnation of Bomber Command's offensive seems to conveniently forget the basic and undeniable fact that it was the *Luftwaffe* which began indiscriminately bombing civilian populations as a legitimate means of waging war.

September 8th was a quieter day after the massive enemy assault of the previous 24 hours, and 222 Squadron was not engaged. The following afternoon, however, saw 222 Squadron in action over Ashford. Pilot Officer Whitbread: -

Whilst on patrol over east Kent we sighted a formation of enemy bombers flying west at 20,000 feet, above cloud. It had an escort of Me 109s, flying above and behind at 26,000 feet, and also another formation of fighters flying to one side, at the same height as the bombers. The fighters were engaged. I had a combat with an Me 109. A burst of roughly four seconds from my guns appeared to shoot off the starboard aileron when the 109 went into a spin. It continued to spin downwards into the cloud layer where it disappeared rom view. My flight leader stated that he had observed the 109 spin down and also the pilot baling out.

In his diary, Laurie wrote: 'One Me 109 claim. Confirmed by Van Mentz.' The enemy fighter belonged to 6/JG 27 and crashed at Beneden; *Unteroffizier* Georg Rauwolf baled out and was captured.

The pathos of action remained constant over the next few days. On September 14th, Laurie wrote to his mother from the Officers' Mess at RAF Hornchurch: -

Dear Mother

Thank you for your letter, received this morning. How nice to have Rex and Doris, and Colin at home together. I am disappointed that I won't be there too. Fancy Ludlow having some bombs!

Everything is going fine down here. We get far less to do now that the weather has broken. There is no sign of us leaving this station yet, so I doubt that I will get any leave until things quieten down again.

I am keeping fit – except that I got a touch of frostbite in the left hand last week. Its better now except from a large blister on the thumb.

Mother, would you see if I've left my RAF navy blue blazer at home? I don't want it but can't find it here. Please tell me in the next letter. I do hope I haven't lost it.

Love to all, Cheerio, Laurie.

The reference to 'frostbite' requires some clarification, as a previously published account states that this was because Pilot Officer Whitbread had been sleeping in his Spitfire (so as to be immediately available at dawn). The truth is, however, that September nights are just not that cold, so the 'frostbite' was actually caused by intense cold whilst flying at high altitude.

As for 'getting far less to do', the next day, September 15th, has gone down in history as 'Battle of Britain Day', the whole fury and might of the enemy being thrown repeatedly at London. On that great day, Pilot Officer Whitbread's Spitfire, N3023, ZD-R, was unserviceable, necessitating in him flying it from Rochford to Hornchurch for repair.

In his diary on September 18th, Laurie wrote 'Seven days leave start?', but none was forthcoming. Instead of travelling home to see his sweetheart, Jane, Pilot Officer Whitbread was patrolling over Canterbury in Spitfire P9878. He did not fly the following day but his usual mount, N3023, was serviceable for September 20th.

By this time the back of the German offensive had been broken, although fierce fighting continued. In a few days time the He 111 would be completely withdrawn from daylight operations as the German bomber fleet concentrated its efforts on safer night bombing. Enemy fighter sweeps, however, had failed to provoke the required response, RAF Controllers recognising that these incursions were no threat unless fighters were scrambled to intercept, so chose instead to let the Germans waste their fuel. This was a disappointment to the enemy fighter pilots who had for so long been frustrated by having to provide close bomber escort. The opportunity to roam freely, hunting prey, was most welcome, but morale took a further plunge when Göring ordered that one *staffel* in each *gruppe* would re-equip as a fighter-bomber unit. Such a statistic represented a significant one third of the available German fighter force, and not surprisingly the majority of senior fighter leaders disagreed with such a move given that the force was already too weak to achieve aerial supremacy over England. At operational level everything had been done to wring extra performance out of the 109s, but instead of being given the long range auxiliary fuel tanks requested for so long, SC250 bombs arrived instead. The tactical thinking, however, was that if the fighter formations contained fighter-bombers, which could not be identified by radar, the RAF Controllers would have to consider every sweep a threat and respond accordingly.

On Friday September 20th, 1940, for the first time, 22 Me 109 fighter-bombers of II/ LG 2, protected by numerous fighters, took off from the Pas-de-Calais bases, London bound. Between Calais and Dover the Germans climbed to 25,000 feet before swooping down on the capital. Believing the enemy sweep to be no threat, Fighter Command's squadrons were kept on the ground, permitting the fighter-bombers to reach London umolested. Diving to 22,000 feet and pressing the bomb release switch, the *Jabo* pilots had already turned for home when their bombs exploded in the City of London and on a rail terminus west of the Thames's great bend. Listening to the British radio frequencies, German intelligence reported a great confusion of orders and counter-orders after the 'fighters' had dropped their bombs.

After the first wave of 'Tip n'run' raiders had caused confusion, a second wave was reported incoming over the Kent coast at 14,000 feet. Unbeknown to the RAF controllers, there were no fighter-bombers in this formation, so the Biggin Hill and Hornchurch Spitfire squadrons were scrambled. 222 and 603 Squadrons were up from Hornchurch at 10.55 a.m., but as they desperately climbed for height over the Thames Estuary, the 109s fell on them. The first Spitfire pilot to fall in action that day was Pilot Officer Whitbread. Reg Johnson: -

My vivid memory is that this sortie was a 'B' Flight commitment only, led by Pilot Officer Broadhurst in Blue Section, followed by Pilot Officer Whitbread, myself and another in Green Section. We climbed to the suicidal height of 14,000 feet and stooged around in tight formation with only one pair of eyes available to scan the sky in front, perhaps over 200 degrees. I do not think that we deserved to be jumped, but we were certainly inviting it. We were banking gently to the left, which allowed me at No 3 to look over the top of No 1, and I shouted the warning "Bandits! 2 o'clock above – attacking!" I turned over and dived straight down. There is no way that Pilot Officer Whitbread could even have seen the enemy, formatting as he was on the aircraft to his left and with three-quarters of his head and back to the attackers. When I left it was his right side facing the 109s, which were already in firing range. I can only assume that having received my warning he too rolled to his right, exposing his left side to the enemy and was hit before his dive commenced.

It was a tragedy.

Spitfire N3203 crashed at 11.15 a.m. in the garden of Pond Cottage, Hermitage Road. Higham, near Rochester in Kent. The occupant, a Mrs Perry, wrote to Pilot Officer Whitbread's father: -

Your son died a great hero. He had three German planes firing all around him and his machine was riddled with bullet holes. It appears he was trying to bale out as he was out of his seat. My husband, who was in the garden, ran to the Spitfire to see if he could be of any help, but the pilot was lying outside the plane. He must have been trying to bale out as the Germans caught him down his left side – he must have then fallen back into the cockpit and came down with the plane as it bumped across the ground, or maybe he got stuck in the plane whilst coming down. Either way he was thrown clear upon impact. He lay just outside the plane and must have died instantly. He did not suffer, so please tell his mother. I know this is very soon after your great grief but perhaps it will help you with a little relief knowing that he did not linger on a suffer after his injury. Will it help you if I say that if I have to lose one of my own boys then I hope that they go the same way. It would be awful if he had endured weeks of suffering only for the Lord to call. I hope God will give us the means to overcome these murderers. I feel sure that your son will not have given his life in vain. It was an awful feeling when the Spitfire was coming down. It gave me an awful shock especially as I thought that it was coming down on my house, but we felt more than sorry when we found that your son was dead. My husband covered him up until the ambulance arrived to take him to the mortuary. Where we live is between the Thames

Estuary and the south-east, so if the Germans try to get to London from either direction we witness the full force of the fighting. We had another plane almost on us today, it crashed in the field in front of our house.

Pond Cottage.

When initially researching this story some years ago, I believed that Pilot Officer Whitbread had been shot down by *Oberleutnant* Hans Hahn, of II/JG 2. More recent research, however, suggests that 'B' Flight of 222 Squadron could equally have been attacked by none other than Major Adolf Galland, *Kommodore* of JG 26 and one of the *Luftwaffe's* foremost *experten*, who shot down a Spitfire in a diving pass. After the initial bounce, 'B' Flight re-formed only to be attacked again, losing two more Spitfires, although both pilots were safe. In such confused circumstances, involving so many enemy fighters, it is impossible to be absolutely certain who was responsible for bringing Laurie Whitbread down, but Galland does appear to be another strong contender.

By the time the Me 109s withdrew, only one of their number remained behind in a foreign field. Fighter Command, however, had lost four pilots killed and several wounded. 222 Squadron's Sergeant Norman Ramsay made this observation regarding his personal attitude to losses at that time: -

People missing or killed at that stage of the battle meant little or nothing to me. I had joined 222 from 610 at Biggin Hill after we had lost 10, yes 10, pilots, so I was well used to disappearing faces. Having been shot down myself I had learned to survive, to get the experience necessary for survival.

Pilot Officer Geoffrey Wellum of 92 Squadron adds: -

On September 20th, 1940, I flew two patrols in Spitfire K9998. After this length of time I can recall nothing of the action, but do remember that during September and October the 109s were always in the Biggin Hill Sector, and caused problems. I recall that they were always above us as we never seemed to be scrambled in time to get enough height. Our climb was always a desperate, full throttle affair, but we never quite got up to them. I did manage to get a crack at two Me 109s on one patrol but although I saw strikes I could only claim them as damaged.

It is perhaps characteristic that Laurie Whitbread had arranged that in the event of his death on active service the official telegram arising should not be delivered directly to his mother but to the Rev. Hulbert, and whose duty it would then be to break the sad news. On October 3rd, 222 Squadron's CO, Squadron Leader John Hill, wrote to Mr Whitbread: -

It is with deep regret that I have to write to you from 222 Squadron and offer our sympathy in the very sad loss of your son.

He was killed instantly by a bullet from an enemy aircraft when doing his bit in the defence of our country. His passing is a great loss to us; he has been in the Squadron since its formation and was always most popular, having a quiet and efficient disposition and charming manner.

Reg Johnson remembered what happened, and why, literally minutes before passing away himself, 43 years later: -

From my now very senior years I remember Pilot Officer Whitbread as a brave man of the highest quality. Naturally courageous, he was always prepared to give his life for his country, but it was taken away from him due to the practice of unsatisfactory tactics.

For me personally it was a great privilege to be a member of 222 Squadron, with which I completed 101 operational sorties. I was shot down twice and parachuted twice, and wounded once. From being the junior reserve pilot I soon became the senior NCO pilot due to my incredible good fortune.

Reg certainly was fortunate: during the Battle of Britain 222 Squadron lost nine pilots killed in action.

Pilot Officer Whitbread was the first Ludlovian to lay down his life in World War Two, and that fact hit the small rural community hard. As a mark of respect he was laid to rest in the local cemetery with full military honours. Annually, St Laurence's church, in the town centre, is illuminated in his honour every September 20th, and a road in Ludlow has been named after this gallant 26-year old.

To me, Laurie Whitbread epitomises that generation of young men who volunteered to defend their country in its hour of need, all possessed of intelligence and tremendous potential. The world, there can be no doubt, is a poorer place for their passing. Laurie's old school master, George Merchant, attended the funeral, and it is to him that we give the last word: -

So we turned and went back and left him alone in his glory, with his name and rank on the gravestone and proud badge of the Royal Air Force that he had carried through peril to the stars.

For some reason I think of him as typical of those 50 boys from the school who died in the same way, a kind of symbol of what they were and what they did and why. I hope nobody will think I have singled him out from the others, it means that I regard them as having done anything less or deserving less to be remembered. He was just the kind of boy you noticed first and remembered afterwards if you saw him talking in a group of his fellows, though he was probably saying less than any of the others.

He was the kind of boy one does not forget and is glad to have known.

Laurie Whitbread's grave on the day of his funeral.

Chapter Four

Pilot Officer 'Robin' Rafter

Pilot Officer William Pearce Houghton Rafter's story typifies the experience of young replacement pilots, with limited training and experience, pitched into the crucible of combat during the Battle of Britain.

Known by his family as 'Robin', this tragic casualty was born on July 17th, 1921, the son of Sir Charles and Lady Rafter whose home was at Elmley Lodge in Old Church Road, Harbourne, Birmingham. Sir Charles was Chief Constable of the Birmingham City Police and served for 37 years; he died in 1935, being survived by his wife, eldest son Charles, Robin, and the boys' elder sister, Elizabeth. When Sir Charles passed away, Robin was at Shrewsbury School, moving to Cheltenham College the following year. At school he was an enthusiastic sportsman, excelling at cricket, rugby, football, squash and swimming. His education complete, on June 26th, 1939, the 18-year old was given a Short Service Commission in the RAF and accepted for flying training.

Robin's *ab initio* flying training was undertaken on Tiger Moths at No 6 Civilian Flying School at Sywell in Northamptonshire. There he achieved his civilian flying licence before moving on to No 12 FTS at Grantham in Lincolnshire on September 2nd, 1939 – just one day before Britain and France declared war on Nazi Germany. Two days after war broke out Robin was transferred to No 10 FTS at Ternhill, in Shropshire, where he was authorised to wear the coveted pilot's brevet on November 3rd, 1939. The 19-year old pilot passed his final exam with 64% and was assessed thus: 'Ground subjects a poor average. Navigation and airmanship weak. A safe pilot but lacks polish. A keen average officer'.

It is a fact that between the wars strategic thinking always supported the view that 'the bomber will always get through'; fighters were considered to be of limited value, even for defence, and yet the role of army co-operation flying was considered essential. Fighter Command was actually responsible for training pilots to serve in such squadrons, and instruction was provided at the School of Army Cooperation at Old Sarum in Wiltshire, which had existed since the Great War. In 1939, the object was to train replacement crews for tactical reconnaissance squadrons flying the twin-engine Bristol Blenheim; shortly after the war started many of these units were sent out to France with the BEF's Air Component. Anticipating the likely need for replacement pilots, a reserve pool was added to the school at Old Sarum, the combined output of which was 72 pilots, 37 observers and 72 air gunners on a six week course which included 40 hours of flying. The school's aircraft establishment was increased to 12 Lysanders, 12 Hectors, 12 Ansons and 15 Blenheims. The site at Old Sarum consequently became too small, and the school was therefore divided: single-engine types remaining there (No 1 School of Army Co-operation) whilst twins went to Andover (No 2 School). No 1 School trained 20 pilots and 20 air gunners per fortnight on a fortnightly course, whilst No 2's course remained six weeks.

Pilot Officer Rafter was posted to No 2 School at Andover on February 1st, 1940, where he completed the twin-engine course before reporting to No 1 School on March 17th. Unfortunately Robin's pilot's flying log book has not survived, but from the logs of other pilots we know that flying exercises on the Lysander including 'pinpointing ponds, photography and vertical pinpoints'.

Now a fully-fledged Army Cooperation pilot, on April 26th, 1940 Pilot Officer Rafter reported for duty at Andover, where he was engaged on supply flights until May 7th. On that day, together with Pilot Officers McCandlish, Tuppin and Walsh, Robin joined his first squadron, No 225, at Odiham. Three days later Hitler attacked the west; by June 3rd, the French and Belgian armies had collapsed, the British forced to retire on and be evacuated from Dunkirk. On June 10th, 225 Squadron moved to operate from Old Sarum, conducting a significant amount of dawn and dusk flying. Robin Rafter's first operational flight was made on between 2030 – 2230 hrs on June 27th, in Lysander N1315, in company with LAC Howes. This 'coastal recco' of St Albans and Selsey Bill was uneventful except for a destroyer, six miles south of Ventnor, which gave no reply when challenged. On July 1st, the Squadron moved to Tilshead. During that month Robin flew six more similar patrols, with LACs Howes and Parr, all of which were uneventful, as were the two operational sorties he made in August.

By this time, however, the Battle of Britain was in full swing, and Fighter Command's casualties were a serious issue. The number of replacements required exceeded the ability of OTUs to produce pilots, even though the courses were cut back to the absolute bare minimum in terms of time and content, so Air Chief Marshal Dowding appealed to other RAF commands and the Fleet Air Arm for help. So it was that on August 22nd, 1940, Flying Officer Hallam and Pilot Officers Rafter answered the call and left 225 Squadron to fly Spitfires at 7 OTU, Hawarden. Their No 6 Course comprised 34 officers, six American officers and four NCO pilots, and three students being re-coursed due to injury.

It is interesting to compare the flying experience of Flying Officer Hallam and Pilot Officer Rafter at this point. The former was 23 and had been commissioned and learned to fly in 1937. After service flying training Pilot Officer Ian Hallam reported to No 2 Army Cooperation Squadron at Hawkinge on April 30th, 1938. By the time his unit moved to France on October 6th, 1939, therefore, Hallam was an experienced pilot who remained on the continent until his squadron was withdrawn in May 1940. In July he joined, on temporary attachment, the Photographic Reconnaissance Unit based at Heston, where he was able to gain air experience on such aircraft as the Spitfire, Harvard, Hornet Moth, Wellington and Hudson. On August 7th, Flying Officer Hallam reported to 225 Squadron and which time he would have met Pilot Officer Rafter. Hallam's logbook indicates that at that time he had over 500 hundred hours experience on single-engined aircraft *alone*; a study of comparable logbooks suggests that Rafter would have had such an amount in *total*. Moreover, Hallam had already logged six Spitfire hours at Heston; for Rafter such an experience at Hawarden would be completely new.

Ian Hallam's logbook indicates that whilst training on Spitfires at Hawarden, he made 14 Spitfire flights between August 23rd and 29th, 1940. These sorties included local familiarisation, formation flying, aerobatics, map-reading, homing practice, No 1 & 5 Attacks, and firing guns into the sea. Upon conclusion of the course, Flying Officer Hallam had accumulated 15 hours on Spitfires, so it is reasonable to assume that Pilot Officer Rafter would have likewise achieved a similar amount of flying time. Originally the operational training course was of four weeks duration, but as the need for replacements increased this was reduced to a fortnight. In reality pilots were passed out when considered competent on type, which was usually between 10 days and three weeks after 10 – 20 hours flying time. Incredibly those hours did not include any air-to-air firing, due to the shortage of both time and ammunition, so dire was the hour. All the OTUs were able to do, therefore, was provide conversion experience to operational type.

Who decided, I wonder, which pilots went to which squadrons? What criteria, if any, was used other than that on paper all were qualified to fly the Spitfire operationally? On August 31st, 1940, Flying Officer Hallam, who, as we have seen was an experienced pilot of several years experience, was posted to 610 'County of Chester' Squadron at Acklington in 13 Group. Based in the north of England 610 Squadron was absorbing replacement pilots and providing further training, so Hallam was able to record a further 21.05 Spitfire flying hours, before being posted south, to 222 'Natal' Squadron in 11 Group, on October 1st. The inexperienced Pilot Officer Robin Rafter, however, was posted straight from Hawarden into the traumatic combat zone to join a heavily engaged squadron in the thick of battle. Whose pen, I wonder, made that stroke and would it not, perhaps, have made common sense to send Flying Officer Hallam south from Hawarden and Pilot Officer Rafter north? On paper, though, both were qualified pilots and that appears to have been the only consideration when postings were chosen.

On Saturday August 31st, 1940, just over a week since reporting at Hawarden to fly Spitfires, Flying Officer BR MacNamara (also a former Army Co-operation pilot) and Pilot Officers FJ MacPhail and WPH Rafter arrived at Hornchurch Sector Station in Essex, joining 603 'City of Edinburgh' Squadron. The scene greeting them must have been horrendous: on that day, the *Luftwaffe* had bombed various airfields, and the Sector Stations at Hornchurch and Biggin Hill had been hit twice. Some of the battered airfields were rendered close to non-operational. The Hornchurch Station Operations Record Book records a vivid picture of events: -

Mass raids continued to be made against our aerodromes, again starting early in the morning. The first two attacks were delivered at 0830 and 1030 respectively and were directed at Biggin Hill, Eastchurch and Debden. The third attack was delivered at Hornchurch, and although our squadrons engaged, they were unable to break the enemy bomber formation, and about 30 Dorniers dropped some 100 bombs across the airfield. Damage, however, was slight, although a bomb fell on the new Airmen's Mess which was almost completed. The only vital damage, however, was to a power cable, which was cut. The emergency power equipment was brought into operation until repair was effected. Three men were killed and 11 wounded. 54 Squadron attempted to take off during the attack and ran through the bombs. Three aircraft were destroyed, one being blown from the middle of the landing field to outside the boundary, but miraculously all three pilots escaped with only minor injuries.

The fourth attack of the day was also directed at Hornchurch, and once again, despite strong fighter opposition and AA fire, the bombers penetrated our defences. This time, however, their aim was most inaccurate, and the line of bombs fell from them towards the edge of the aerodrome. Two Spitfires parked near the edge of the aerodrome were written off, and one airman was killed. Otherwise, apart from the damage to dispersal pens, the perimeter track and the aerodrome surface, the raid was abortive and the aerodrome remained serviceable. Our squadrons, which had a very heavy day, accounted for no less than 19 of the enemy and a further seven probably destroyed. 603 Squadron alone were responsible for the destruction of 14 enemy aircraft. Although we lost a total of nine aircraft, either on the ground or in combat, only one pilot was lost.

On what was clearly a particularly bitter day of fighting, 603 Squadron was in action four times, not suffering a casualty until the final sortie. At 6.20 pm, Pilot Officer 'Sheep' Gilroy was shot down but baled out safely. Unfortunately his Spitfire crashed into 14 Hereford Road, Wanstead, killing the occupant's pet dog. Over Woolwich, 10 minutes later, an Me 109 of I/JG 3 shot down and killed Flying Officer Waterston. Flying Officer Carbury was more fortunate and returned safely to base after his Spitfire's compressed air system was hit by a 109's 20 mm rounds. The enemy fighters were on a *Freie Hunt*, sweeping over Kent; Flying Officer Carbury, simultaneously with Flight Lieutenant Denys Gillam of Kenley's 616 Squadron, attacked and shot down 2/JG 77's *Staffelkapitän*, *Oberleutnant* Eckhart Priebe who baled out and was captured near Elham. Fighter Command, however, lost a total of 39 pilots during that furiously contested day.

603 Squadron was an Auxiliary unit raised at Turnhouse near Edinburgh in 1925. Having flown Wapiti, Hart, Hind and Gladiator biplanes, in September 1939, by which time the Squadron had been called to full time service, 603 received Spitfires. The Squadron's pre-war pilots were all wealthy individuals who flew for pleasure at the weekends, and personnel comprised both friends and relatives from the local area. After war broke out, 'A' Flight was deployed to Dyce, to afford the Royal Navy some protection, and 'B' Flight at Montrose, where a vulnerable FTS was based, the Squadron therefore being responsible for the great stretch of coastline between the Firth of Tay

and Aberdeen. German aircraft, however, faced a long flight across the inhospitable North Sea to attack targets in Scotland, and so these tended to be probing raids by either single or pairs of bombers. The crucial thing to remember, however, is that these raiders were operating well beyond the range of fighter cover and were therefore unprotected. When northern based squadrons moved south, however, and met 109s, the change in operational conditions could only be described as traumatic. On August 27th, 1940, Squadron Leader 'Uncle' George Denholm led 24 pilots of 603 Squadron south to Hornchurch; only eight would survive the Battle of Britain.

In Scotland, 603 Squadron had been accustomed to keeping just one section of three pilots at readiness; at Hornchurch three *squadrons* were kept at this state throughout daylight hours. In their naivety, some of 603 Squadron's young pilots remained exuberant: Pilot Officer 'Broody' Benson wanted to 'shoot down Huns, more Huns, and then still more Huns!' and was certain that 'Now we'll show the bastards!' Shortly after arrival, 603 Squadron was scrambled; by the end of that first day, two pilots, including Pilot Officer Benson, were dead. There would be no let up, and from the following day onwards half a dozen of the Squadron's pilots would sleep in their dispersal hut as security against a surprise dawn attack. They would rise at 4.30 a.m., on what could well be the last morning of their young and promising lives, and by 5.00 a.m. their Spitfires' engines would shatter the silence as ground crews warmed them up. The first raid usually came in around breakfast time and from then until about 8 p.m. the Squadron was continuously engaged. Bacon, eggs and beans were sent across from the Mess, but pilots ate as and when they could.

Even before 603 Squadron had flown south that fateful August day in 1940, the character of the Auxiliary unit had already started to change. Three RAF Volunteer Reserve pilots had joined the Squadron, the pilots of which had previously been exclusively commissioned officers. Amongst those lowly Non Commissioned Officer pilots was Sergeant Jack Stokoe: -

During my Spitfire training at Aston Down I logged between 10 – 15 flying hours. Fortunately I then went north, to 603 Squadron in Scotland, which meant that I was able to further get to grips with the Spitfire. When we arrived at Hornchurch I was therefore fortunate to have a total of around 70 hours on Spits. Had I gone straight from Aston Down to Hornchurch I would not have rated my chances of survival very highly.

Jack Stokoe was an aggressive and competent fighter pilot who immediately opened his account against the *Luftwaffe*. On August 29th, he flew on four patrols, damaging a 109 but having his own control wires shot away. The following day Jack destroyed a 109 and damaged another, but again his own machine was hit: a cannon shell hit the windscreen and the pilot's left hand was peppered with shrapnel. On September 1st, he sent a 109 down in flames over Canterbury, and damaged to more the next day; Jack Stokoe: -

I was attacking an enemy aircraft and remember machine-gun bullets, or maybe cannon shells, hitting my Spitfire, followed by flames in the cockpit as the petrol tank exploded. I thought 'Christ! I've got to get out of here and *quick*!' I undid the straps and opened the hood, but this turned the flames into a blowtorch. I was not wearing gloves, as during our hasty scramble I had forgotten them, but had to put them back into the flames to invert the Spitfire so that I could drop out (no ejector seats in those days!). I remember seeing sheets of skin peeling off the backs of my hands before I fell out of the aeroplane. I was then concerned regarding whether the parachute would function or whether it had been damaged by fire, but I pulled the ripcord and fortunately it opened perfectly.

I landed in a field, but the Home Guard queried whether I was an enemy agent but a few choice words in English soon convinced them I was genuine! I was then rushed to into the emergency hospital at Leeds Castle, suffering from shock and severe burns to my hands, neck and face.

I was in hospital for six weeks, during which time my parents received a telegram to say that I was 'Missing in Action', such was the confusion of that hectic period. I returned to operational flying six weeks later, on October 22nd.

During those early days of action with 11 Group, 603 Squadron had to learn quickly or be damned. Having fallen prey to the experienced 109 pilots, Squadron Leader Denholm's Spitfire pilots rapidly determined not to let themselves be 'bounced'. 'Uncle George' would fly on a reciprocal of the course given by the Controller, until at 15,000 feet when he would turn the Squadron about, still climbing. This way 603 Squadron often saw the enemy striking inland below them, and, enjoying the advantage of height, were in a perfect position to intercept. Breaking away from the officially accepted vic

Sergeant Jack Stokoe, a spirited and successful Spitfire pilot in spite of being wounded several times.

of three aircraft, Denholm devised a new system whereby a pair of Spitfires would fly together, offering mutual support. Recent research by John Alcorn (see Chapter One) suggests that 603 was actually Fighter Command's top scoring squadron in the Battle of Britain; if this is so, and I for one believe it to be so, George Denholm's tactical awareness and application of original thought must take the lion's share of credit for this accolade. Moreover, unlike many squadron commanders, 'Uncle George' also led his Squadron, virtually without exception, on every sortie during the Battle of Britain, in addition to performing numerous administrative tasks. After an engagement, Squadron Leader Denholm remembered that 'the Squadron would come home either individually or in ones and twos in intervals of about two minutes. About an hour after landing I used to check to see if anyone was missing. Sometimes a phone call would be received from a pilot who had perhaps forced landed elsewhere, or baled out and was safe, which was always news well received. Other times we would be informed by recovery team of the identity of a crashed Spitfire and pilot.' The Oxford undergraduate Pilot Officer Richard Hillary, who had joined 603 Squadron in June 1940, wrote of the attitude towards casualties in his classic first-hand account 'The Last Enemy': 'At the time, the loss of pilots was somehow extremely impersonal; nobody, I think, felt any great emotion as there simply wasn't time for it'.

The day after Sergeant Stokoe went down over Leeds Castle, Pilot Officer Hillary fell victim to *Hauptmann* Erich Bode, *Kommandeur* of II/JG 26, and also dropped from the fight in flames. Miraculously Hillary was thrown clear of his blazing Spitfire and although terribly burned managed to deploy his parachute. Two hours later he was rescued from the Channel by the Margate lifeboat, close to death. Cared for by the remarkable surgeon Sir Archibald McIndoe, Hillary subsequently became a 'Guinea Pig' at East Grinstead's now famous Burns Unit. Tragically his suffering and recovery would be for nothing: whilst training to be a night fighter pilot Hillary would be killed in 1943.

Whilst all of this dangerous drama was going on high over southern England, during the first four days at Hornchurch Pilot Officer Rafter watched his Squadron scramble time and time again, returning all too often with casualties. In 1989, Air Vice-Marshal Harry Hogan, who commanded 501 Squadron throughout the Battle of Britain, told me that 'some of our replacement pilots were straight from OTUs and these we tried to get into the air as soon as possible, to provide a little extra experience, but we were just too tired to give any dogfight practice at all. They were all very green, youngsters who were often completely bewildered and lost in action'. With 603 Squadron so heavily engaged, however, taking casualties in terms of both pilots killed and wounded, and Spitfires either damaged, requiring repair either on site or at a MU, or destroyed, there neither experienced pilots available to train new pilots or aircraft to spare for anything other than operational flying. So it was, therefore, that Pilot Officer Rafter's first flight with 603 Squadron was an operational one.

At 9.34 a.m. on Thursday, September 5th, 1940, Squadron Leader Denholm led 12 Spitfires off from Hornchurch, his three new replacement pilots, including Pilot Officer Rafter, in the formation. The Squadron had been scrambled in response to a major threat approaching Dungeness, where two large German formations crossed the English coast and set a north-westerly course. Squadron Leader Harry Hogan's 501 Squadron was already airborne from Gravesend, and spotted the raiders whilst patrolling between Canterbury and the Kentish coast: 30 Do 17s escorted by 70 Me 109s all incoming at 20,000 feet. Hogan's Hurricanes valiantly charged the 109s, but over Maidstone the two large enemy formations separated into numerous smaller groups, the progress of which the Observer Corps found impossible to plot. One of these smaller raids struck out for Biggin Hill, 30 Me 109s of II/JG 3 weaving 6,000 feet above the bombers. The *Gruppenkommandeur* himself, *Hauptmann* Erich von Selle, was leading the 109s, and in his *Stabschwarm* were two of his main staff officers: *Leutnant* Heinrich Sanneman, the *Gruppe* Technical Officer, and Oberleutnant Franz von Werra, the Adjutant.

Squadron Leader Robin Hood's 41 Squadron had been scrambled from Hornchurch at 9.10 a.m. and vectored to patrol Canterbury. When the Germans crossed the coast and headed north-west, the Squadron was vectored south. The Spitfires were flying high, at 27,000 feet, enjoying the benefit of being 1,000 feet above Von Selle's 109s. Between Maidstone and Romney a flight of Hood's Spitfires fell on the escorting enemy fighters: Flight Lieutenant Norman Ryder damaged a 109, Pilot Officer Ben Bennions hit another, which he later reported having seen 'streaming glycol and going down about eight miles south of Maidstone', and Sergeant Carr-Lewty watched his victim crash into a wood south-east of Canterbury. Flight Lieutenant Webster hit two 109s, the engine of one bursting into flames, but neither were seen to crash; he then attacked another 109 which rolled over and went in near Maidstone. Flying Officer Boyle set about another 109 that was attacking two Spitfires, but only Squadron Leader Hood and Pilot Officer Wallens got through to the bombers, both damaging Do 17s. Seconds after Hood's Spitfires had attacked the 109s, 603 Squadron arrived on the scene and joined the fray (Flight Lieutenant Norman Ryder of 41 Squadron reported having seen 'XT' coded Spitfires during the combat).

Just take a moment to visualise this scene: around 100 fighters in total cutting and thrusting, whirling, twisting and turning in some kind of bizarre but deadly aerial choreography. What was Pilot Officer Robin Rafter's impression of this vivid and incredibly dangerous scene have been, as a mere 19-year old with comparatively limited flying experience and minimal flying hours on Spitfires? Opposing the Spitfires were some of the most experienced and successful combat flyers in the world at that time, do not forget, so the reader will not, I am sure, be surprised to learn that Pilot Officer Rafter lasted just a matter of seconds after joining the fray. He later wrote this awesome account of the action in a letter to his mother: -

Oberleutnant *Franz von Werra.*
Goss/Rauchbach Collection

Well, I was over Kent at a little over 25,000 feet on a lovely morning of the 5th September when I sighted a huge formation of Jerries. I very nearly shot a Spitfire down by mistake, but then saw on the starboard side, underneath me, an Me 109. I got all fixed and started my dive onto the Me 109 and was nearing it when I saw in my mirror a couple of Me 109s on my tail. Well, I took what evasive action I could, but found two a bit of a problem. I started to get away from them when my tail must have been damaged as all movement on the control column was to no avail, thus putting my machine out of control so far as I was concerned. Well, by this time I had a little piece of shrapnel in my leg, and probably owe my life to the fact that my machine was out of control, as the Jerries evidently found difficulty in getting their sights on me as my machine was going all over the place. Luckily I was very high up and it then occurred to me to bale out. My oxygen tube had already become detached, but I had great difficulty in undoing the pin of my harness to loosen myself out of my seat. I eventually got the pin out, but could not get out of the aircraft. By this time the Jerries had ceased firing at me, but I had no idea where I was over. The next part of my experience was rather a miracle. The machine's nose dropped violently, thus having the effect of throwing me forward, the force so great that I went through the canopy, thus unknowingly injuring my head. You can't imagine my surprise! I was then at 15,000 feet and floating about in the air rather like a cork. You will understand why when I explain that instead of diving at 400 mph, I had rapidly slowed down to about 180 mph, as the human body never falls faster, that being the 'terminal velocity'. I then felt so light I had to look to ensure that I was wearing a parachute. Luckily I had given it a slight inspection that morning. I pulled the cord and the 'chute opened up and I breathed once more.

Now the most terrifying experience happened, I floated down right through the aerial battle that was taking place. I came through it without a scratch, but then I noticed an Me 109 coming towards me, and you've no idea what a damned fool you feel suspended in mid-air with an enemy fighter buzzing around you.

Well, he never fired at me, as a Spitfire came along and drove him off; whether he would have done or not cannot be said. Next worry was where I was going to land as there were a lot of trees near. I avoided them and landed in a nice field. My Spitfire, which was new, crashed in a ploughed field some way away. The LDV accosted me with a shotgun as I was wearing my RAF battledress which must have confused them a bit. I was treated by a local first aid post then taken to hospital.

That afternoon they performed a slight operation, stitching up the back of my head, which had a slight cut, and my right cheek, which is invisible now. They also took me the piece of shrapnel from my right leg which entailed a rather deep incision, but I am okay now and had all of the stitches out yesterday. I have been up and about for the last three days. I am coming out at the end of this week and will soon be back to get my own back on the Jerries! There is a saying that you are not a fighter pilot until you have been shot down once. Well, you have nothing more to fret about and you've heard everything there was, and see how simple it all was, and how well I was cared for? I'm still as good as new, with no facial disfigurement. Might even get a few days leave to see you. You must remember that I got off lightly and many more have received worse than me.

It is interesting that only pilots who claimed victories made out after action reports. Those pilots who were shot down, without claiming a kill, did not, and yet their experiences can often be the key to crucial discoveries. Of course actual combat reports became available to the public during the 1970s, and have provided an absolutely crucial reference for historians. The foregoing account, however, as a personal letter from a son to his mother, although preserved remained in the family's private hands and so has never been available in the public domain. Back in 1990, however, a friend of mine with a removal business mentioned that he had recently moved an elderly lady whose 'brother was a Spitfire pilot and she has his bits and pieces'. Swiftly I followed up this lead and was soon in touch with the lady concerned, Mrs Elizabeth

A chunk of Merlin engine recovered from the crash site of the Spitfire Pilot Officer Rafter abandoned on September 5th, 1940.

Barwell, who, it transpired, was Robin Rafter's sister. Amongst the items she had so carefully preserved was the original hand written and a typed copy of her brother's letter, and, so far as I can accurately ascertain, this correspondence had not been shared outside the family. Having read the letter I was interested to see if any 603 Squadron combat reports might suggest who drove off the 109 that was circling Pilot Officer Rafter during his parachute descent. Imagine my delight when I found the following report at the Public Record Office, submitted by Pilot Officer Stapleton: -

I was diving to attack them (the bombers) when I was engaged by two Me 109s. When I fired at the first one I noticed glycol coming from his radiator. I did a No 2 attack and as I fired was hit by bullets from another Me 109. I broke off downwards and continued my dive. At 6,000 feet I saw a single-engined machine diving vertically with no tail unit. I looked up and saw a parachutist coming down circled by an Me 109. I attacked him (the 109) from the low quarter, he dived vertically towards the ground and flattened out at ground level. I then did a series of beam attacks from both sides, and the enemy aircraft turned into my attacks. He finally forced landed. He tried to set his radio on fire by taking off his jacket, setting fire to it and putting it into the cockpit. He was prevented by the LDV.

Now this is where things got really interesting! Pilot Officer Rafter's Spitfire crashed at Marden, in Kent, some 24 miles south-east of Biggin Hill. Three Me 109s forced landed in England as a result of damage sustained during the same action, one at Wichling (32 miles east of Biggin Hill), one at Aldington (16 miles south-east of Wychling) and another at Loves Farm, Winchett Hill, Marden. This enemy fighter came down at 10.10 a.m. and very close to where Rafter's Spitfire crashed. That particular Me 109 is known to have been <+- of Von Selle's II/JG 3 *Stabschwarm*, and the pilot was captured in identical circumstances to those described by Pilot Officer Stapleton. The enemy pilot was none other than *Oberleutnant* Franz von Werra, later to become infamous as the only German prisoner to escape Allied custody.

In 1958, Kendal Burt and James Leasor published their book recounting Von Werra's adventures, 'The One That Got Away', this subsequently being made into a feature film with Hardy Kruger starring as Von Werra. Burt and Leasor, however, incorrectly accredited Von Werra's demise on September 5th, 1940, to Flight Lieutenant Webster of 41 Squadron, who reported having attacked an Me 109 which 'turned over and crashed near Maidstone'. Such a description does not suggest a forced landing, which the authors described Von Werra as having made that day. Other authors have similarly incorrectly accredited Von Werra to Flight Lieutenant Pat Hughes of 234 Squadron, but in reality Hughes is not even a contender given that his action was fought over the Isle of Sheppey, many miles from Marden. Another source correctly credits Pilot Officer Stapleton with shooting down Von Werra, but states that the latter's 109 had already been damaged when attacked by the 603 Squadron pilot. Indeed, that damage, it is claimed, was caused by 41 Squadron's Pilot Officer Bennions, who reported attacking a 109 which he subsequently saw 'streaming glycol and going down eight miles south of Maidstone'. From Stapleton's report, however, there is no doubt that Von Werra's aircraft was not at all damaged when he attacked it; had the 109 been any less than 100% operational I very much doubt that the pilot would be hanging around in the combat area to buzz a parachutist.

My findings were published in 1993, in my third book, 'Through Peril to the Stars' (Ramrod Publications), and, there can be no doubt, was the first time that the correct sequence of events leading up to Von Werra's capture were published. Early in 1994, I traced Squadron Leader Jerry Stapleton himself, who had only very recently returned to live in the UK, as I recall. Prior to our contact the Squadron Leader had absolutely no idea that it was he who had shot down the infamous Franz von Werra, but remembered the combat: 'It was right on the deck. I recall having to shoot carefully so as to avoid hitting people working in the fields'. Naturally Squadron Leader Stapleton was delighted to learn that he had brought down 'The One That Got Away', and I was pleased to provide him with a copy of the combat report he had last seen over 50 years previously.

As for Franz von Werra, after escaping from Allied custody in Canada he resumed operational flying and significantly increased his score over Russia. In August 1941 his unit, I/JG 53, was withdrawn to Holland; on October 25th, whilst leading a *Schwarm* of Me 109Fs on a coastal patrol, Von Werra's engine failed, sending 'The One That Got Away' to a watery grave in the North Sea.

The wounds suffered by Pilot Officer Rafter on September 5th, 1940, led to some weeks recovering in hospital. On October 2nd, he was transferred from Maidstone to the Officers' Hospital at Torquay, where, on October 11th, came devastating news: his elder brother, Pilot Officer Charles Rafter, had been killed when the wing of his 214 Squadron Wellington hit a hangar shortly after take off from Stradishall. Robin returned to home for the funeral, Charles being buried next to the boys' distinguished father in Birmingham.

Squadron Leader Jerry Stapleton at the time he corresponded with the author regarding September 5th, 1940.

On October 29th, 1940, Robin Rafter was discharged from hospital and sent home for a week's leave with his bereaved family. On November 7th, he returned to RAF Hornchurch, although still categorised as 'non effective, sick' and unable to fly. He was considered fit on November 26th and reported back to 603 Squadron, which was still at Hornchurch.

The Battle of Britain was now over; by the end of September 1940, the German bomber force had been unable to any longer sustain such heavy losses at the hands of Fighter Command, so was withdrawn from the daylight battle. At night, however, the enemy bombers were able to operate with impunity, so embryonic were Britain's nocturnal defences, and the night blitz would claim many lives that winter. The German defeat in the Battle of Britain was largely due to the fact that the bombers were of a medium capacity only, designed to support the army in a tactical capacity, and lacked the range and payload to achieve a strategic decision. Moreover, the Me 109 was designed and

Flying Officer Charles Rafter (left) & Pilot Officer Robin Rafter leaving Elmley Lodge after their last home leave together.

intended as a short range defensive fighter, not as a long range escort fighter, and was completely unsuited, therefore, to the role into which it was pressed during the summer of 1940. Given these factors and the onset of winter weather, unsuitable for a seaborne invasion, Hitler had to accept that the opportunity to invade in England had passed. In February 1944, *Hautpmann* Otto Bechtle, the Operations Officer of KG 2, gave a lecture in Berlin regarding the air war against England 1940-43. Failure in the Battle of Britain was due, he maintained, to one factor: 'the enemy's power of resistance was stronger than the medium of attack'. 'Churchill's Few' had, therefore, given Hitler his first reversal of the war, and by maintaining the British Isles as the last bastion of freedom in the west kept the spirit of and hope for democracy alive.

Pilot Officer Robin Rafter posing with a painting of his late father, Sir Charles (who died in 1935), whilst home for his brother's funeral.

When Pilot Officer Rafter returned to active duties, although the crisis had passed, the threat had not. By day German fighters continued to sweep over southern England and, due to the inclusion of fighter-bombers in their formations, could not be ignored by Fighter Command. The RAF pilots found themselves mounting standing patrols from dawn to dusk, and many survivors would actually recall this period as the most exhausting.

On November 29th, 1940, Pilot Officer Rafter made his second operational flight with 603 Squadron. Squadron Leader Denholm led nine Spitfire Mk IIAs south-east at 9.50 a.m. Off Ramsgate the Squadron Tally Ho'd a lone Me 110 of *Stab*/StG.1 engaged on a reconnaissance flight. The 603 Squadron's Operations Record Book comments that the Spitfire pilots 'were frustrated as being in search of bigger game'. Nevertheless Denholm's Spitfires virtually used the hapless enemy machine for target practice, and its destruction was subsequently shared between all nine pilots. The 110 soon crashed into the sea, killing the pilot, *Oberleutnant* Pytlik, whose gunner, *Oberleutnant* Fryer, remains *vermisst*.

After the action, 603 Squadron returned to Hornchurch at low altitude. Flying at 2,500 feet, however, Pilot Officer Peter Olver was shocked to see Pilot Officer Rafter's Spitfire, P7449, suddenly drop out of formation and crash in a meadow at Kingswood, Sutton Valence, Kent; there was no parachute. Many years later, Peter wrote and told me that 'I do remember Rafter, mostly I expect because of the horror I felt at him flying to the deck for no apparent reason. In those days if a pilot failed to return, you could usually be 100% certain that an Me 109 had sneaked up unseen, but during this operation there had actually been no such enemy fighters in the area'. According to Group Captain Denholm 'I can only vaguely recall Pilot Officer Rafter, probably because he was with us for such

Pilot Officer Peter Olver.

a very short time, but I cannot recall his accident. After an action the Squadron never returned to base as a cohesive unit, but ones and twos, so the only witness to the crash would have been whoever was flying with him. Cases like this were often due to the oxygen system failing, causing the pilot to black out, but Rafter would have had no need to use oxygen at such a low altitude.'

So what caused the crash? Could Rafter's Spitfire have been damaged by return fire from Pytlik's Me 110? This is possible, but had the young pilot known that his machine had been damaged, surely he would have reported this over the radio after the action? Perhaps, then, the Spitfire was damaged without the pilot's knowledge? That being so, and if the pilot was uninjured, why did he not shout up over the R/T that he had lost control of his aircraft? Why did he not bale out? So many questions, but Robin Rafter's (sadly now late) sister, Elizabeth Barwell, believed she had the answer: -

I have always been of the opinion that Robin blacked out as a result of the head injury sustained on September 5th. He was still not 100%, in my opinion, but was so keen to get back to his squadron and into the air again. I will always be absolutely convinced that this was the case.

Ironically, on the eve of Pilot Officer Rafter's death, 603 Squadron held a dinner party at the Dorchester Hotel to celebrate its successes against the enemy.

The 19-year old Pilot Officer Robin Rafter was buried with his father and brother in Birmingham. In more recent times their graves were seriously damaged in an act of mindless vandalism.

All that now remains: Pilot Officer Rafter's 'wings', medals, photographs and the all-important letter written from Maidstone Hospital after he was shot down on September 5th, 1940. These items were given to the author by the pilot's sister, Mrs Elizabeth Barwell, who has sadly since died.

*The grave of Sir Charles Rafter and his pilot sons at
Harborne Church, Birmingham.*

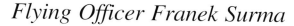
Chapter Five

Flying Officer Franek Surma

Francizsek Surma was born on July 1st, 1916, at Rybnik, in the Galcowicz district of Poland. His parents, Francizsek and Tekla Surma were peasant farmers and had three daughters, all of whom were older than 'Franek' and doted on the baby of their family. A clever boy, Franek won a scholarship to attend the grammar school at Galkowicz and of which the Surmas were justly proud. A model son, even after long days of studying Franek would always help out on the farm. In 1928 he continued his education in Zory, and at that time decided to become a pilot. Eight years later he enlisted in the Polish Air Force and volunteered for aircrew training. According to his personal air force file, Franek Surma was passed as category 'A' fit for duty, and considered 'very physically fit and an excellent mathematician.'

Every Polish service pilot also had to complete basic infantry training, so although Cadet Surma was on the strength of the Air Force Officer Cadet Training School at Deblin, he completed his infantry experience with No 4 Company of the Polish Infantry Cadet School. That complete, Franek started *ab initio* flying training in July 1937. By April 1939, he was a Cadet Staff Sergeant, and at Deblin his flying instructor was Joseph Szlagowski, who was featured on the excellent documentary 'Churchill's Few' in 1980.

In July 1939, Officer Cadet Surma received his 'wings', a silver eagle clutching a laurel wreath, and his file at that time records that he was 'well above the average both physically and intellectually. He shows initiative and enthusiasm, and is a good example to his comrades to whom he displays maximum loyalty'. Posted to the Krakow Squadron, Surma flew the little P.11c fighter: a dream had come true.

Franek Surma in his Polish Air Force uniform at his niece's christening shortly before the outbreak of WW2.

On Friday, September 1st, 1939, peace was shattered when Hitler invaded Poland with 63 divisions, the spearhead of which comprised no less than 15 *panzer* divisions. The Germans enjoyed the benefits of modern technology and tactics whilst the 56 Polish divisions responded with the equipment and thinking of 1925. Both armies were largely horse drawn, but the Poles even had horses in the front line: sabre brandishing cavalry against steel *panzers*! The struggle would be bitter but brief, and could only end in defeat for the gallant Poles. In the air it was the same: totally obsolete Polish fighters and bombers were decimated by modern enemy combat machines. After two weeks the Polish Air Force had taken some 90% losses in both aircraft and aircrew, and was consequently unable to continue operations. On September 17th, what Polish aircraft remained serviceable were flown across the border into neutral Roumania, and many Polish Air Force personnel also managed to escape. The original plan was to train the Poles in Roumania on British aircraft types, but as both German and Russian influence in that country was so strong this proved impossible. Leaving the Roumanians to their fragile neutrality, the Poles travelled westwards, the majority by boat and via Constanza, Beirut, Malta and Marseilles.

In France, Lyon was made the central collecting area for the free Poles, and in March 1940 Polish pilots began being absorbed into French Air Force squadrons. Although the French aircraft types were superior to those in which the Poles had met the Nazis over Poland, they were still inferior to the German machines. Having struck against the west on May 10th, 1940, the Germans dominated the battle, both on the ground and in the air. Again the hapless Poles found themselves on the losing side and were again forced to flee, this time across the Channel to England. No possible means of escape from the continent was overlooked by the Poles, whose only aim was to remain free and eventually liberate their homeland. In Britain, Blackpool became the central collecting point for the Poles, where slowly administration managed to review the status of escapees and ensure that no 'Fifth Columnists' were amongst them. Fortunately pilots with combat experience, including Franek Surma, had made it safely to England; as Fighter Command's losses increased their services would soon be sorely needed by the RAF.

Franek Surma's route to England in 1940 was via Roumania, Syria and France. He was initially billeted at No 51 Pool, Eastchurch, where his combat experience marked him out for immediate posting to No 6 OTU at Sutton Bridge. There Pilot Officer Surma of the Royal Air Force, as he now was, learned to fly the Hawker Hurricane. The difficulties, however, for these Polish exiles must have been immense, not least having to learn a new language spoken both on the ground and in the air. The language barrier, particularly regarding the Poles and Czechs, was of great concern to Air Chief Marshal Dowding. Although by the summer of 1940 there were two Polish and two Czech squadrons in Fighter Command, albeit with British commanding officers and administrators, the language difficulty stayed Dowding's hand in committing them to the fray. On August 30th, 1940, however, Flying Officer Ludwik Paskiewicz destroyed a German bomber whilst on a training flight, as a result of which his Squadron, No

303 based at Northolt, was declared fully operational; the other three foreign squadrons were swiftly added to the board.

By that time, the experienced foreign pilots chosen for early RAF flying training, like Pilot Officer Surma, were also starting to reach the squadrons. On August 20th, Surma reported to North Weald, where he flew Hurricanes with 151 Squadron, a regular RAF unit that had already fought determinedly during the Battle of France and early stages of the Battle of Britain. The young Pole's first operational flight was on August 25th, when his Flight was deployed to operate from the forward base at Rochford. Five days later he opened his account against the *Luftwaffe*, claiming an He 111 'probable' over the Thames Estuary. On September 1st, 151 Squadron was taken out of the line, having suffered 11 pilots killed during the Battle of Britain alone, and flew north to Digby. After a period of leave it was decided that the Squadron's two Poles, Pilot Officers Surma and Jan Orzechowski, being fresh to the fray, should report to 607 'County of Durham' Squadron based at Tangmere.

607 Squadron was an Auxiliary Air Force unit and had also fought in the Battle of France, taking heavy casualties since returning to the combat zone a few days previously. Having joined 607 on September 10th, Surma made his first operational flight from Tangmere four days later. The Squadron was making up to six sorties a day at this time, which must have been exhausting, and on September 17th, Surma chased an Me 109 off Sergeant Lansdell's tail. Although the Pole managed to get off several quick bursts the enemy fighter made off into cloud. During that action, Pilot Officer Harry Welford was shot down, possibly by *Hauptmann* Neumann of 1/JG 27, but, although slightly wounded, he safely forced landed at Bethersden. In 1988, he remembered 607 Squadron's Polish pilots: -

Jan Orzechowski was a short, stocky and rather serious man. He smoked cigarettes incessantly and used a cigarette holder. The Polish officers tried to strike a certain pose, I suppose, to keep up with us rather casual Britishers. They were extremely good pilots, but quite mad and totally fearless. Franek Surma, who was with me in 'B' Flight, was a bit more relaxed and met us half way, probably because he spoke more English than the others.

An item picked up at Harry Welford's crash site in the 1970s by enthusiast Don Wiltshire.

Harry Welford pictured in 1940, and in 1995, shortly before his death.

On Thursday, September 26th, 1940, the Germans heavily bombed Supermarine's Spitfire factory at Woolston. The defending squadrons were scrambled and battle was soon joined. Heavy combat ensued over the Isle of Wight, Portsmouth and at sea, six – 12 miles south of the Needles, between 3.50 and 4.30 p.m. 607 Squadron arrived on the scene just as the raiders started bombing. After the initial head-on charge, the Squadron was split up and pilots acted independently. Some 15-20 miles out to sea, south of St Catherine's Point, Surma found 15-20 Ju 88s at 15,000 feet: -

I saw a bomber break away from the enemy formation and tried to overtake him. At the same moment I saw an Me 109 gliding down above and behind the Ju 88s. I followed the enemy aircraft for a considerable distance and, when several miles south of St Catherine's Point I made two or three long bursts from 100 – 150 yards on the tail of the enemy aircraft, which immediately went into a dive and crashed into the sea.

Unfortunately, however, the raid on Woolston was a complete success: the Supermarine works were gutted; at least 36 civilian workers were killed and 60 seriously injured. Aircraft production at the site was brought to a standstill that September, but the following month, to the great credit of Supermarine's work force, 139 Spitfires were built in October, compared to the August high of 149.

Harry Welford: -

The Woolston factory after the raid on September 26th, 1940. Compare this to the picture on page 17.

I do recall an amusing anecdote concerning Franek Surma and the events of September 26th, 1940. We had a very intrepid and garrulous fighter pilot in Jim Bazin's 'B' Flight called 'Chatty' Bowen, who seemed to enjoy continued success in combat. Franek envied Chatty's success and wished that he could borrow some of his luck. Chatty was known to carry a stuffed toy elephant as a mascot, and Franek pleaded with and cajoled Chatty into lending it to him for a sortie. After much argument and persuasion from other members of the Flight, Chatty agreed to lend Franek the mascot to fly with, but only on a sortie he was not flying himself. Franek was instructed to return the mascot to Bowen's Hurricane the moment he landed. Later, Surma returned jubilant as he had destroyed a 109, and as promised he returned the mascot to his rigger, who replaced it in the cockpit of Bowen's Hurricane. Chatty, however, just couldn't find the mascot on his next trip and cursed Surma for not returning it. On that sortie Chatty was shot down and it was assumed that his change of luck was due to Surma not having returned the toy elephant. The twist to the tale is that when the salvage team recovered the wreck of Bowen's Hurricane from the Isle of Wight, they discovered the elephant in the cockpit; it was believed that the mascot had fallen from the gunsight and jammed the rudder pedals!

The time that Franek and I were together in 'B' Flight was extremely short, only six days, but the loss of life occurred so rapidly that the experiences of a lifetime could be crammed into a few days. Franek was the sort of chap who was immediately popular and when we had a beer in the evening he would teach us how to say 'Nostravia', which means 'Good health' in Polish. He impressed me. The story about the mascot I probably got second hand off a Squadron chum whilst I was in Ashford hospital, as the incident occurred after I was shot down, but the story is certainly true to the characters of both Chatty and Franek. Before I was wounded Franek was trying to borrow the mascot, and used to infuriate Chatty, who was a senior pilot whilst Surma was very junior, beyond all reason by calling him his 'Lovelee boy'!

Franek Surma, left, tormenting 'Chatty' Bowen at dispersal! Note than Bowen is wearing a German lifejacket, a highly prized trophy.

Franek Surma resting between sorties at 607 Squadron's dispersal.

By October 11th, 1940, 607 Squadron was pulled out of the line, having lost 11 pilots killed that summer. On October 17th, Pilot Officer Orzechowski was posted to the new all Polish 306 Squadron, whilst Pilot Officer Surma went to another RAF fighter squadron, No 46, at Stapleford. He arrived on October 18th, along with several other replacement pilots, but three days later was posted to 257 Squadron at North Weald.

257 Squadron had only been formed at Hendon the previous June. Initially equipped with Spitfires these were soon exchanged for Hurricanes. During the early stages of the Battle of Britain, the Squadron flew from Northolt and suffered heavy casualties. This led to a change in command, and the charismatic Squadron Leader Robert Stanford-Tuck revitalised the Squadron. Reg Nutter was a sergeant pilot at the time, and remembers Tuck: -

I found him to be a very charismatic leader and this, combined with his exceptional combat record, immediately gave one a good deal of confidence in him. His style of leadership contrasted greatly with that of his predecessor, Squadron Leader Harkness. Tuck would make suggestions to the Ground Controller as to how we might be better placed to intercept, but Harkness would follow all instructions explicitly. There is no doubt that before Tuck's arrival the Squadron's morale was at a low ebb; under his leadership, however, there was a tremendous improvement. In many ways he was an individualist, but he would nevertheless go out of his way to give sound advice to other pilots.

On October 28th, Surma engaged an He 111 in an inconclusive combat over Romney and Folkestone. The enemy bomber was credited as a 'probable', but the following day Pilot Officer Surma was not so lucky.

On the afternoon of Tuesday, 29th October, the Me 109 fighter-bombers of II/LG 2 attacked North Weald at low level, supported by JG 26 Me 109 fighters. Flight Lieutenant Peter Brothers was at tea in the Officer's Mess when the raiders struck: -

We all dived under the table! My car, an open 3-litre Bentley, was parked outside and I was livid to find that a near miss bomb had filled it with soil, which took forever to clean out!

As the raid came in, 12 Hurricanes were actually taking off. Sergeant Goodwood's aircraft left the ground but was then slapped back down by a bomb blast; the pilot was burned to death. Flight Lieutenant Blatchford got up safely and engaged, but was hit by a 109 and forced to crash land back at North Weald. The 257 Squadron Intelligence Officer, Flying Officer Geoffrey Myers, described what happened to Pilot Officer Surma: -

Red 2, Pilot Officer Surma, saw the bombs falling as he was taxying over the aerodrome. A bomb exploded on his left hand side as his aircraft was running up. The explosion jerked him, but he took off satisfactorily. He noticed four enemy aircraft flying over our hangar between 4-5,000 feet, and also saw many planes on his right, which he took to be Hurricanes.

When he climbed to about 3,000 feet he heard an explosion in his cockpit, which filled with white smoke. His plane went into a spiral dive, he no longer had control so opened the Perspex. After a moment the Hurricane came out of its dive and levelled out, but soon began diving to starboard. After trying to bring it out of this second dive without success, he attempted to bale out. By this time he had lost height to 1,500 feet. After struggling to get out of the cockpit he baled out at about 1,000 feet and made a safe parachute descent, landing in a tree top near an inn at Matching. After quickly convincing the Home Guard that he was Polish and not German, he was given two whiskies and driven back to the aerodrome. He had lost both of his flying boots when jumping out of the plane, received a black eye but was otherwise unharmed.

Pilot Officer Surma had been shot down by *Hauptmann* Gerhard Schöpfel, *Kommandeur* of III/JG 26.

Shortly before he died in 1987, Wing Commander Stanford-Tuck commented that: -

Of course I knew Franek Surma very well and there are many stories I could tell you of him. He was a wonderful little chap – but wild! He was also a loyal and thoroughly trusty wingman.

The Poles held their Commanding Officer in similar high esteem: Surma presented Tuck with a miniature set of Polish 'wings', which his Poles asked him to wear on his tunic; this he did, until shot down and captured in 1942.

Characteristically, after his lucky escape on October 29th, Pilot Officer Surma was flying again on November 2nd. By that time the Battle of Britain was over, but the opposing fighter forces would continue to clash over the Channel and southern England until the following February, and the night *blitz* continued apparently unchecked.

On November 11th, the Italian Air Force sent 50 aircraft to attack a convoy off Lowestoft. 257 Squadron intercepted and decimated the Breda 20 bombers and CR42 biplanes. Although Surma was not involved, another Pole, Pilot Officer Carol Pniak, actually forced an Italian bomber to surrender and made it land at Woodbridge in Suffolk!

November 1940 continued with more convoy patrols from Martlesham Heath. December saw little activity, the weather causing problems on December 6th: Sergeant Bennet's Hurricane was tipped on its nose by high winds whilst taxying, and Surma, in V7052, stalled on approach to Clacton, landing in a field short of the runway. The verdict was that he had misjudged the wind strength, which was over 40 m.p.h.

On December 16th, 1940, Pilot Officer Surma was posted to 242 Squadron, also flying Hurricanes at Martlesham. This largely Canadian squadron was commanded by Squadron Leader Douglas Bader, who had been given the task of improving morale following the beating suffered by 242 in France. This he did, and the great man subsequently led the Squadron throughout the Battle of Britain. During the winter of 1940/41, however, 242 was also providing aerial cover for Channel convoys, and Pilot Officer Surma flew 17 such routine patrols between December 27th, 1940 – February 28th, 1941. Of the young Polish fighter pilot, Squadron Leader Bader reported 'A very competent fighter pilot who understands English well on the R/T'.

On March 14th, 1941, Pilot Officer Surma took leave of 242 Squadron to join a Polish unit, 308 'City of Krakow' Squadron, which was flying Hurricanes at Baginton, near Coventry. 308 Squadron had been formed at Speke in September 1940, moving to Baginton later that month in order to afford some protection to both Coventry and the Armstrong-Whitworth factory, which was adjacent to the airfield. The Poles' first kill had been a lone reconnaissance bomber on November 24th, 1940, which was appropriately celebrated during the Squadron's Christmas bash at Leamington Spa's Clarendon Hotel'. By March 1941, combat experienced Polish pilots who had fought in British squadrons during the Battle of Britain were identified and posted to Polish squadrons, as was the case with Pilot Officer Surma. Joining him in 308 Squadron would be other veterans, including Flight Lieutenant Marian Pisarek and Pilot Officer Jurek Poplawski, who became a particular friend. Many years later, Wing Commander Poplawski wrote to me from his home in Argentina: -

Franek Surma and I were close friends. We were both veterans of the Battle of Britain, although he was a much more distinguished pilot than me, and we were of a similar age. He was a rather quiet and deep person, perhaps even a little reserved. Perhaps we were all like that, trying not to think of tomorrow. It would be wrong to say that we were not afraid, after all we were just ordinary human beings, and as such we all knew what fear was. But we also had an unwritten code of conduct in our lives, a sense of duty that helped us control our fear. That code was possibly the most important influence on our lives. Franek and I discussed it a lot.

Because the night blitz was reaching its zenith, enemy reconnaissance aircraft were regularly active over the Midlands during daylight hours. At 11.25 a.m. on Wednesday 26th March, 1941, Pilot Officer Surma led Pilot Officer Bozek and Sergeant Kremski off from Baginton to intercept one such intruder. The Ju 88 was sighted over Leamington and attacked, the German pilot immediately jettisoning his bombs. Much to the delight of 308 Squadron, the combat progressed until it was over the airfield at 3,000 feet, but the raider somehow escaped, albeit trailing smoke. The three Poles were credited with a third of a probable each.

Above: 308 Squadron gathered at the 'Baginton Oak'.

Left: Jurek Poplawski.

On April 2nd, 1941, the Poles received great news: their Hurricanes were to be replaced with Spitfires! These were not the new Mk Vs, however, or even Mk IIs, but obsolete and tired Mk IAs of Battle of Britain vintage. Two days later the CO, Squadron Leader Jan Orzechowski, took two other pilots to Kirton-in-Lindsey and collected three Spitfires from 65 Squadron, which was resting there before returning to 11 Group. On April 6th the Poles tried out their new aircraft, the Squadron diary commenting that the 'pilots take to new machines at once. Very manoeuvrable and lighter to handle than the Hurricane.'

The Baginton control tower in 1988.

At 1.40 p.m. on Sunday May 11th, Pilot Officer Surma and Sergeant Widlarz were scrambled to investigate a 'bogey' at 27,000 feet over Kidderminster in Worcestershire. No aircraft were found, however, and the Poles were informed by Ground Control that the radar plot had transpired to be a friendly Blenheim. It was a perfect day for flying with excellent visibility, and so the two Spitfires continued on patrol, the two pilots no doubt enjoying the sheer thrill of flight.

Over Malvern, the engine of Pilot Officer Surma's Spitfire, R6644, suddenly burst into flame. Having shut off the fuel supply to minimise the risk of fire spreading, the pilot checked his instruments and noted a severe drop in oil pressure. Standing Orders dictated that in such circumstances the pilot should make a forced landing and save the aeroplane, and it is likely that Surma, an experienced pilot, intended to do just that – until his windscreen became covered in oil, obliterating his essential forward vision. Smoke also started pouring into the cockpit, making it clear that the wisest course of action would be to abandon the Spitfire over rural Worcestershire. Waiting until the aircraft was clear of the built up area of Malvern below, Surma inverted the aircraft and dropped out, leaving R6644 to its fate. The parachute opened safely and as the pilot descended he saw his Spitfire crash in an open field east of Malvern Link. Not surprisingly, in sleepy wartime Worcestershire the high drama over Malvern had attracted great interest.

An R series Spitfire's markings are applied at Eastleigh.

Schoolboy Harry Cleaton: -

I was walking along the main Worcester Road in Malvern, between Great Malvern and Link Top on the Malvern Hills. I had just reached the leathercraft factory and sat down on a low stone wall to admire the view. I could see a Spitfire over Malvern Link, flying towards Worcester, but it was trailing a thin plume of black smoke and losing height rapidly. This was an astonishing sight, and then the pilot baled out! I ran all the way to North Malvern Police Station, in Newtown Road, but when I arrived, breathless, the local bobby, PC Jack Calder, was just leaving on his push bike to find the crash site.

Mr Davies, Malvern's Chief Air Raid Warden, was walking his dog along Pickersleigh Road when R6644 passed over him, trailing smoke. He ran to the nearest house, No 9, and called Malvern Police Station, giving the Station Officer a running commentary of events until the aircraft disappeared from his view.

Schoolboy Jimmy Thomas: -

We had been playing an early season game of cricket on Malvern Link Common and were walking home when we saw the Spitfire. When the pilot baled out we just couldn't believe it! The Spitfire pitched down vertically, and we reckoned that both plane and pilot would make landfall in the Madresfield area. We immediately jumped on our push bikes and pedalled off furiously in that direction!

Bill Pritchard, a 21-year old milkman working for Bennett's Dairy of Worcester: -

I was driving my milk truck down Jennet Tree Lane, which leads from Malvern Link to Callow End and knew nothing of the crashing Spitfire until there was an explosion in the field to my right, near the junction of Jennet Tree and Hawthorn Lanes. Naturally I was absolutely startled and stopped immediately. Good job I did, as a length of aluminium three feet long hit the road directly in front of me; had I still been driving it would have gone straight through my windscreen! I realised then that it was an aircraft and not a bomb that had caused the explosion, so I climbed over a newly laid hedge and hurried to the crash site, although I realised that if the pilot was still in the plane he would be beyond any help. As I made across the field I was puzzled by someone shouting at me, but looking around there was no-one else on the scene but me. Then I looked up and saw the pilot coming down on his parachute, shouting at me to keep away from the burning wreckage because of dangerous exploding ammunition. The parachutist drifted over me, towards the cottage at the junction of the two lanes, so I returned to my truck, picked up the piece of aircraft in the road and took it home as a souvenir.

Inside the nearby cottage, Mrs Probert was having lunch with her daughter, Vi, who was enjoying a rare weekend off from her work in the Land Army, and two evacuees. Vi remembered: -

We were startled by the explosion and all four of us dashed outside to investigate. We could see a pall of smoke rising and assumed a stray bomb to be the cause. As we turned around to go back inside we were amazed to suddenly see a parachute disappearing over the back of our cottage! We ran into the adjacent field and watched an airman land before gathering up his parachute. Our instinct was to go to him and help, but then we had second thoughts as he could have been a German! I can't remember what was said between us but I do recall that he had a foreign accent which sounded a bit German.

Having collected up and removed his parachute, Pilot Officer Surma walked across the lane and looked at the wreckage of his Spitfire, which was burning fiercely in a small crater whilst other debris was scattered on the surface over a wide area. By now literally hundreds of people were arriving, by various modes of transport, from the directions of both Malvern and Callow End. Local lad Neville Grizzell had just enough time to give the pilot a Woodbine before the Pole was ushered away by a doctor and PC Calder. Hurrying to the scene along Hawthorn Lane were a group of airmen from a searchlight site, who took charge of the situation and confirmed Surma's identity.

Vi Probert, top left, in her Land Army days, and two photographs of Franek Surma taken at Bosworth Farm after the crash.

The area was farmed by the Page family, who took the pilot to Bosworth Farm where he was made most welcome until transport arrived to return our hero to Baginton.

The airmen and police then had to fend off souvenir hunters. Young air cadet Ken Davies, son of the Chief Air Raid Warden, was rapidly on the scene and managed to purloin a much-coveted piece of Spitfire wreckage. Harry Cleaton was not so fortunate, as en route his push bike suffered a puncture, meaning that he could not get to the crash site until the following day. By then the site was so well guarded, the recovery team being on site, that the young schoolboy was unable to acquire a souvenir. These events, however, would remain indelibly etched upon the memories of all who had witnessed the drama take place.

Shortly after Pilot Officer Surma and Spitfire R6644 parted company over rural Worcestershire, 308 Squadron moved from Baginton to Chilbolton in Hampshire. There the Poles exchanged their Spitfire Mk Is for Mk IIs, and undertook gun firing pratice at Chesil Beach with 118 Squadron. On June 24th, 308 Squadron moved again, this time to RAF Northolt, the home of No 1 Polish Fighter Wing. Flying from Northolt the Squadron provided cover to convoys off Portland Bill, Swanage and Bournemouth, but, more importantly, Northolt was within striking distance of enemy occupied France; it was in that direction that the Polish Wing would be engaged.

Two days before 308 Squadron arrived at Northolt, Hitler invaded Russia. No longer were the Nazis' territorial ambitions aimed westward, at Great Britain, but eastwards. This meant that although there was no longer a prospect of any renewed attempt to invade Britain that year, the British government was under pressure from the Russians to open a second front. Moreover, there was a new offensive attitude prevalent at Fighter Command HQ, Dowding's successor, Air Chief Marshal Sir Sholto Douglas, being keen to 'Lean into France'. The idea was that small formations of medium bombers would attack various targets in north-west France, in daylight and escorted by huge numbers of Spitfires which would take on smaller numbers of enemy fighters and destroy them. The initiative would be called the 'Non-Stop Offensive', and in readiness for this undertaking Fighter Command had re-organised itself into 'wings' of three squadrons, each with a dedicated Wing Commander (Flying) and based at Sector Stations. The squadrons had also been largely re-equipped with the Spitfire, it having been recognised as the superior British fighter of the period. For the Spitfire pilots it was to be a hectic 'season'.

On June 27th, 1941, 308 Squadron flew its first sweep over France, during which Pilot Officers Surma and Szyszka shared the destruction of an Me 109 whilst strafing the *Luftwaffe* airfield at St Omer. The Poles were in action daily, either sweeping or supporting bombers in complex Circus operations involving hundreds of aircraft. Although there were combat successes, there were casualties too: on July 12th, Flying Officer Stanislaw Wielgus, one of 308 Squadron's original members, was shot down and killed over the Channel; the following day, amidst torrential rain and thunder, his body was washed ashore on the south coast. July 17th saw 308 Squadron's new CO, Squadron Leader Marian Pisarek, run into 'pretty big trouble'; 306 and 308 Squadrons had taken off together but became separated over France: North of St Omer, Pisarek's 12 Spitfires were jumped by 60 Me 109s, probably of III/JG 26. Pisarek ordered his pilots into a defensive circle before resuming formation, with weavers, and zig-zagging back to the coast. Owing to repeated enemy attacks, defensive circles had to be resumed several times, but somehow the Poles kept together and fended the Germans off. Three 109s were claimed destroyed and two probables, but two 308 Squadron Spitfires, having taken off late and straggling behind the main formation, were missing. Pisarek keeping his tiny force intact, however, whilst scoring victories against an overwhelming enemy force is the stuff of legends. The two missing pilots, Pilot Officer Maciejowski and Sergeant Hegenbarth, courted disaster by flying alone over France and paid the price: the former was captured, the latter killed.

A 308 Squadron Spitfire lands at Northolt after a sweep.

On July 22ⁿᵈ, 308 Squadron participated in a sweep of Dunkirk, St Omer and Gravelines. Enemy aircraft were shot up on the ground at St Omer and Guines, and on the return flight Pilot Officer Surma destroyed a 109E which he caught attacking a Spitfire between Guines and the French coast. The combat took place at just 200 feet, and the Spitfire pilot clearly saw the 109 crash into the ground.

July 26ᵗʰ saw 308 Squadron's pilots released for 24 hours, the Squadron diary commenting that 'The pilots will soon be engaged on a sweep of a different kind!' Throughout August 1941 the Squadron would be further engaged, claiming more victories and suffering further casualties. On August 29ᵗʰ, Squadron Leader Pisarek led 308 Squadron as top cover on a Circus to Hazebrouck; over the coast, the Poles were attacked by 'Masses of Jerries'. Once more skilful leadership kept the Spitfires together and got them home safely without loss.

Squadron Leader Marian Pisarek.

In early September 1941, 308 Squadron upgraded its Spitfire Mk IIs for the newer Mk VB, which boasted a more powerful Merlin and two 20 mm cannons. Some of 308 Squadron's Mk IIs were cannon-armed 'B's, but the engine was the same as that which powered the purely machine-gun armed, and therefore lighter, Mk IIA. The improved performance of the Mk VB, therefore, was most welcome and would become Fighter Command's workhorse until the Spitfire Mk IX arrived in 1943, just in the nick of time, to counter the FW 190 menace. On September 16ᵗʰ, Pilot Officer Surma made his first flight in a Spitfire Mk VB, AB930, ZF-J. That day, 308 Squadron's 'A' Flight (six Spitfires) engaged 30 Me 109Fs over Gravelines. Surma, by now promoted to Flying Officer, was leading Red Section and destroyed a 109 which his wingman, Sergeant Warchal, confirmed destroyed. Surma's friend, Pilot Officer Poplawski, claimed a kill in unusual circumstances by forcing a 109 down into the sea without firing a shot!

On September 20th, the Polish Wing flew as escort cover wing on Circus 100, to Rouen. Over the target Surma and his wingman, Sergeant Jan Okroj, became separated. The latter was flying Surma's usual AB930 and was attacked by three Me 109s. From long range their cannon shells damaged his tail unit; somehow Okroj outran his assailants and forced landed at Thorney Island. The Spitfire was so badly damaged, however, that it was sent to Heston Aircraft Ltd for repair. During that sortie Flying Officer Surma destroyed two more 109s, both of which crashed in flames, before engaging a third enemy aircraft: -

As I was too low to re-join the Squadron I flew low to the Channel. About 10 miles out to sea I caught sight of the bombers – they were on my starboard side. As it was quiet I managed to join a squadron on the port side, by which time I could see the English coast, and saw an Me 109F making off after attacking a Spitfire. Behind the Me were three Spitfires in line astern. I manoeuvred to cut off the Me's escape but the Spitfires abandoned their quarry for some unknown reason. The enemy aircraft climbed and I tried to get on his starboard side and into the sun. At that moment the German turned to port and looked back, and as I was at the same height he saw me. This Me had its undersurfaces painted in the same blue as our Spitfires, and the upper surfaces were camouflaged in green and brown, as our aircraft used to be, no doubt to confuse us.

The German pulled over on his back, I followed and got him below me. We started a dogfight but he kept on circling and made several attempts to reverse our positions. The Me was superior in engine power and climbed away very easily. My only possible tactics were to turn either to port or starboard to cut in on him. All this time the enemy aircraft was gaining height and attempting to shoot me down, but his ammunition was wasted as I took care to keep out of his axis of fire. I was unable to fire at him as I was unable to get into a sufficiently favourable position to do so. As the position became a stalemate we both broke off at the same time.

This combat is of particular interest, because I doubt that Flying Officer Surma engaged an Me 109F, more likely it was another Spitfire as German pilots did not paint their machines to represent Spitfires. Also, could that explain why the three Spitfires broke off their pursuit? Did the pilot Surma attacked realise that his assailant was another Spitfire, I wonder, or did he too assume this to be a 109? 'Friendly fire' was an understandable mistake in the heat of battle, especially at this time when the Me 109F was still a comparative newcomer to the action and was so dissimilar to its predecessor, the angular Me 109E, but more like the curvaceous Spitfire. Such a scenario was not uncommon, even for experienced and successful fighter pilots.

September 27th, Flying Officer Surma probably destroyed a yellow-nosed Me 109F during a Circus to Amiens, and Poplawski destroyed another, which he later reported as 'burning nicely as it crashed into a row of houses west of Amiens.' The 109, however, had previously riddled the Pole's Spitfire with bullets, damaging the Spitfire so badly that Jurek had to crash land at Biggin Hill.

On Circus 107, which took place on October 12th, the Northolt and Kenley Wings escorted bombers attacking St Omer, 308 Squadron flying as forward support at 24,000 feet. Flying Officer Surma: -

I was leading the right hand four aircraft. Having been warned over the R/T that our aircraft had been engaged by 109s, we wheeled round, re-crossing the French coast south of Le Touquet. Over the Channel I saw two Me 109s flying far apart in line astern, as though following a combat. I took evasive action by flying into the sun and the Me's passed below, unaware of my presence. I dived on the tail of the second Me and fired three short bursts into its tail from above at 100 – 150 yards range. The leading Me took evasive action and dived out of sight. My victim turned over onto its back and I fired another burst from about 80 yards. Whilst it was in that position white smoke poured from the Me 109, which then went into a steep dive. Bright flames then came from the Me, which went into a steep dive. Bright flames then came from the 109 which was burning fiercely as it crashed into the sea.

Pilot Officer Stanislaw Wandzilak of 308 Squadron prepares for an operation.

The following day saw Pilot Officer Poplawski notch up 308 Squadron's 50th victory when he destroyed a 109 between Mardyck and St Omer. Another important occasion occurred on October 28th, when Flying Officer Surma was awarded Poland's highest gallantry decoration, the Virtuti Militari, Vth Class. He was now an 'ace' fighter pilot, having destroyed five enemy aircraft, probably destroyed two more, damaged another with a third share in a damaged Ju 88. In an impressive ceremony at RAF Northolt, the 25-year old Pole received his medal from General Sikorski, leader of the Polish people in exile.

The Polish Wing up from Northolt on another sweep in 1941.

During the first week of November 1941, 308 Squadron flew on several Ramrod operations, supporting 'Hurribombers', and a Polish Wing sweep to St Omer on November 7th. By now the season was drawing to a close, as winter weather set in, but the tempo of operations remained fairly constant. The next operation was a highly complicated Circus, No 110, to bomb the railroad repair facility at Lille. The Polish Wing's squadrons were designated top (308), medium (315) and close (303) escort. At 11.05 a.m., the Polish Wing Leader, Wing Commander Rolski, led the Wing off from Northolt, completing an orbit of the airfield before setting off to rendezvous with the bombers over Manston. 308 Squadron was the first to arrive and started an orbit whilst waiting for the other Spitfires, and the Blenheim bombers, to arrive. On cue the two other Polish squadrons arrived simultaneously with the bombers and all set course for France. Unfortunately whilst completing their turn, 308 Squadron had been blinded by the bright sun and lost sight of the 'beehive'. Wing Commander Rolski could see that 308 was turning the wrong way, but was unable to communicate via R/T due to the essential requirement for silence at this stage of an offensive operation. Instead the Wing Leader violently rocked his wings to attract attention, but to no avail. Eventually Squadron Leader Pisarek had no option but to break radio silence and inform Ground Control that his Squadron had missed the rendezvous. 'Ops' then vectored Pisarek towards the bombers, and 308 Squadron set off in hot pursuit.

The main formation soon crossed the French coast west of Dunkirk, passing over Bethune before hitting the target and turning for home over Arras. Covering the bombers' withdrawal were five 10 Group Spitfire squadrons; although these units were in their correct position whilst the bombers were outward bound, they were ahead of their prescribed co-ordinate on the return journey, throwing the bombers and escorting squadrons into confusion. The Blenheim's passage over France had already attracted accurate flak and after leaving the target eight 109s were spotted beneath the Allied formation. Although the Germans repeatedly attacked from below and behind, all of the Blenheims were brought home safely. Also in the air were a further seven 11 Group fighter squadrons and one from 12 Group and between them claimed four Me 109s and one FW 190 destroyed, three 109s damaged and a 190 damaged.

Fighter Command also suffered casualties, however. 308 Squadron, unable to locate the main formation after missing the rendezvous, was vectored to patrol from Dunkirk to Calais, between 16-25,000 feet. Towards the end of their patrol time, when fuel reserves were a consideration, the Squadron was jumped from above by a large force of Me 109Fs from I/JG 26. The Poles were immediately split up and obliged to disengage and head back across the Channel. After losing their attackers, 308 Squadron's pilots, in ones and twos, found and joined the main formation, also travelling home.

Back at Northolt, Pilot Officer Poplawski reported as follows: -

I went to the assistance of a Spitfire that was being attacked by an Me 109F. I got on the Me's tail and from 200 yards above I gave a short burst from my cannons. I saw an explosion in the starboard wing and the Me turned onto its side with the starboard wing down. I fired another burst from both my machine-guns and cannons. Volumes of black smoke appeared from the Me which started to dive down sideways. As four Me 109s were approaching to engage me, and were higher, I decided to join a formation of our aircraft in the distance.

Pilot Officer Stabrowski: -

I saw a Spitfire being attacked by an Me 109F and went to its assistance, engaging the enemy aircraft from above and astern. I gave it a burst of fire from both cannon and machine-gun at 300 yards. The Me wobbled badly and I knew that I had hit it. I followed up my attack and fired three more bursts. The Me quivered and wavered more and more, thick black smoke pouring from the underside of the fuselage. It dived towards the sea near the French coast. Being short of ammunition and petrol, and a long way from base. I could not chase the Me and so returned to England.

The only German fighters lost that day were two FW 190s, the pilot of one of which was killed. Three more enemy aircraft were damaged in crash-landings, which could have been combat related and one of which may even have been the 109 clearly damaged by Poplawski

Spitfire AB930 showing damage from Circus 100. It was in this aircraft that Franek Surma was reported missing from Circus 110.

and Stabrowski, who appear to have attacked the same enemy aircraft simultaneously but independently.

Circus 110 was a disaster for Fighter Command, which lost 14 pilots, including three squadron commanders and a wing commander, and at least 17 Spitfires. One of those squadron leaders belonged to the Polish Wing, Squadron Leader Szczeszniewski, who was captured. The only other Spitfire failing to return to Northolt was AB930, flown by Flying Officer Surma who was posted 'Missing'. The squadron diary summarised the day as 'very depressing'.

Franek Surma's body was never found. The gallant Pole is not forgotten, however, and his death was far from the end of this inspirational story.

In May 1985, 44 years after Franek Surma baled out of R6644 over Malvern, I was working at Malvern Police Station, a 23-year old uniform patrol officer of two years experience. By coincidence, although I did not know it at first, I lived in the police authority owned property that was formerly North Malvern Police Station, and from which PC Jack Calder had hurried to

Pilot Officer Stabrowski.

Madresfield on that far off Sunday lunchtime. Fascinated by wartime aviation my whole life, and extremely moved by the sacrifices by young airmen during the Battle of Britain in particular, a friend's chance remark, shortly after I moved to Malvern, that a Spitfire had crashed at Madresfield and that the pilot was a Polish Battle of Britain veteran, changed the course of my life.

The friend who first told me about the Surma crash was 18-year old local aviation archaeologist Andrew Long, with whom I had researched on a casual basis for the last four years. Andy had collated the basic details of the crash, and knew in which field it happened. I became so fascinated by the whole story, however, that we soon traced eyewitnesses via the local media and were piecing together a detailed story. Moreover, the Spitfire's Form 78, detailing the units with which it served, provided us with the basic data required to undertake further research at the Public Records Office. A list of pilots who had once flown R6644, which had an impressive total of 266 flying hours, was subsequently obtained and research commenced to trace any survivors or the relatives of casualties. The story of Franek Surma himself particularly interested me as I was so moved by the fact that he had no known grave. Over the next year our project grew enormously, and we received permission from the MOD, the landowner, Madresfield Estate, and the tenant farmer, Mr Nugent at Lower Woodsfield, to excavate the crash site of R6644. From that point on the project became bigger and more ambitious still!

Crop rotation dictated that the site could not be excavated until September 1987, so in October the previous year Andy and I co-founded the Malvern Spitfire Team to undertake the project. We also decided to make the excavation a public one, to raise money for the RAF Association's Wings Appeal, and involved the local branch. Significantly we all wanted to provide a marker to Franek Surma, a more personal one than the imposing Polish Air Force Memorial at Northolt, on which his name was inscribed. We decided to build a cairn of granite, hewn from the nearby Malvern Hills, in Jennet Tree Lane, near to where Pilot Officer Surma landed by parachute. Needless to say there was a complex and typically inefficient paper chase by the local authorities before permission was granted, but we persevered and got there in the end. Support was also forthcoming from the local Air Training Corps Squadron, No 1017, and the MOD Participation Committee approved a fly past by the Battle of Britain Memorial Flight and a Tornado GR1 of 65 Squadron (with which unit R6644 had flown). The icing on the cake was when the Polish Air Force Association in Great Britain honoured us by accepting our invitation to unveil the memorial. It was a privilege indeed to learn that two Polish Battle of Britain veterans, both of whom remembered Franek Surma, would perform the honours: Squadron Leaders 'Gandy' Drobinski and Ludwik Martel.

Top of my research priority was to try and ascertain what had happened to Flying Officer Surma on November 8th, 1941. I was very pleased indeed when Jurek Poplawski was traced to his home in Buenos Aires; protracted correspondence developed between us, and in 1987 the Wing Commander had this to say of Circus 110 and Franek Surma: -

The Polish Air Force Mememorial at Northolt.

The whole flight lasted 1 hour & 55 minutes. I believe that it was Franek's Spitfire being attacked by at least one 109. The German attack was both sudden and shocking in its ferocity. We tried to assist the Spitfire but I soon had a warning of 'Break left!' from Squadron Leader Pisarek, which I did. Apparently there were even more 109s coming down to attack and so, as I was also short of fuel, I couldn't hang around. Therefore I did not see what ultimately happened to either Franek or the 109 that I had attacked. I also remember that there was another 109 between me and that which was shooting at the Spitfire, but that is really all I can remember of that action, which was fairly early on in my operational career. I flew throughout the war, and so much happened later, in Normandy and Germany, for example, that it is difficult to recall that fleeting moment in 1941 with any more clarity.

Sadly Squadron Leader Pisarek was killed later in the war when leading the Polish Wing, but his wingman on Circus 110, a new pilot, Pilot Officer Kazek Budzik, was found very much alive and well in Nottingham: -

That was my first operational flight and Pisarek told me to stay close to him, which I did. As Pisarek shouted 'Break' to Poplawski then I must have been with him in the area that Surma was killed, but I must admit that as I was so inexperienced and concentrating so hard on staying with Pisarek that I didn't see much of what was going on around me. I do remember a 109 flashing across my windscreen and Pisarek yelling at me to fire. Of course Surma was an experienced pilot, an ace. I hardly knew him but I remember thinking at the time that he had been very unlucky to be killed like that.

Another 308 Squadron combatant was Sergeant Jan Warchal, whom I met by chance at the Spitfire Jubilee Airshow at Duxford in 1988, although he was unable to recall anything of the combat. Sadly all of the other 308 Squadron participants had either been killed during the war or had died since 1945.

308 Squadron's combat report mentions a parachute seen in the area of Dunkirk, but the time does not correspond with Poplawski and Stabrowski's combat reports. If Pilot Officer Surma baled out but was not picked up, it is possible that his body was washed up on either the French or British coast and subsequently buried as an unknown airman. Team members scoured Commonwealth War Grave and cemetery records on both sides of the Channel but no likely contenders could be found. On that basis we must assume that Pilot Officer Surma went to his death in the English Channel, imprisoned in Spitfire AB930.

So who shot down Franek Surma? German combat records indicate that the enemy pilot responsible was *Hauptmann* Johannes Seifert, the 25-year old *Kommandeur* of I/JG 26. Seifert was an *experten*, already decorated with the *Ritterkreuz*; he would be killed in action against American Lightnings in 1943. It was the end of another mystery.

Hauptmann *Johannes Seifert of I/JG 26.*

'Operation Spitfire', the recovery of Spitfire R6644 and the unveiling of the Surma Memorial took place on Saturday, 11th September 1987 and remains one of the most moving experiences of my life. It seemed that the whole of Worcestershire had turned out to support us, and a significant amount of cash and publicity was raised for the 'Wings Appeal'. The excavation indicated that the Spitfire had hit a layer of very hard clay and granite just a few feet below the surface, shattering all major components. Indeed, the recovery team in 1941 had done a very good job! Nevertheless many small artefacts were found, the biggest being a piston and liner, the most impressive being the tiny De Havilland badge from the extreme front of the aircraft's propeller spinner cap. All of the finds were laid out for display on a long table whilst team-member Bob Morris, an engineer with 66 (Spitfire) Squadron during the Battle of Britain, identified the nuggets of history for our 100 special guests and innumerable members of the public.

The recovery of Spitfire R6644 starts at last!

Malvern Hills District Council hosted a civic reception for our Polish and other VIP guests, whose number included many former Spitfire personnel, in a marquee at the crash site. It was a poignant occasion, made more so when the Council Chairman, Mrs Lyn Norfolk, explained that her own father remained missing in action from World War Two. Squadron Leader Martel spoke on behalf of the Polish delegation and, moved close to tears, described how honoured he was to have been invited to such a unique event, and how indescribably moved both he and his colleagues were that so many people had turned out to remember a young Polish flier whom they had never met. 'Perhaps', he said, 'the motto of the Malvern Spitfire Team is true: "The Legend Lives On".'

Although bad weather grounded the Battle of Britain Memorial Flight at St Athan, Jennet Tree Lane was absolutely packed when the time came for Surma's memorial to be unveiled.

Battle of Britain Spitfire fitter Bob Morris, a keen member of the Malvern Spitfire Team, examines finds with Squadron Leaders Drobinski and Martel. Above is a piston and liner from Spitfire R6644's Merlin engine, the largest single item recovered.

The two Polish pilots walked with the team and the guard of honour, provided by the local ATC squadron, the few yards to the memorial. It was incredible to see the huge crowd of people part ahead of us, and I will never forget the words that Squadron Leader 'Gandy' Drobinski said to me that day: 'In 1945 we Poles were not invited to participate in the great victory parade, such was the situation with Stalin, and we could not even go home. Britain gave us a home and, all these years later, you have now given us our victory parade. It was worth the wait'.

Around the cairn were clustered journalists and television cameras, and during the dedication service Rev. Eric Knowles said that 'Flying Officer Surma's sacrifice is an example to us all of how to serve our country, our friends and our God.' Squadron Leaders Drobinski and Martel solemnly stepped forward and removed the Polish Air Force ensign from the memorial. The atmosphere was incredibly charged, the crowd silent as wreaths were laid by the Polish Air Force Association, RAF Association and the Malvern Spitfire Team. As the last wreath was set down a strong gust of wind suddenly shook the tree beneath which the memorial was built; in the prevailing atmosphere it was easy to imagine that this was Franek Surma's spirit coming to rest. I certainly hope it was.

In June 1988 the artefacts recovered from R6644's crash site became the centre-piece of a major exhibition featuring the Malvern Spitfire Team's research at Tudor House Museum in Worcester. The opening event was attended by numerous Battle of Britain pilots and

Squadron Leaders Martel & Drobinski look solemnly on whilst Mr Tadek Krysztik, secretary of the Polish Air Force Association, prepares to lay a wreath at the Surma Memorial, also pictured with additional floral tributes from the RAFA & Malvern Spitfire Team.

Squadron Leaders Marttel & Drobinski; 1940 & 1987.

other VIPs, but the ribbon could only be cut by one man, so far as we were all concerned: Kazek Budzik, Squadron Leader Pisarek's wingman on Circus 110. The exhibition was a huge success, attracting 10,000 visitors in just a few months. Consequently the time allocated to our exhibition was extended, and it then became a travelling show, seen at numerous aviation and cultural centres across the UK.

Efforts to trace the Surma family had so far failed, but early in 1989 I enlisted the help of Polish Spitfire enthusiast Kryzstof Choloniewski, who placed an appeal on my behalf in the Krakow newspaper. Out of the blue, in February 1989, a letter arrived in my post which remains the most moving piece of correspondence I have ever received; it was from Franek Surma's two surviving sisters, Elzbiete Morcinek, aged 80, and Otylia Paszek, aged 76: -

We were delighted and extremely moved to learn of your project, the knowledge of which affected us considerably. At last we will learn the whole truth regarding the fate of our dear brother. We are the only surviving family of Franciszek Surma and came from a long line of peasant farmers, 'Franek' being the youngest child. We all adored him, as did everyone who knew him. He was a very good child, very obedient and hard working. At school in Zory he passed his exams and decided to become a pilot. On this issue he opposed his parents' wishes for the one and only time. None of us agreed with us his plans, for we considered joining the air force to be a very dangerous affair and so were afraid for our little brother. Our concern made no difference as he was decided and would not consider any alternative. We do not regret now that we did not succeed in changing his mind as we now know that he was a hero. Two of our family, in fact, were killed by German pilots: the Germans bombed a school in Wieszniowice in Czechoslovakia and hit a house on the opposite side of the street, where our sister lived and who was killed instantly.

After Franek completed his education at Zory he moved to Krakow and joined the air force. At this time he wrote about attending a course at the Reserve Officers Cadet School for infantry at Rozane. He also attended cadet schools in Rawicz and Deblin.

We were always delighted to see Franek when he was on leave and our parents would organise parties. He looked wonderful in his uniform, He was an extremely cultured, intelligent and gallant young man. We were all very interested to learn of his flying exploits and listened to his stories with bated breath. On one of his few visits he even brought home a parachute to show us how safe it was to jump.

Two days before war broke out he made several aerobatic and low passes over every house occupied by a member of our family. We remember running out of the house in a state of great excitement! We all knew that this was Franek but we were scared to death by his aerobatic antics! In Galkowice there stood a large oak tree and this shook violently as Franek passed overhead, so low was he. We understood that this was a sign to say that our little brother was going away.

During the war we received a letter from Franek via Holland. He let us know about the dispatch of two other letters and some money. Only one of those letters reached us. Via Portugal we received parcels from him, known as 'Signs of Life', containing tins of sardines. Our joy was not for the food but the knowledge that the sender was still alive. Can you imagine our great joy? Those were the only happy moments in those cruel days. After the war ended we received another parcel, which made us happy because we assumed that Franek was still alive. But we waited in vain for him to come home. Finally we asked the Red Cross to try and discover whether he was still alive. Eventually we received confirmation that our dear brother had failed to return from an operation in 1941 and was probably killed in the cold waters of the English Channel. We also received his medals and photographs. The news of this tragedy drove us all to the utmost depths of despair.

Since that time, more than 40 years have now passed and we are happy that Franek's memory is alive, not only with us. At our 'Memory Room' in Gadawe his photograph is displayed in a place of honour. Also you, in far away England, have not forgotten him. We are so proud of our brother. We are also astonished at your achievements as such a young man, and want to shake your hand for all you have done. Kindly express our gratitude to everybody who has contributed to the commemoration of Franek Surma. We are most grateful to his friends, the chaplain and the people of England. It is hard to express our thanks in words; there are no words that could adequately express the feelings of two old people who have kept alive in their hearts the memory of their dear brother.

Through your project you have awakened our memories and shown how wonderful people can be. Many special thanks go to you and we will be praying for your success in life, prayers for someone now very dear to us. May God take care of you and your organisation. We are so happy that there is still someone to light a candle for Franek on All Souls Day. We are happy because the memorial erected to him serves as his grave, a symbol he can see from heaven. We have always worried about Franek having no known grave, but now we are at peace, thanks to you.

More words are really superfluous, but even that was not the end of the tale.

In 1992 I was a Local Beat Officer at Malvern Police Station, responsible for the areas of Malvern Link, Madresfield, North and West Malvern. My colleagues and I were constantly

Dilip Sarkar with guests at the Tudor House exhibition in June 1988: From left to right: Bob George (616 Sqn), William Walker (616 Sqn), Roger Boulding (74 Sqn), Mrs Helen Budzik, Gandy Drobinski (303 Sqn), Kazek Budzik (308 Sqn), Ken Wilkinson (19 Sqn), John Down (616 Sqn), Bob Pugh (616 Sqn), Tony Pickering (501 Sqn), Hugh Chalmers (65 Sqn) & John Lumsden (33 Sqn).

bemused at how to deal with petty crime and nuisance caused by bored teenagers. We had already tried to show them that there was an alternative to anti-social behaviour through finding an interest. The problem was, however, that many of the local youth initiatives suffered from an almost crippling lack of funding, and this needed to be put right. Over the years since the Surma Memorial was unveiled, I had often thought about what Eric King said in his dedication, that Surma's story was an example to us all of how to serve our country, family, friends and God. Franek Surma could become, I felt, an inspiration to young people, and so it was decided to found the Surma Memorial Trust for Youth, the concept being to raise and distribute funds to projects working to improve the quality of life for youth in our local area. The initiative received wholehearted support from the West Mercia Constabulary and local authorities, and the Trust was soon registered as a charity.

At the time I was planning to publish my second book, 'The Invisible Thread: A Spitfire's Tale', telling the story of Spitfire R6644 and Franek Surma, and my friend of many years, the aviation artist Mark Postlethwaite G.Av.A., was painting a picture of R6644 high over the Malvern Hills for the cover. Local businesses sponsored production of a print, and Battle of Britain veterans and related personalities, such as TV presenter and former Spitfire pilot Raymond Baxter, kindly agreed to sign them. This was another terrific concept: young and old working together for a positive and common purpose. I hoped that the youngsters would start to view elderly people, the wartime generation, with much greater understanding and respect. It was unanimously agreed that all proceeds from print sales should be donated to the Surma Trust.

In September 1992, the book, print and Trust were all launched at Great Malvern's prestigious Abbey Hotel. Situated in a cul-de-sac, the RAF Exhibition Flight set up a Spitfire Mk XVI outside the Hotel, and over 30 former pilots attended the event, which was a massive success. The public turned out in droves, and when David Pennel displayed his Spitfire Mk IX overhead, the whole town was brought to a standstill. It really was another absolutely incredible experience, all in the name of Franek Surma.

At the launch alone we raised £4,000 from print sales, and over the next couple of years or so that figure rose to £20,000. That money was distributed by the Trustees amongst numerous local youth initiatives, and definitely made a positive difference. In 1998, policing arrangements changed and I became a 'Rural Beat Manager', a 'local' bobby responsible for the town of Upton-upon-Severn and 39 villages! My work in Malvern over, it was decided to use the Trust's remaining funds to buy computer equipment for Malvern Youth Centre, where a plaque would be erected telling the Surma story. So it was that we were joined there one winter's evening by Mrs Barbara

R6644: The Invisible Thread *by Mark Postlethwaite G.Av.A.*

Sykes, niece of Polish Battle of Britain pilot Flying Officer Franek Gruszka, who unveiled the plaque and in so doing brought a great adventure to a close.

The story of Franek Surma changed my life forever, because it made me want to spend my life researching and writing about not only the stories of wartime casualties but equally the memories of survivors, and making sure that these incredible people were not forgotten. So it was that I turned my back on a promising police career and dedicated my life to this crusade.

Without doubt the entire Surma project was very special indeed, not just to me but to literally hundreds of connected people all over the world. That is appropriate, because there can be no doubt that Flying Officer Franciszek Surma was a very special young man indeed.

At The Invisible Thread's launch, Abbey Hotel, Great Malvern, Worcester-shire, 1992; from left: Dr Gordon Mitchell, Wg Cdr Jimmy Jennings AFC DFM, Mr Fred Roberts, Flt Lts Hugh Chalmers AE, Peter Hairs MBE, Tadek Turek VM, Michael Graham DFC, Mr Bob Morris, Mr Bob Morton, Sqn Ldr Buck Casson DFC AFC, Flt Lts William Walker AE, Kazek Budzik VM KW, & Flt Lts Richard Jones AE & Ken Wilkinson AE.

Chapter Six

Sergeant Peter Rose

Peter Garratt Rose was born on May 17th, 1916, at Burton-on-Trent in Staffordshire. His father, John Frederick Rose, had served in the local county regiment during the Great War, after which his services were retained to assist with administration on the continent. There Major Rose was joined by his family, which remained with him in France until he left the army in 1920. Back in England, Peter Rose became a pupil at Burton Grammar School, where he was an accomplished member of the school rowing club. In 1930, Peter was coxswain and steered the school crew, in which his elder brother, John, rowed at stroke, to victory in the Burton Regatta, winning the Leander Challenge Vase. In 1932, Peter rowed at bow and was again in the winning team. That year he left school, joining both his father and elder brother at the local brewing company Bass, Ratcliff & Gretton Ltd. Major Rose was the company accountant, and spent 50 years of his life there; John worked in the Engineering Department and Peter was a clerk in the Bottling Department.

Peter Rose had always wanted to fly, so, much against his mother's wishes, he joined the RAF VR in 1936, learning to fly at Burnaston, near Derby. Unfortunately this meant that the close rowing relationship he enjoyed with brother John had to end, so much did flying training interfere with practice on the River Trent. On June 13th, 1939, Peter was called up for full time service as the world awaited the inevitable war with Nazi Germany.

John & Peter Rose on the Trent in 1939.

After 'square bashing' and ground schooling at No 3 Initial Training Wing (ITW), Sergeant Rose's service flying training was successfully completed before he reported to No 7 OTU, Hawarden, to fly Spitfires. By this time the Battle of Britain was drawing to a close; when Sergeant Rose reported to his first operational fighter squadron, No 65, the unit was resting at Turnhouse after being heavily engaged flying from Hornchurch.

Sergeant Rose then flew with 65 Squadron at Tangmere, moving with the Squadron to Kirton in February 1941. There 65 rested again and trained replacement pilots whilst providing convoy protection patrols. Such was the monotony, however, that Peter transferred to No 1 Photographic Reconnaissance Unit (PRU), based at Benson, 'to escape the boredom of patrolling the east coast'.

A famous photograph of certain 65 Squadron pilots at Tangmere in February 1941. All are in best blue because due to bad weather flying had been scrubbed and they were off into Chichester - until official photographers turned up! From left to right: Sergeants Orchard & Chalmers, Flying Officers Finucane & Wigg, Sergeants Rose & Mitchell. Sadly Sergeant Orchard was killed the following day.

65 Squadron pilots at dispersal, Kirton, 1941. Peter Rose second from left, seated.

The PRU started out as the Photographic Development Unit (PDU), the first operational flight of which was made by Squadron Leader Sidney Cotton on March 10th, 1939, this being a sortie in a Lockheed Hudson to photograph Mannheim. The unit then operated Blenheims before receiving Spitfires in October 1939. The weight of camera equipment and full fuel tanks, however, meant that these Spitfires could not carry arms and therefore relied upon height and speed for protection. All equipment deemed superfluous was stripped out, empty gun ports were blanked off and panel join lines were even filled with plaster, thus ensuring a completely smooth finish. These alterations increased the Spitfire's speed from around 362 to 390 m.p.h. Cotton had also developed a special duck egg green paint called 'Camotint', in which all PDU aircraft were painted. With wing mounted cameras fitted, the first Spitfire photographic reconnaissance flight was made to the German city of Aachen on November 18th, 1939. During the Battle of France in May and June 1940, PDU Spitfire pilots flew 557 sorties, losing 12 aircraft. After Dunkirk the unit re-formed at Heston as No 1 PRU and would find the Spitfire to be a superb aerial reconnaissance machine when fitted with long focal length oblique cameras. Indeed, the Spitfire remained in service as a photographic reconnaissance machine until long after the cessation of hostilities in 1945, by which time it had undergone numerous adaptations throughout the whole spectrum of marques. Clearly, however, the PRU pilots' role was a very dangerous, not to mention unsung, one, flying unarmed aircraft deep over enemy territory and returning with essential intelligence.

Saturday, May 3rd, 1941, dawned cloudless, and remained fair, with good visibility. Throughout the day, No 1 PRU carried out a number of sorties to photograph the industrial Ruhr Valley. Two Spitfires failed to return.

Sergeant Rose was making only his second trip with No 1 PRU since have transferred to Heston less than three weeks previously. At 1 p.m., a Spitfire was seen in difficulty over the village of Soumagne, near Liege in Belgium. The aircraft concerned was R6805, flown by Peter Rose, and the Merlin engine could be heard by those on the ground to be running very roughly. The aircraft was then seen spinning and the pilot baled out.

49-year old Leonard Melon was the village policeman who rapidly donned his uniform and stepped outside his front door to see a parachute drifting south-west. In the same direction he could see the Spitfire's funeral pyre billowing high in the sky. Melon immediately set off on push bike to the scene, being met whilst en route by many excited villagers who told him that the aircraft had crashed near the hamlet of Maireux, in a field owned by the Demollin-Spronck family. There a crowd had already gathered and the officer saw that a single-engined aircraft had buried itself deep in the sloping field. In an orchard some distance from the blazing wreckage he found the body of a young aviator. Eye-witnesses told him that as the parachute descended, both wings had suddenly been torn from the aircraft, one of these scything through the parachute's shroud lines. The hapless pilot then plunged to earth, his descent unchecked.

A German photograph of Peter Rose's crash site.

Dr Robert Berlemont was also at the scene and pronounced life extinct. Beside the body lay a collection of keys and two identification tags: one stated 'RAF No 748692 P Rose', the other 'Do Not Remove. No 58849'. German troops soon appeared and seized the items as Leonard Melon covered the corpse with a blanket. The Germans ordered Melon to remain at the crash site and guard it whilst they examined the body and picked through the smouldering debris of Sergeant Rose's Spitfire. Later, Melon was joined by his colleague from the nearby village of Melen, and with the help of German soldiers they loaded the pilot's body onto a cart and went to the mortuary. Melon then returned to the crash site and mounted an overnight guard with police officers from neighbouring Olne.

On Monday, May 5th, 1941, Sergeant Rose's funeral took place in the village church at Fecher. For some reason the Germans had refused to allow the body to be buried in the local cemetery, so some two thousand patriotic Belgian mourners accompanied the coffin to the crash site. 300 students from Liege University were in the congregation and carried wreaths in both Belgian and British national colours. The coffin was draped in a British Union Jack, and covered in floral tributes. At that point truckloads of German soldiers appeared, broke up the gathering and confiscated the coffin.

After the gathering had dispersed, the body was given back to Leonard Melon to bury. Instead of doing so at the crash site, however and as instructed by the Germans, the policeman interred Sergeant Rose, by cover of darkness and in secret, in the Spronck family plot at Soumagne Cemetery.

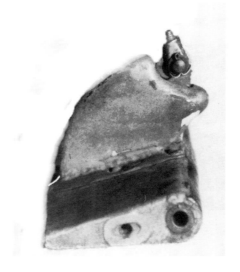

Peter Rose's grave in Soumagne, and a tail aileron trim tab from his Spitfire, preserved in the village.

In 1948, Major and Mrs Rose visited Soumagne and were told the full story by Monsieur Spronck, who presented the grieving parents with their 25-year old son's flying helmet. Later the Commonwealth War Graves Commission decided that Sergeant Rose should be exhumed and re-buried at a new communal war cemetery some distance away. Both the villagers and Major Rose protested, and eventually the Commission agreed that Sergeant Rose could remain at Soumagne providing he was given his own grave. The villagers then erected a memorial to their own war dead, burying the young pilot nearby. A kerbstone surround was paid for by the village, and the Commission erected Sergeant Rose's headstone, inscribed with the words 'This Was a Man'. John Rose observed 'How well they chose their words; how adequately they describe a most lovable brother'.

In October 1988, John Rose and his family arrived unannounced in Soumagne and were moved to discover fresh flowers on Peter's immaculately kept grave. Each successive generation of children in Soumagne are told the story of 'their' young pilot, whose courage and sacrifice represented hope in those terrible days of occupation. What a pity that in England our children are not inspired with the same respect and awareness of the debt we will always owe all of those servicemen who gave their lives for freedom.

The inscription on Sergeant Rose's headstone comes from Shakespeare's Julius Ceaser, Act V, and is both a poignant and moving epitaph to this tragic young man from Staffordshire: -

> His life was gentle; and the element so
> Mixed in him that nature might stand up and
> Say to all the world: "This was a Man."

The crash site today.

Chapter Seven

Wing Commander Douglas Bader DSO DFC
&
Flight Lieutenant 'Buck' Casson DFC

To Dilip
with Best Wishes
from
'Buck' Casson

The name of Douglas Bader will forever be inspirational, for, though no less flawed than any other human being, here was a *real* hero.

A public school boy captivated by the thought of powered flight, and whose uncle was adjutant of the RAF College, Cranwell, Bader was commissioned into the RAF between the wars. He achieved his ambition and became a fighter pilot. A gifted sportsman, Bader had not only played cricket to a high standard but also was expecting to play rugby for England, it became apparent that the young pilot had a natural aptitude for aerobatics. Although a member of the RAF Aerobatic Team, such daredevil flying proved his undoing. Having disregarded various warnings from his Flight Commander, Harry Day, against low flying, Bader crashed at Woodley aerodrome, near Reading, attempting a slow roll at virtually zero feet. The reckless manoeuvre was executed for no other reason than to show off to civilian pilots. As Bader himself later said, "Made a balls of it, old boy, that's all there was to it!" Indeed he had. The young airman's legs were so badly crushed that both were amputated, and he lingered near death for several days. But the incredibly tough Bader spirit could not be crushed. Remarkably he recovered and not only mastered comparatively primitive and clumsy artificial limbs, but amazingly passed a flying test! Unfortunately the King's Regulations did not provide for disabled pilots, so, rejecting the offer of a desk job, Douglas Bader, aged 23, left the service that he loved so much in 1933.

That very year, however, saw the Nazi dictator Adolf Hitler achieve power in Germany, starting the countdown to the Second World War. Bader, working in the office of the Asiatic Petroleum Company's aviation department, recognised not only that war was inevitable, but that England would soon need trained service pilots like himself. The RAF would not back down, however, and refused to offer Bader a flying appointment. Undeterred, Bader maintained pressure on the Air Ministry, until, on August 31st, 1939, Air Vice-Marshal Portal, the Air Member for Personnel, confirmed that in the event of war, he would be reinstated to flying duties. Three days later Britain and France declared war on Nazi Germany.

Having passed a medical and flying test, Douglas Bader was re-commissioned as a Flying Officer and pilot. After a refresher course at the Central Flying School, Bader joined 19 Squadron at Duxford on February 7th, 1940. At last he was flying Spitfires! When Hitler attacked the west, however, on May 10th, 1940, Air Chief Marshal Sir Hugh Dowding far-sightedly preserved his Spitfire force for home defence, committing only Hurricane squadrons to the losing battle being fought in France. By then Bader had been promoted to Flight Lieutenant and was a flight commander in 222 Squadron, still flying Spitfires. When the British Expeditionary Force was left with no option but to retire on and evacuate from Dunkirk, the Spitfires were at last deployed and clashed with the Me 109s during Operation DYNAMO, the air operation covering the withdrawal. On June 1st, 1940, Bader scored his first aerial victories when he destroyed an Me 109 and damaged an Me 110 over Dunkirk; the die had been cast.

On June 24th, 1940, Bader was promoted to Acting Squadron Leader and left 222 Squadron to command 242, a demoralised unit of largely Canadian Hurricane pilots who had been badly mauled during the Fall of France. Leading by example, Squadron Leader Bader soon demonstrated that he was no disabled passenger and whipped his new squadron back into shape. Based at Coltishall in 12 Group, however, Bader soon became frustrated as the forward squadrons of 11 Group bore the brunt of the Battle of Britain. His energetic personality did not permit an idle role, and Bader was unable to understand the (sound) concepts of Dowding's System of Home Defence, in which 12 Group's role was to protect 11 Group's airfields whilst their fighters were engaged, and not otherwise sally forth southwards against the enemy. On August 30th, 1940, 242 Squadron was ordered to reinforce 11 Group and intercept a German raid on aircraft factories to the north-west of London. Bader's Hurricanes fell on the unescorted enemy bombers and, he believed, alone executed great damage. This led Douglas Bader to believe that had he been commanding more fighters in the air then even greater losses would have been inflicted upon the enemy. This was, however, a fallacy, as contemporary combat records prove that a number of 11 Group fighters, both Spitfires and Hurricanes, were successfully involved in the same engagement which was not, therefore, the solo 242 Squadron execution that Bader believed.

Squadron Leader Bader already enjoyed a unique relationship with Air Vice-Marshal Sir Trafford Leigh-Mallory, the Air Officer Commanding No 12 Group, who, amazingly, had never been either a fighter pilot or leader. 'LM', however, saw merit in Bader's suggestion that he should lead several squadrons forward over 11 Group and against the enemy, even this was contrary to the System. That System, which was tried and tested, was, it must be remembered, created by two of the RAF's most experienced fighter leaders, Dowding and the AOC 11 Group, Air Vice-Marshal Keith Park. Both men had significant experience of flying fighters during the Great War, and Dowding also possessed a terrific scientific understanding which had enabled the early harness of radar into the System. That Leigh-Mallory and the very junior officer Acting Squadron Leader Douglas Bader should challenge the thinking of Dowding and Park was insubordinate to the extreme. But so it was that the ambitious Leigh-Mallory, and ever impatient but enthusiastic Bader, saw the 'Big Wing' concept as a means of ensuring that 12 Group played a fulsome role in the Battle of Britain, which would no longer be the private concern of 11 Group.

On September 7th, 1940, Squadron Leader Bader led the Hurricanes of 242 and 310 (Czech) Squadrons, and the Spitfires of 19, into action as a 'Wing' over London for the first time. Bounced by 109s whilst climbing over the Thames Estuary, the engagement was not the great success that both Leigh-Mallory and Bader had hoped for, but as the days went on the Wing's perceived success increased. This led Leigh-Mallory to deploy two further squadrons to fly with the 'Big Wing', namely the Spitfires of 611 and the Hurricanes of 302 (Polish). The evolving tactics led to the higher performance Spitfires taking on the German fighter escorts, whilst the Hurricanes attacked the bombers. The Big Wing's claims were subsequently impressive, and led to many congratulatory signals being received by Squadron Leader Bader. Unfortunately, no one seems to have checked these claims against the actual German aircraft lying wrecked across southern England. Had they done so, a massive discrepancy would have become immediately apparent. The fact of the matter was that ambition and enthusiasm concealed the truth: the more fighters are in action, the more confused a battle becomes, and thus several pilots can simultaneously attack and claim the same aircraft destroyed. These claims were made in good faith, however, the speed of combat having deceived the human eye and each pilot being unaware of the presence or involvement of other friendly fighters.

Unfortunately Leigh-Mallory had friends at the Air Ministry, whereas Dowding and Park ad neglected such politics in favour of defending the country. People in high places began taking notice of the Big Wing's claims, and became convinced that such tactics were better than those of Park's, which carefully employed penny-packet formations. The adjutant of 242 Squadron was also an MP who had the Prime Minister's ear, and this officer was responsible for betraying his Commander-in-Chief at top level. Although the Battle of Britain was won by Dowding and Park, towards its close they were both called to account for their tactics at the Air Ministry. The meeting was unprecedented, and what was virtually a 'kangaroo court' heard evidence from the exponents of both tactical doctrines. That having been said, Squadron Leader Bader was the most junior officer present, and vigorously expounded his Big Wing theory, whilst Dowding and Park were not invited to bring along one of their many squadron commanders, any one of which had far more combat experience than Bader.

The result of the 'Meeting of Infamy' was that the two real architects of victory in the Battle of Britain were shamefully treated. Dowding was sacked as Commander-in-Chief of Fighter Command, and Park was moved into Training Command. His place at the helm of prestigious 11 Group was taken by Leigh-Mallory, and Sholto Douglas, a Leigh-Mallory and Bader supporter, took over from Dowding. And so it was that the fundamentally flawed Big Wing prevailed, and convinced high RAF commanders that the Wing, of three squadrons, should become the basic fighter formation in both attack and defence. Strangely enough, shortly after the Battle of Britain a simulated exercise took place in which Big Wings responded to a recreated German raid that had actually taken place during the summer of 1940. The result was a disaster: confusion reigned, and the enemy successfully bombed all targets.

After the change at the helm of Fighter Command, the outlook shifted from the defensive over to the offensive. The idea was to 'Reach out' and take the war to the enemy over occupied France. The concept was simple: wings of Spitfires would sally forth across the Channel and engage German fighters, which would be destroyed en masse. A new operational command post was created, that of 'Wing Commander Flying'. Following on from Douglas Bader's role at Duxford in 1940, experienced fighter squadron commanders were promoted to be Wing Leaders and appointed to various Sector Stations. Naturally Bader himself was a top choice, and his old friend Leigh-Mallory even gave him a choice of venue for the coming season: Biggin Hill or Tangmere? The dedicated Bader decided that Biggin Hill was too close to the distractions of London for his young pilots, and so opted for Tangmere, nestling near the south coast near Chichester. And so, in March 1941, Wing Commander Douglas Bader took leave of his beloved 242 Squadron and became Wing Leader at Tangmere.

Wing Commander Bader at the 616 Squadron dispersal, Westhampnett, 1941.

On the south coast Bader found 616 Squadron, commanded by Billy Burton, another Cranwell graduate and actually the 1937 Sword of Honour winner, with which he was already familiar: during the closing stages of the Battle of Britain 616 had reinforced the Big Wing. Burton's squadron was at Westhampnett (now known as Goodwood), which was shared with the Spitfires of 610 Squadron, led by former 616 Squadron Battle of Britain stalwart, Squadron Leader Ken Holden. At nearby Merston was the Wing's third Spitfire squadron, 145, commanded by the indomitable Canadian Stan Turner, who had flown with Bader during the Battle of Britain.

Spitfires take off from Westhampnett on another sweep, summer 1941.

'Dogsbody' soon chose to lead the Wing at the head of 616 Squadron, and chose a young Sergeant pilot from the Volunteer Reserve stable as his wingman. Alan Smith remembers that day: 'Wing Commander Bader came stomping into the dispersal hut, and looked around at we pilots gathered therein. He already knew Cocky Dundas and Johnnie Johnson, so said to me "Who are you?" I nearly jumped out of my seat! "Smith, Sir", I replied, "Sergeant Smith".

"Good", said Douglas, "I want you to fly as my Number Two". I just couldn't believe it, it was like God asking me to keep an eye on heaven whilst he popped out for a minute!'

The Wing Leader's initials, 'DB', were painted on the fuselage of his personal Spitfire, and Bader's radio call sign therefore became 'Dogsbody'. His leading section of four Spitfires inevitably became 'Dogsbody Section'.

Soon the Tangmere Wing was frequently flying fighter sweeps over France, regularly engaging the enemy. These sweeps were not necessarily successful, however, as the Germans knew only too well that a fighter is only going to cause damage if another fighter is sent to intercept. So, the *Luftwaffe* very sensibly chose either to remain on the ground, the RAF fighters just wasting time and petrol, or carefully chose to attack only when the tactical situation was entirely in their favour. Interestingly, this was a reversal of the Battle of Britain situation, the RAF pilots facing a two-way sea crossing on a single engine and fighting over enemy occupied territory. Moreover, and most importantly, the Spitfire, designed as a defensive fighter and in which capacity it excelled, was being used as an offensive fighter, for which it was possessed of insufficient range. The Me 109, however, now found itself fighting the defensive battle for which it was designed, as opposed to having also been pressed into an equally unsuitable offensive role during the Battle of Britain. Clearly, the Fighter Command 'Non-stop Offensive' of 1941 was not going to be the pushover that the RAF's optimistic high commanders expected and required.

During the Battle of Britain, RAF fighter controllers had likewise not responded to German fighter sweeps over southern England, but were forced to do so when fighter-bombers, indistinguishable from normal fighters on the radar screen, began to be included in the enemy formations. After bombs had unexpectedly rained down on London during the morning of September 20th, 1940, Fighter Command had not only been forced to respond to every enemy incursion, but had to mount standing patrols over the south coast. The tables were now turned however, and the RAF started sending small formations of light bombers to attack certain targets in north-west France. These raiders, which the Germans could not ignore, were escorted by wings of Spitfires and it was hoped that this tactic, the 'Circus' operation, would help achieve the required end result. In reality, however, there were no targets in France that were crucial to the German war effort and which would therefore generate the kind of reaction hoped for by Sholto Douglas and Leigh-Mallory. Although the Germans started to respond to these nuisance raids, they still chose when, where and how to attack. The initiative was completely theirs, and do not underestimate the fact that the German day fighter force at that time possessed some massively skilful and experienced *experten*.

Down at Tangmere, however, Bader's Spitfire pilots had observed the German fighters flying, as Johnnie Johnson later put it to me, 'in this lean and hungry looking formation'. Flying Officer Hugh 'Cocky' Dundas of 616 Squadron discussed this with Wing Commander Bader, and persuaded him that it was worth an experiment to emulate the enemy *Schwarm*. So it was that one morning in May 1941 found four Tangmere Spitfires stooging up and down the Channel, imitating the German formation, and hoping to get bounced. Sure enough the 109s took the bait, but Bader timed the break into fighting pairs slightly wrong and Dundas was shot down, crash-landing at Hawkinge. But the experiment had convinced Bader that the 'Finger Four' was the best tactical formation. From then on the Tangmere Wing practised the method until the Spitfire pilots got it right. Ron Rayner, who joined the Wing when 41 Squadron relieved 145 at Merston in July 1941, told me that "the 'Cross-over' or 'Finger-four', as we called it, was absolutely brilliant. It made such a massive difference which cannot be emphasised enough".

Flying Officer Hugh 'Cocky' Dundas.

Sergeants West, Brewer, Mabbett & Pilot Officer Hepple pose with Spitfire 'DB', P9766; note the nose art!

Whilst the Spitfire pilots' experience increased with the improving weather, so too did the tempo of the air war over France: on June 22nd, 1941, Hitler made a surprise attack on Russia, Operation BARBOROSSA, and soon the Soviets were clamouring for Allied support. As with Poland two years earlier, the Western Allies were unable to provide direct military assistance, so the only option was to try and tie down *Luftwaffe* units on the Channel coast. The sweeps and circuses, supplemented by rhubarbs and ramrods, continued unabated that fateful summer, but RAF losses were high and the Germans continued to defend the west with just two fighter groups, JG 2 *Richthofen* and JG 26 *Schlageter*.

As can be imagined, Wing Commander Bader ensured that the Tangmere Wing was kept busy and in the thick of the press. But, by August 1941, he was tired. Other Wing Leaders had already been rested, but, characteristically, Bader had refused all such offers, preferring instead to see out the 'season' at Tangmere. His pilots had christened the Wing 'Bader's Bus Company', and morale was high. The RAF fighter pilots, operating over France in large numbers, had submitted grossly exaggerated combat claims, the majority of which were allowed by Intelligence Officers without any accurate means of verification (due to the combats having taken place over France or the Channel and there not being access to any wrecked enemy machines). The Spitfire pilots believed, therefore, that they were doing well, blissfully unaware of the actual German losses and combat claim ratio which was, in fact, in the enemy's favour by a ratio of 2:1. Churchill and the War Cabinet knew the truth, of course, through ULTRA decrypts, but could not permit the facts to become common knowledge. And so it was that the 'Non-Stop Offensive' continued unabated, but became known by the Germans as the 'Non-sense Offensive'.

By this time, Douglas Bader had been decorated with both the DSO & bar, and the DFC; he was a celebrity. Naturally the media had capitalised on the morale-boosting story of the legless fighter 'ace', and so, Douglas Bader's contribution to the war effort was not only from the cockpit of a Spitfire but also via the propaganda war. The public eagerly read the newspapers, listened to the wireless and watched the cinema news reels for news of their heroes. Uppermost amongst the august were fighter pilots: as in the Great War the public saw in their knightly deeds something romantic and noble, and so the exploits of the 'aces' were enthusiastically followed. Douglas Bader became a household name.

On the morning of Monday, August 9th, 1941, the teleprinter clattered away at Tangmere as the Form 'D' came through from 11 Group HQ, detailing the Wing's task for that day. This was another complex Circus, No 68, involving many aircraft to Gosnay. The Tangmere Wing was to provide Target Support. Directives issued that August stipulated that the Target Support Wing's role was to 'clear the road to the target area, also to cover the withdrawal of the bombers and escort Wings. There are usually two Target Support Wings, one being routed the same direction as the bombers, to arrive over the target three minutes earlier, and the other is given a different route, but also arriving three minutes in advance of the bombers.'

For Wing Commander Bader and the Westhampnett Spitfire squadrons, 616 and 610, Target Support was a routine sortie, although not, of course, without the usual hazards. Although Squadron Leader 'Elmer' Gaunce DFC's 41 Squadron had arrived at Merston just two weeks previously, the Squadron had already flown numerous practice sweeps when based at Catterick and at least one offensive patrol over France from Redhill. Circus 68, therefore, represented nothing other than a typical sortie and was not beyond the capabilities of any of the Tangmere Wing's three Spitfire squadrons.

Sergeant Alan Smith, Wing Commander Bader's usual 'Dogsbody 2', had a head cold and so was unable to fly. Imminently to be commissioned, and as his name was not 'on the board', Alan prepared to go into London and buy a new uniform. His place as the Wing Leader's No 2 was taken by a New Zealander, Sergeant Jeff West, a pilot with one-and-a-half Me 109s destroyed and one damaged to his credit. Clearly West was not without experience: frequently that summer he had flown No 2 to Flight Lieutenant EP Gibbs, until that officer was shot down over France on July 9th, 1941.

For this Target Support sortie to Gosnay, 'Dogsbody' Section therefore consisted of:-

Dogsbody: Wing Commander Douglas Bader DSO* DFC.
Dogsbody 2: Sergeant Jeff West.
Dogsbody 3: Flight Lieutenant Hugh Dundas DFC.
Dogsbody 4: Pilot Officer 'Johnnie' Johnson.

Also leading 'Finger Fours' within the 616 Squadron formation of three sections, would be the squadron commander, Squadron Leader 'Billy' Burton (Yellow Section), and the 'B' Flight commander, Flight Lieutenant Lionel 'Buck' Casson (Blue Section). Across the other side of the airfield, Squadron Leader Ken Holden DFC and 610 Squadron also prepared for the morning sortie.

Take-off came at 1040 hrs, 'Dogsbody' Section leading Westhampnett's Spitfires for yet another sortie into very hostile airspace. High over Chichester, Squadron Leader Holden swiftly manoeuvred 610 Squadron into position above and slightly to port of 616. As Target Support, the Wing had no bombers to meet prior to setting course for France, although the Spitfires were still routed out over Beachy Head. As the Wing left Chichester, however, there was no sign of 41 Squadron.

The Beachy Head Forward Relay Station recorded the Tangmere Wing's R/T messages that day. As the Wing neared 'Diamond', 41 Squadron had still not appeared. Group Captain Woodhall, at Tangmere, was the first to speak, making a test call:-

'Dogsbody?'

'OK, OK'.

Bader then made R/T test calls to the commanders of both 610 and 41, using their Christian names as was his usual practice:-

DB: 'Ken?'
KH: 'Loud and clear'.
DB: 'Elmer?'

There was no response from Squadron Leader Gaunce which provoked an acid remark from the Wing Leader to 'Woody'. Unable to wait, 616 and 610 Squadrons set course for France and Gosnay, adopting their battle formations in the process. Still climbing, Wing Commander Bader waggled his wings insistently, indicating that 'Dogsbody 3', Flight Lieutenant Dundas, should take the lead. Dundas slid across, tucking his wing tip just two or three feet from Bader's. From this close proximity, Dundas saw the Wing Leader mouth two words: 'Airspeed Indicator', meaning that the instrument on Spitfire Mk VA W3185 was unserviceable. The Wing had to climb at the right speed to ensure Time on Target at the appointed time, which was crucial. Dundas gave a 'thumbs up' and moved forward to lead the Spitfires to France. On the rear of his hand he had fortunately written the time at which the Wing was due over the French coast in addition to the speed which had to be maintained. The 21-year-old Flight Commander then 'settled down to concentrate on the job'.

Sir Hugh Dundas later recalled that the 'sun was bright and brilliant, unveiled by any layer of high haze or cirrus cloud.' Realising that the white cumulus cloud below provided a background which would immediately reveal the silhouettes of any aircraft, Dundas correctly anticipated that under such conditions 'Dogsbody' would wish to climb as high as possible, and so adjusted both his throttle setting and rate of climb accordingly, taking the Spitfires up to 28,000 feet.

Then, more radio messages:-

DB: 'Ken and Elmer, start gaining height'.
KH: 'Elmer's not with us.'
Unidentified, garbled voice on the R/T, believed to be Squadron Leader Gaunce.
DB: 'Elmer from Dogsbody. I cannot understand what you say, but we are on our way. You had better decide for yourself whether to come or go back'.

Squadron Leader Ken Holden DFC.

Further garbled message followed by 'Woody' advising 41 Squadron that, 'Walker Leader, Dogsbody is 20 miles ahead of you'.

Following the last radio transmissions, at least the Wing was now aware that more Spitfires were bringing up the rear, even if some distance away. The Spitfires cruised over the Channel, towards France, with 610 Squadron above and behind 616. Dundas led the Wing over the French coast right on cue (although there is conflicting evidence regarding whether the coast was crossed south of Le Touquet, known as the 'Golf Course', or Boulogne, slightly further north). This crucial timing observed, Bader accelerated ahead and informed 'Dogsbody 3' over the R/T that he was resuming the lead. The Spitfires' arrival over the coastal flak belt was greeted by dangerous little puff-balls of black smoke which made the formation twist and turn. 'Beetle' then called 'Dogsbody' informing that the beehive itself was 'on time and engaged'. As the Spitfires forged inland, therefore, some distance behind them the bombers and various cover Wings were now bound for France and action.

Group Captain AB 'Woody' Woodhall.

Slightly below the condensation trail level, a 610 Squadron pilot reported seeing contrails 'above and to our left'. Squadron Leader Holden consequently led the squadron higher still whilst 'Beetle' (B) reported:-

B: 'Dogsbody from Beetle. There are 20 plus five miles to the east of you.'
DB: 'OK, but your transmitter is quite impossible. Please use the other.'
B: 'Dogsbody is this better?'
DB: 'Perfect. Ken, start getting more height'.
KH: 'OK, Dogsbody, but will you throttle back? I cannot keep up'.
DB: 'Sorry Ken, my airspeed indicator is u/s. Throttling back, and I will do one slow
     Left-hand turn so you can catch up.'
KH: 'Dogsbody from Ken, I'm making "smoke" (contrails) at this height.'
DB: 'OK, Ken, I'm going down very slightly.'

'Beetle' then advised 'Dogsbody' of more bandits in the vicinity. 616 Squadron's Flying Officer Roy Marples (RM) saw the enemy first: 'Three bandits coming down astern of us. I'm keeping an eye on them, now there are six.'

DB: 'OK'.
B: 'Douglas, another 12 plus ahead and slightly higher.'
RM: 'Eleven of them now'.
DB: 'OK, Roy, let me know exactly where they are.'
RM: 'About one mile astern and slightly higher'.
B: 'Douglas, there is another 40 plus 15 miles to the north-east of you.'
DB: 'OK Beetle. Are our friends where they ought to be, I haven't much idea where
     I am.'
B: 'Yes, you are exactly right. And so are your friends.'
RM: 'Dogsbody from Roy. Keep turning left and you'll see 109s at nine o'clock.'
DB: 'Ken, can you see them?'
KH: 'Douglas, 109s below. Climbing up'.

By this time, 616 and 610 Squadron had progressed into a very dangerous French sky indeed, Beetle having already reported some 72 bandits, representing odds which outnumbered the Spitfires by nearly 3:1. Clearly this was not to be an uneventful sortie. Tension mounting, the Spitfire pilots switched on their gunsight reflectors and gun buttons to 'Fire'. Anxiously they searched the sky, an ever watchful eye being kept on the 109s positioned 1,000 feet above the Wing, waiting to pounce. Bader himself dipped each wing in turn, scrutinising the sky below for the 109s reported by Ken Holden.

DB: 'I can't see them. Will you tell me where to look?'
KH: 'Underneath Bill's section now. Shall I come down?'
DB: 'No, I have them. Get into formation. Going down. Ken, are you with us?'
KH: 'Just above you'.

As Dogsbody Section dived on the enemy, Flight Lieutenant Casson followed with three other aircraft of 'B' Flight.

'Dogsbody 3', Flight Lieutenant Dundas, had 'smelt a rat' in respect of the *Schwarm* of 109s that Dogsbody Section was now rapidly diving towards. Finding no targets to the Section's right, 'Dogsbody 4', Pilot Officer Johnson, skidded under the section and fired at an Me 109 on the left. By this time the whole of Dogsbody Section was firing, although Dundas, still unhappy and suspecting a trap, had a compelling urge to look behind. Suddenly Pilot Officer 'Nip' Hepple shouted over the R/T:-

'Blue 2 here. Some buggers coming down behind, astern. Break left!'

The Spitfire pilots hauled their aircraft around in steep turns. The sky behind Dogsbody Section was full of Me 109s, all firing - without Hepple's warning the Spitfires would have been instantly nailed. As the high 109s crashed into 616 Squadron, Squadron Leader Holden decided that it was time for his section to join the fray and reduce the odds. Informing Flight Lieutenant Denis Crowley-Milling of this decision, Holden led his Spitfires down to assist. Buck Casson, following Bader's Section, was well throttled back to keep his flight together. Also attacking from the rear, Casson managed a squirt at a *Rotte* of 109s. Flying Officer Marples, No 3 in Casson's section, then shouted a warning of even more 109s diving upon the Wing, whilst Squadron Leader Billy Burton urged the Spitfires to 'Keep turning', thus preventing the 109s (which could not out-turn a Spitfire), getting in a shot. Suddenly the organised chaos became a totally confused maelstrom of twisting, turning fighters:-

'BREAK! FOR CHRIST'S SAKE BREAK!'

The Spitfires immediately 'broke' - hard. 'Johnnie' Johnson remembers:-

There was this scream of '*Break*!' - and we all broke, we didn't wait to hear it twice! Round, then a swirling mass of 109s and Spitfires. When I broke I could see Bader still firing. Dundas was firing at the extreme right 109. There was some cloud nearby and I disappeared into it as quick as possible! I couldn't say how many aircraft were involved, suffice to say a lot. It seemed to me that the greatest danger was a collision, rather than being shot down, that's how close we all were. We had got the 109s we were bouncing and then Holden came down with his section, so there were a lot of aeroplanes. We were fighting 109Fs, although there may have been some Es amongst them. There was an absolute mass of aeroplanes just 50 yards apart, it was awful. I thought to myself "You're going to collide with somebody!" I didn't think about shooting at anything after we were bounced ourselves, all you could think about was surviving, getting out of that mass of aircraft. In such a tight turn, of course, you almost black out, you cannot really see where you are going. It was a mess. I had never been so frightened in my life, never!

Chased by three Me 109s, the closest just 100 yards astern, Pilot Officer Johnson maintained his tight turn, spiralling down towards the safety of a nearby cloud which his Spitfire dived into with over 400 m.p.h on the clock. Pulling back the throttle and centralising the controls, the altimeter stabilised, but, speed having dropped to less than 100 mph, the Spitfire stalled. Beneath the cloud, 'Dogsbody 4' recovered control. Having requested and received a homing course for Dover, he headed rapidly for England. Over the R/T, Pilot Officer Johnson could still hear 616 and 610 Squadrons' running battle:-

'Get into formation or they'll shoot the bloody lot of you!'
'Spitfire going down in flames, 10 o'clock.'
'YQ-C (616 Squadron Spitfire). Form up on me, I'm at three o'clock to you.'
'Four buggers above us', this from Hepple.

Left: A Spitfire Mk V taking hits from an Me 109.

Right: An Me 109F under fire from a Spitfire.

'All Elfin aircraft (616 Squadron) withdraw. I say again, all Elfin aircraft withdraw.'

'Use the cloud if you're in trouble', from Billy Burton.

'Are you going home, Ken?', also from Burton.

'Yes, withdrawing', from Holden.

'Ken from Crow. Are you still about?'

'I'm right behind you, Crow'.

'Are we all here?'

'Two short.'

' Dogsbody from Beetle. Do you require any assistance?'

'Beetle from Elfin Leader. We are OK and withdrawing.'

'Thank you Billy. Douglas, do you require any assistance? Steer three-four-zero to the coast.'

The silence from 'Dogsbody' was ominous.

Flight Lieutenant Casson remembers:-

I watched Wing Commander Bader and 'A' Flight attack and break to port as I was coming in. I was well throttled back in the dive, as the other three had started to fall behind and I wanted to keep the flight together. I attacked from the rear, and after having a squirt at two 109s flying together, left them for a single one which was flying inland alone. I finished nearly all of my cannon ammunition up on this boy who finally baled out at 6,000 feet, having lost most of his tail unit. The other three 'B' flight machines were in my rear and probably one of the lads saw this.

I climbed to 13,000 feet and fell in with Billy Burton and three other aircraft, all from 'A' Flight. We chased around in a circle for some time, gaining height all the while, and more 109s were directly above us. Eventually we formed up in line abreast and set off after the Wing.

Billy's section flew in pairs abreast, so I flew abreast but at about 200 yards to starboard. We were repeatedly attacked by two Me 109s which had followed us and were flying above and behind. Each time they started diving I called out and we all turned and re-formed, the 109s giving up their attack and climbing each time.

About 15 miles from the coastline I saw another Spitfire well below us and about half-a-mile to starboard. This machine was alone and travelling very slowly. I called up Billy on the R/T and suggested that we cross over to surround him and help the pilot back as he looked like a sitting duck. I broke off to starboard and made for the solitary Spitfire, but then, on looking back for Billy and the others, was amazed to see them diving away hard to the south-west for a low layer of cloud into which they soon disappeared. I realised then that my message had either been misunderstood or not received. Like a greenhorn, I had been so intent upon watching Billy's extraordinary disappearance to the left, and the lone Spitfire to my right, I lost sight of the Me 109s that had been worrying us. I remember looking for them but upon not discovering their position assumed that they had chased Billy instead. I was soon proved wrong, however, when I received three hits in both fuselage and wing. This occurred just as I was coming alongside the lone Spitfire, which I could not identify as it was not from Tangmere. I broke for some cloud at 5,000 feet, which I reached but found too thin for cover, and was pursued by the 109s.

I then picked out two more 109s flying above me and so decided to drop to zero feet, fly north and cross the Channel at a narrow point as I was unsure of the damage sustained and the engine was not running smoothly. I pressed the teat and tried to run for it, but the two Me 109s behind had more speed and were rapidly within range, whilst the other two flew 1,500 feet above and dived from port to starboard and back, delivering quick bursts. Needless to say I was not flying straight and level all this time!

In the event I received a good one from behind, which passed between the stick and my right leg, taking off some of the rudder on its way. It passed into the petrol tank but whether the round continued into the engine I do not know. Petrol began leaking into the cockpit, oil pressure was dropping low, and with the radiator wide open I could smell the glycol overheating.

As the next attack came, I pulled straight up from the deck in a loop and on my way down, as I was changing direction towards the sea, my engine became extremely rough and seized up as white glycol fumes poured forth. There was no option but to crash-land the aircraft.

I tried to send 'Dogsbody' a hurried message, then blew up the wireless and made a belly landing in a field some 10 miles south of Calais. The 'Goons', having seen the glycol, were decent enough not to shoot me up as I was landing, but circled about for a time and gave my position away to a German cavalry unit in a wood in a corner of the field. One of the pilots waved to me as he flew overhead, and I waved back just before setting fire to the aircraft. Due to the petrol in the cockpit, and because I was carrying a port-fire issued for this purpose, igniting the aircraft was easy. No sooner had I done this than a party of shrieking Goons armed with rifles came chasing over and that was the end of me!

What eventually happened to the lone Spitfire which I went to help out I have no idea. As the 109s followed me, I assume that he got away okay, I certainly hope so.

Buck Casson's crashed Spitfire.

I will never forget that day, one which I have gone over so often in my daydreams.

Flight Lieutenant Casson had been the victim of *Hauptmann* Gerhard Schöpfel, *Gruppenkommandeur* of III/JG26. In 1996, Herr Schöpfel recalled:-

My IIIrd *Gruppe* attacked a British bomber formation, after which my formation was split up. With the British on their homeward flight, I headed alone for my airfield at Ligescourt, near Crécy. Suddenly I saw a flight of Spitfires flying westwards. I attacked them from above and after a short burst of fire the rear machine nosed over sharply and dived away. Whilst the other aircraft flew on apparently unaware, I pursued the fleeing Spitfire as I could see no sign of damage. The British pilot hugged the ground, dodging trees and houses. I was constantly in his propwash and so could not aim properly. Because of the warm air near the ground my radiator flaps opened and so my speed decreased, it thus took me a long time to get into a good firing position. Finally I was positioned immediately behind the Spitfire and it filled my gunsight. I pressed the firing button for both cannon and machine-guns, but - click! I had obviously exhausted my ammunition in the earlier air battles. Of course the British pilot had no way of knowing this and I still wanted to strike terror in him for so long as he remained over French soil. I thus remained right behind him, at high speed. Suddenly I was astonished to see a white plume of smoke emit from the Spitfire! The smoke grew denser and the propeller stopped. The pilot made a forced landing in a field east of Marquise. I circled the aircraft and made a note of the markings for my victory report, watched the pilot climb out and waved to him. Just before being captured by German soldiers, he ignited a built-in explosive charge which destroyed the centre-section of his aircraft.

I returned to my field and sent my engineering officer to the site to determine the reason for the forced landing. He found, to my amazement, that the Spitfire had taken a single machine-gun round in an engine cylinder during my first attack. Had I not pressed on after running out of ammunition, and therefore forcing the pilot to fly at top speed, he would probably have reached England despite the damage. Just a few weeks before, in fact, I myself had made it back across the Channel after two of my engine's connecting rods had been smashed over Dover. On this occasion over France, however, the British pilot, a flight lieutenant, now had to head for prison camp whilst I recorded my 33rd victory.

Hauptmann
Gerhard Schöpfel.

Whilst 'Buck' Casson was to spend the rest of the war as a prisoner, Gerhard Schöpfel running out of ammunition had clearly saved his life. With petrol splashing into the cockpit, another hit would no doubt have ignited the Spitfire into a blowtorch. Luck, it would appear, played no mean part in survival.

Returning to the French coast, Pilot Officer Johnson saw a lone Me 109 below. Suspecting it to be one of the three which chased him into the cloud just a few minutes previously, Johnnie anxiously searched the sky for the other two: the sky was clear. From astern, 'Dogsbody 4' dropped below the 109 before attacking from its blind spot, below and behind. One burst of cannon shells sent the enemy fighter diving earthwards emitting a plume of black smoke.

Pilot Officer Johnson came 'out of France on the deck, low and fast', his Spitfire roaring over waving civilians, just feet above their fields. At the coast, German soldiers ran to their guns, but in a second the fleeting Spitfire was gone. Climbing over the Channel, 'Dogsbody 4' realised that something might have happened to Wing Commander Bader:-

As I was crossing the Channel, Group Captain Woodhall, who obviously knew that there had been a fight from the radar and R/T, repeated 'Douglas, are you receiving?' This came over the air every five minutes or so. I therefore called up and said 'Its Johnnie here, Sir, we've had a stiff fight and I last saw the Wing Commander on the tail of a 109'. He said, 'Thank you, I'll meet you at dispersal'.

The silence from 'Dogsbody' over the R/T clearly meant one of two things, either that his radio was u/s, or he had somehow been brought down. Air Marshal Sir Denis Crowley-Milling, then a flight commander in Ken Holden's 610 Squadron, recalled that: -

The greatest impression I have of August 9th, 1941, is the silence on the R/T. Douglas always maintained a running commentary. Had the worst happened? The colourful language and running commentary had suddenly ceased, leaving us all wondering what had happened. Was he alive or dead? Had his radio failed? I know we were above thick cloud on the way home and asked the Tangmere Controller to provide a homing bearing for us to steer. This was way out in accuracy, however, and unbeknown to us we were flying up the North Sea, just scraping in to Martlesham Heath with hardly any fuel remaining - it was indeed a day to remember!

So confused had been the fighting, so numerous the aircraft in this incredible maelstrom over St Omer, that only Wing Commander Bader himself had the answers to the questions regarding his present state and whereabouts. After the first downwards charge, 'Dogsbody' had found himself alone after flattening out at 24,000 feet. In front of him were six 109s flying in a line abreast formation of three pairs. Flying alone, Bader knew that he should leave this enemy formation and adhere to the instructions which he had even issued to his pilots as formal instructions: get out and get home. He considered these 109s to be 'sitters', however, and in a split-second greed won over discipline and good judgement. Alone over France, Wing Commander Bader stalked the middle *Rotte*. He later reported:-

I saw some more Me 109s. I arrived amongst these, who were evidently not on the lookout, as I expect they imagined the first formation we attacked to be covering them. I got a very easy shot at one of these which flew quite straight until he went on fire from behind the cockpit - a burst of about three seconds.

As two 109s curved towards him, 'Dogsbody' broke right, violently, although anticipating, with some bravado, that his course would take him between a pair of 109s. Suddenly something hit Spitfiire 'DB'. Due to the close proximity of the enemy aircraft, Bader assumed that he had collided with a 109. The Spitfire went completely out of control, diving earthwards, it's control column limp and unresponsive. As he looked behind, Bader's impression was that the entire fuselage aft of the VHF aerial had gone, although he was later to report that it was 'probably just the empennage'.

At 24,000 feet, 'Dogsbody' was unable to consider escape due to the lack of oxygen outside the cockpit at that height. His dilemma, however, was that the doomed fighter was already travelling in excess of 400 m.p.h, so would soon be subjected to forces so great that baling out would become impossible. Yanking the canopy release mechanism, the hood was sucked away, the cockpit immediately being battered by the airflow. Without legs though, would he be able to thrust his body upwards to get out? As he struggled to get his head above the windscreen, he was nearly plucked out of the cockpit, but half way he became stuck - the rigid foot of his artificial right leg jamming in the cockpit, the grip vice-like. Ever downwards the fighter plunged, the pilot helpless and continuously battered by the rushing wind, half in and half out of his crashing aeroplane. Desperately gripping his parachute's 'D' ring, Douglas Bader struggled furiously to get out. Eventually, at about 6,000 feet, the offending artificial leg's restraining strap broke. Free at last, the pilot was plucked out into mid-air; as the Spitfire continued its dive, he experienced a moment of apparently floating upwards. That terrible buffeting having thankfully ceased, in the silence he was able to think - hand still gripping the 'D' ring, he pulled; there was a slight delay before the parachute deployed and then he was really was floating, gently to earth beneath the life-saving silk umbrella.

At 4,000 feet Wing Commander Bader floated through a layer of cloud, emerging below to see the ground still far below. Alarmed by the roar of an aero-engine, he saw an Me 109 fly directly towards him, but the bullets he must have half expected never came as the enemy fighter flashed by just 50 yards away. It may surprise many people to know that such a parachute descent, made due to enemy action or some other mishap whilst flying actively, was often the first a pilot would actually make, there being no formal parachute training. Consequently, Bader had never before had to consider the practicalities of landing with artificial legs, or indeed one such leg, as he drifted earthwards. Having had some minutes to ponder this matter, suddenly French soil rushed up to meet him and he hit the ground hard, in an orchard near Blaringhem, to the south-east of St Omer. For Wing Commander Douglas Bader, the air war was over; his personal period of operational service had lasted just 18 months.

Johnnie Johnson recalled the scene back at Westhampnett:-

Group Captain Woodhall was waiting for me on the airfield, and when Dundas, West, Hepple and the others came back the consensus of opinion was that the Wing Commander had either been shot down or involved in a collision.

In his flying log book, Johnnie Johnson wrote that on this penetration over France there had been 'more opposition than ever before.' Squadron Leader Burton's log book recorded 'Had a bad time with 109s on way out and had to get into cloud.'

As the clock ticked on, it became clear from fuel considerations that the two Spitfires reported missing during the radio chatter over France were unlikely to return to Westhampnett. Reasoning that if flying damaged machines the pilots might land at one of the coastal airfields, Tangmere telephoned each in turn, receiving negative responses from all.

Douglas Roberts was a Radio Telephone (Direction Finding) Operator at the Tangmere 'Fixer' station which was, perhaps oddly, located on West Malling airfield in Kent:-

It was there that on August 9th, 1941, we were told that Wing Commander Bader was missing and so listened out for several hours. Our system was basic when compared to modern equipment today, but nevertheless very efficient. The aerial system was a double dipole which, when rotated, would indicate either a true bearing or a reciprocal. Despite our diligence, nothing was heard from 'Dogsbody'.

Had either of the two missing pilots reached mid-Channel, then there was an excellent chance that they would be picked up by air-sea rescue. If their dinghies had drifted closer to the French coast then it was more likely that the Germans would get to them first, unless their positions could be discovered and a protective aerial umbrella established. Consequently Dundas, Johnson, Hepple and West were soon flying back over the Channel, searching. At Le Touquet, Dundas led the section north, parallel to the coast and towards Cap Griz-Nez. Avoiding flak from various enemy vessels, especially near the port of Calais, a steep turn at zero feet returned the Spitfires to Le Touquet. At one point Hepple broke away to machine-gun a surfacing submarine, but otherwise the only item to report was an empty dinghy sighted by Sergeant West. To Johnnie Johnson, that empty, life-saving, rubber boat was somehow symbolic of their fruitless search. With petrol almost exhausted, the section landed at Hawkinge. No news had yet been received of either missing pilot. Immediately the aircraft were refuelled, the 616 Squadron pilots took off, intending to head back across the Channel to France. Shortly after take-off, however, Group Captain Woodhall cancelled the sortie, fearing that a second trip was too risky as the enemy might now be waiting. Swinging round to the west, Dundas led the Spitfires back to Westhampnett.

For Hugh Dundas, the thought of Bader dead was 'utterly shattering'. Having been shot down himself during the Battle of Britain, and only narrowly escaping with his life, Dundas, then 20, had found Douglas Bader a massive inspiration. In November that year, his own brother, Flight Lieutenant John Dundas DFC of 609 Squadron, was killed in action over the Solent; John's death affected him deeply, so when Douglas Bader arrived at Tangmere he no doubt helped fill a great void in this impressionable young man's life. The two were certainly close, and Dundas was to remain devoted to Douglas Bader until his own death in 1995. 'Buck' Casson's loss was also a serious blow to Dundas's morale: they had joined the squadron together at Doncaster and, until that day, were the last remnants of the old pre-war pilots. When the fact dawned on him that he was now the only member of the old guard left, Dundas found this a 'terrifying thought.' Regarding Bader, as a loyal lieutenant, Dundas felt some degree of responsibility. He drove back to Shopwyke House 'alone and utterly dejected.'

With no news other than the fact that her husband had apparently vanished, Group Captain Woodhall had the unenviable duty of driving over to the Bay House and informing Mrs Thelma Bader. John Hunt, a young Intelligence Officer, was already there, having arrived to give some support only to discover that Thelma had yet to receive the bad news, which 'Woody' tempered by stating that Douglas Bader was 'indestructible and probably a prisoner'. Later, Hugh Dundas arrived and with Jill, her sister, persuaded Thelma to take some sherry, which she only brought up again. As Dundas drove back to Shopwyke House he cried. Back at the mess, he and Johnnie Johnson shared a bottle of brandy. Despair had overtaken the inner sanctum.

The Bay House at Bognor, where the inner sanctum awaited news of 'Dogsbody'.

Just as the Target Support detail had been 'routine' for the Tangmere Wing, so too was August 9th, 1941, for JG26, dispersed around various airfields in the Pas-de-Calais. Having urgently responded to the 'Alarmstart', it was 109s from the 'Schlageter' Geschwader that the Tangmere Wing had fought that day high above Béthune. After the action, which developed into a running battle between Béthune and the French coast, the German pilots claimed a total of seven Spitfires destroyed. In reality the figure was five, three Spitfires of 452 (Australian) Squadron having also failed to return (with one pilot killed), lost somewhere between Béthune and Mardyck. However, although JG26, the only *Luftwaffe* unit to engage Spitfires that day, only lost two 109s (including one pilot killed) during the engagement, the RAF pilots claimed a staggering 22 Me 109s destroyed, 10 probables and eight damaged.

Amongst the successful German pilots was JG26's *Kommodore*, *Oberstleutnant* Adolf Galland, who had recorded victory number 76, a Spitfire north-west of St Pol, at 11.32 a.m. Shortly afterwards, *Oberleutnant* 'Pips' Priller, *Staffelkapitän* of 1/JG26, arrived at Audembert to tell Galland about this captured legless 'Adler', urging Galland 'you must come and meet him.' Whilst in hospital, at the *Clinique Sterin* in St Omer, Bader was actually visited several times by two JG26 pilots; he shared a bottle of champagne with them in the doctor's room and concluded that they were 'types' whom he would have liked in the Tangmere Wing. Previous accounts have stated that the Germans recovered Bader's missing leg from his Spitfire's crash site, but in fact French eyewitnesses confirm that the artificial limb in question fluttered down on its own and landed close to Wing Commander Bader's parachute. The villagers handed the article in to the German authorities, after which Galland's engineers made running repairs on the leg to afford the Wing Commander some mobility. A few days later,

Galland sent his *Horsch* staff car to fetch Bader for a visit to the *Geschwaderstabschwarm*.

Whilst visiting JG 26, Wing Commander Bader was interested to know what had happened when he was brought down. His explanation was a collision with an Me 109, although he had not actually seen the aeroplane with which he had supposedly collided. Galland was puzzled, however, as none of his aircraft had been involved in such a collision. One 109 pilot had been killed: *Unteroffizier* Alfred Schlager who crashed at Aire, some 10 miles south-east of St Omer. The Germans therefore conceded it possible that Bader may have collided with Schlager who had not survived to make any report. More likely, though, so far as Galland was concerned, was that Wing Commander Bader had been shot down by one of two pilots, either *Oberfeldwebel* Walter Meyer (6/JG 26) or *Leutnant* Kosse (5/JG 26) who had recorded their 11th and seventh victories respectively above the area of St Omer that morning. According to Adolf Galland, for Bader it was an 'intolerable idea' that his master in the air was an NCO pilot. Tactfully, therefore, a 'fair-haired, good looking flying officer' was selected from the victorious German pilots and introduced to Bader as his champion. Kosse was the only officer of that rank to make a claim that morning, and so it is likely that it was he who Bader met at Audembert. However, neither German pilot's victory

Wing Commander Bader being entertained by Adolf Galland (second left) and his JG 26 officers.

report was conclusive. As Galland later wrote '*it was never confirmed who shot him down*'.

Amongst the officers present at the reception thrown for Bader by JG 26 was *Hauptmann* Gerhard Schöpfel. In 1995, he recalled the occasion:-

My meeting with Wing Commander Bader was memorable and one which I well recall. Our *Oberst* Joachim-Friedrich Huth had lost a leg in the First World War, and when the report about Bader being shot down reached him he was sure that spare artificial legs existed in England. There followed a number of telephone calls, during which Bader's capture was reported to the Red Cross, and it was decided that an RAF aircraft should be offered free passage to deliver the spare legs to our airfield at an appointed time and date. So far as I know, this was initially confirmed by England.

When the Red Cross had announced that Wing Commander Bader was a prisoner, on August 14th, 1941, there was absolute euphoria within Fighter Command, and in particular, of course, at Tangmere. Group Captain Woodhall broadcast the news over the station tannoy.

Sir Denis Crowley-Milling remembered:-

The loss of Douglas Bader had left us all stunned. A few of us, including Dundas and Johnson, were with Thelma Bader in their married quarters at Tangmere when the telephone rang. After speaking, Thelma came back to join us and very calmly said 'Douglas is safe and a prisoner'.

When the signal was received from Germany offering free passage for an RAF aircraft to deliver Wing Commander Bader's spare legs, Group Captain Woodhall responded so enthusiastically that he even offered to fly a Lysander to Audembert himself. However, the Air Ministry rejected the proposal out of hand.

Gerhard Schöpfel continues:-

On the appointed time and date for an RAF aircraft to arrive with the legs, I was at the *Geschwader-gefechtsstand* in Audembert, having flown in from my base at Ligescourt, home of my III/JG26. Soon after our meeting, Bader wanted to inspect one of our Me 109s. Galland invited him to climb into a *Geschwader-maschine* and Bader commented that he would like to fly it, but of course this could not be allowed.

Many photographs were taken by the Germans of this visit, which numerous non-flying JG 26 personnel would later recall as the most memorable incident of their entire war. Amongst the snapshots is a photograph of Bader sitting in the cockpit of a 109, a German officer standing on the adjacent wing. In 'Reach for the Sky' and other books the object in this officer's left hand has been described as a 'pistol' - other photographs from the same series show that in fact *Oberst* Huth is holding his gloves!

Gerhard Schöpfel:-

When told of our arrangement via the Red Cross regarding his spare legs, he was not surprised when no plane arrived as he felt that high authority in England would take time to sanction such things. He hoped, however, that his own Wing would find a way.

One or two days later, our radar announced a Beehive approaching. The Blenheims flew over St Omer where they dropped a few bombs on our I *Gruppe*. Also dropped, however, was a crate containing Bader's legs which was attached to a parachute.

On August 19th, 1941, the 'Leg Operation' took place when, during a Circus to Longuenesse, an 82 Squadron Blenheim dropped the spare legs by parachute. The Tangmere Wing flew close cover, as Ron Rayner recalled:-

I flew with 41 Squadron on that particular sortie and I remember it distinctly. The legs were dropped over St Omer and not without ceremony, it being announced over the R/T that Wing Commander Bader's legs had been delivered. We were weaving around the Blenheims and we were acting as individual aircraft, not a cohesive formation as was usual. Then we continued on to the target before turning round for home.

Woodhall signalled the Germans and so consequently the crate in question was recovered, the legs therein being duly presented to Bader. Galland was most upset that the British had responded so unchivalrously, however; to his mind, 'bombs and charity did not go together'. For Galland, however, his meeting with Wing Commander Bader was to gain an even more-bitter aftertaste.

On August 17th, 1941, whilst Wing Commander Bader still occupied *Chambre 21* in the *Clinique Sterin,* a local French girl who worked at the hospital in an auxiliary capacity, Lucille Debacker, handed Bader a note. The content was astonishing: a Frenchman was to wait outside the hospital every night from midnight until 2 a.m., poised to guide *'Le Colonel'* to a local 'safe' house. Incredibly the note was even signed, by a Frenchwoman, Mme. Hiècque, in her own name. The Hiècques were a working-class French family who lived at the *quai du Haut-Pont* in a long row of terraced houses overlooking the St Omer canal. Gilbert Petit, a young friend of the Hiècque family, was employed at the SNCF railway station in the town. Each night he waited patiently in the shadows of an alleyway across the road from the hospital, risking being caught out after curfew. Within, Bader had received bad news: he was imminently to be taken to Germany. Having been given his new legs, on the night of

August 20th, he knotted bed sheets together, lowered the makeshift rope out of a window at the rear of the building and climbed down. Squeezing through a small gap between the chained gate, Bader met Petit and together they made their way through the cobbled streets, darkness their cloak. Having avoided at least one German patrol, the fugitives eventually reached the sanctuary of the Hiècque household, Bader in great pain from his stumps. *'Le Colonel'* was given a bed upstairs, before drifting off into sleep he thought 'That's foxed the bloody Huns. I'll be seeing Thelma in a couple of days!'

The following day, Mme. Hiècque walked to the hospital and saw many German soldiers searching for the escaped prisoner. Upon her return, she told Bader that *'Les Boches sont tres stupides!'* Bader, however, appreciated the consequences for these French patriots if he was found in their house. Mme. Hiècque was supremely confident, however, that the Germans would never find him, and awaited word from Gilbert that the Underground had been contacted and an escape plan formulated. That afternoon, *'Le Colonel'* was taken out into the back garden and watched a tangled mass of contrails overhead as yet another drama took place above St Omer. The Hiècques and their neighbours shouted enthusiastically, *'Vive les Tommies! Vive les Tommies!'*, giving Bader another view of the sweeps he had flown so often.

The Hiecque's canalside house was actually some distance from the *Clinique Sterin*, and the Germans, being convinced that Bader could not walk far, had cordoned off the area of St Omer around the hospital which they now searched intently. The hospital staff were questioned, but one female lacked Lucille Debacker's courage and resolve: Hélène Lefevre betrayed the conspirators. At about 5.30 p.m. there was an urgent bang at the Hiècque's door - *'Les Boches!'* M. Hiècque bundled Bader into the back garden, hiding him in a chicken run. Within a minute the Germans were in the house and seconds later a bayonet was thrust repeatedly into the straw covering the escapee. Realising that the next stab would probably penetrate his neck or back, Bader stood up, raising his hands. As the Germans escorted him out of the front door to a waiting car, he tried to persuade the *Stabsfeldwebel* who had arrested him that the old couple had no knowledge of his presence, his arrival having been during the night and via a back garden gate. It was then that he noticed Hélène Lefevre leave the German vehicle, and realised that they had all been betrayed.

Bader's escape attempt made life 'very unpleasant' for Adolf Galland. There was an inquiry into the escape and even Bader's visit to Audembert came under scrutiny. Gerhard Schöpfel continues with the German view:-

After Wing Commander Bader received his new legs, we heard that he had escaped by knotting some bed sheets together and climbing out of an upstairs window. For a man with two artificial legs this must have taken incredible guts and will power. Really, however, in view of the strenuous activity involved, which included hiking over the Pyrenees, he actually had little chance of getting away with it. He was soon found in a house by the canal in St Omer. Our *Geschwader* was told that on a subsequent train journey into captivity proper, the guards took both his legs away to prevent another audacious escape attempt!

At the end of the month, the 616 Squadron Operations Record Book concluded that August was:-

A disappointing one from the operational point of view owing to the poor weather conditions. Although 16 offensive sweeps were carried out over France, their effectiveness was in several cases hampered by too much cloud, making it difficult for the squadrons in the Wing to keep together. Wing Commander Bader DSO (& Bar) DFC, and Flight Lieutenant Casson were shot down on August 9th and are now prisoners of war. This was a serious loss to the RAF, the Wing and the Squadron.

In the overall scheme of things, August 1941 was indeed a disappointing month for Fighter Command: 98 Spitfires and 10 Hurricanes were lost. However, JG 2 and JG 26 combined had lost just 18 pilots, i.e. the loss ratio was exactly a staggering 6:1 in the *Luftwaffe's* favour.

Following the loss of its first Wing Leader, the Tangmere Wing itself would never be the same again. Johnnie Johnson:-

When Douglas was shot down it really was his own fault. He was tired, ready for a rest. Leigh-Mallory had asked him to come off Ops, as "Sailor" Malan, leader of the Hill Wing, had already done having recognised in himself the signs of strain. Douglas wouldn't go, of course, and so the AOC agreed to let him stay on until the end of what was called the "season", the end of September when the weather started failing. Peter Macdonald, our adjutant, a former MP who had served with Douglas in 1940, also recognised the signs of strain and had insisted that Douglas, Thelma and he go off on a week's golfing to St Andrews - they were, in fact, booked to go on August 11th. Douglas was tired and irritable; he couldn't see things quickly enough in the air. On the day in question, when Ken Holden sighted the 109s and Bader was unable to see them, he should have let Ken come down and attack as he had suggested. In not allowing this, he lost us six, maybe even seven seconds, by which time the high 109s were down on us. But of course Douglas was a bit greedy and would not therefore allow this. When I was a Wing Leader later in the war such a situation often arose and it made sense for me, if I couldn't see the enemy, to stay put and cover those who could whilst they attacked. This is what should have happened.

All of these years later, is it possible, I wonder, to establish from the remaining clues, what or who exactly caused Wing Commander Bader's demise over France that fateful day?

Johnnie Johnson back at Tangmere: Bader's Bus Company: Still Running!

On August 9th, 1941, Circus 68 was directed against Gosnay, near Béthune, an oft-visited target lying some 20 miles south-east of St Omer. The first thing to go wrong for the Tangmere Wing, however, was that as 616 and 610 Squadrons took off and made for the English coast, Wing Commander Bader discovered that his Airspeed Indicator was unserviceable. It was accepted practice that any pilot whose aircraft developed a defect should turn back, for example on July 10th, 1941, the 610 Squadron diary records that one of its pilots returned 'after five minutes with a u/s ASI'. For Douglas Bader, however, it was unthinkable that the Wing should go into danger without him. Wing Commander Bader pressed on, therefore, although he handed over the lead to Flight Lieutenant Dundas upon reaching Beachy Head. By that time though, his actions had probably contributed to the next problem: 41 Squadron not making the rendezvous. A former 41 Squadron pilot, Ron Rayner, has pointed out that although the squadron had arrived at Merston just two weeks previously, it had already flown many practice sweeps from Catterick and indeed a number over France. The squadron commander, Squadron Leader Gaunce DFC, was both an experienced and exceptional fighter pilot and leader. It was also unusual for a squadron not to arrive at its appointed position on time. In this case, however, 616 and 610 Squadrons had taken off from Westhampnett and 41 from Merston, the idea being that the three squadrons would join over Chichester. The likelihood is, however, that as Wing Commander Bader had no ASI, between taking off and handing over to Dundas, he had actually flown too fast for 41 Squadron to catch up. After Wing Commander Bader resumed the lead over France, we have evidence, in fact, that he did indeed fly too fast, as the transcribed radio messages indicate: Squadron Leader Holden asked Dogsbody to 'slow down'. The u/s ASI, coupled with the fact that the Wing Leader did not turn back as he ought no doubt explains why the Tangmere Wing went into action that day as 24 Spitfires instead of 36.

On Circus 68, Fighter Command lost five Spitfires in total: Wing Commander Bader and Flight Lieutenant Casson from the Tangmere Wing, and three from 452 (Australian) Squadron. In addition, 452 Squadron suffered two more aircraft damaged. Two of 452 Squadron's pilots were captured and one was killed. Available information records their attack as having been 'Delivered about 1130 hrs between Mardyck and Béthune, mostly above 20,000 feet but some at 10,000 feet.'

Mardyck is virtually part of Dunkirk, Béthune being some 30 miles to the south-east - a lot of sky in which to pinpoint a combat over 60 years later!

Both 315 and 603 Squadrons also suffered one Spitfire damaged each. JG 26 provided the sole German opposition to Circus 68, the *Geschwaderstab* and all three *Gruppen* making contact with the enemy. This represented 100 - 120 Me 109Es and Fs, a substantial force indeed. Consequently the German pilots made claims for seven Spitfires destroyed, a figure which tallies almost exactly with the actual RAF losses of five Spitfires destroyed and four damaged. The German victory claims were as follows:-

Pilot	**Victory No**.	**Unit**	**Opponent**	**Time & Location.**
Oblt. Schmid	- 16 -	*Geschwaderstab*	- Spitfire -	1125 hrs, 10 km E of St Omer
Obfw. W. Meyer	- 11 -	6/JG26	- Spitfire -	1125 hrs, St Omer.
Obfw. E. Busch	- 6 -	9/JG26	- Spitfire -	1125 hrs, location not known.
Uffz. H. Richter	- n/k -	*Geschwaderstab*	- Spitfire -	1130 hrs, N of Dunkirk.
Obstlt. A. Galland	- 76 -	*Geschwaderstab*	- Spitfire -	1132 hrs, NW of St Pol.
Lt. Kosse	- 9 -	5/JG26	- Spitfire -	1145 hrs, St Omer.
Hptm. G. Schöpfel	- 31 -	*Stab* III/JG26	- Spitfire -	1145 hrs, E of Marquise.

Regarding German losses, it is perhaps worth mentioning that these are sourced from the *Luftwaffe* Quartermaster General's Returns, which were not for propaganda purposes but for internal audit. This original source can therefore be considered to be as complete and accurate as our own records. On the day in question, an Me 109F-2 of III/JG 26 crashed on take-off at Ligescourt, and an FW 190 crash-landed near Le Bourget, the latter incident not believed to be combat-related. The only other losses are as follows:-

3/JG 26 - Me 109F-4 (8350) - Crashed near Aire, *Uffz*. Albert Schlager killed.
II/JG 26 - Me 109E-7 (6494) - Pilot n/k, baled out near Merville.

As we have seen, Wing Commander Bader's impression was that he had collided with an enemy aircraft. Certainly Johnnie Johnson has graphically described the close proximity of the enemy, the maelstrom of fighters being just '50 yards apart', but Bader was not lost during these initial seconds of mayhem. Having levelled out from the diving charge, Bader then went off alone, stalking a section of Me 109s. Again he had broken the rules. Frank Twitchett of 145 Squadron once explained to me: 'if separated over France, the only sensible thing to do was get down on the deck and get home fast.'

When repatriated in 1945, Wing Commander Bader reported that after his subsequent attack, during which he set a 109 alight rear of the cockpit:-

In turning away right-handed from this, I collided with an Me 109 which took my tail off, it appeared as far up as the radio mast but was actually only the empennage.

However, in a letter dated August 5th, 1981, Group Captain Sir Douglas Bader wrote:-

My impression was that I turned across a 109 and that it collided with the back of my Spitfire, removing the tail. On the other hand, if the pilot of the Me 109 had fired his guns at that moment, he could have blown my tail off. The result would have been the same.

The crucial question that must therefore be asked, is did Wing Commander Bader collide with an Me 109, or was he actually shot down? None of Galland's pilots had been involved in a collision, however, so the only candidate for such an occurrence was JG 26's single fatality, *Unteroffizier* Albert Schlager whose aircraft crashed near Aire-sur-la-Lys. The evidence, however, suggests that *Unteroffizier* Schlager was not involved in a collision, but actually shot down by Pilot Officer 'Nip' Hepple, whose combat report states: -

I was Yellow 3 when 616 Squadron took off from Westhampnett at 1040 hours. Shortly after crossing the French coast south of Boulogne the Squadron went into a left hand orbit. After a few minutes about 20 Me 109Fs were seen to the east of us and several thousand feet below, climbing up over white cloud. W/C Bader into attack in a steep dive, when I got down to their level the e/a had split up.

I climbed up to the right and saw an Me 109F come up in front of me. He appeared to be on the top of a stall turn and so I gave him a long burst, closing to point blank range. I saw on the side of his a/c, as he turned to the left, a large '6' just behind the cross on the fuselage. He then went into a very slow gliding turn to the left and I had a vivid view of his hood flying off and the pilot jumping out of his machine. I watched him falling and turning over and over until he had dropped down to some low white cloud; his parachute had still not opened so I assume he was killed. This a/c is claimed as destroyed.

The camouflage was a dirty grey and black, in addition to the usual cross there was a '6' behind it. The tail was painted orange and the spinner black and white. I was flying an aircraft with 'Watford' and its coat of arms marked on it.

To assist recognition in the air, German fighters were specifically marked on the fuselage with either a thick horizontal or wavy line adjacent to the black cross. In the case of I *Gruppe*, however, no such marking was carried, and Schlager's 109F was of I/JG 26's 3rd *Staffel*. Hepple remarks on the number six painted on the fuselage, but makes no mention of any line marking, which would have been highly visible. Hepple's reference to an 'orange' tail was more likely red, and specifically the vertical rudder. Unfortunately we do not know what identifying colour 3/JG 26 used at this time, which could assist with identifying Hepple's victim, and nor are we aware of what individual number Schlager's aircraft was. The German pilot, however, baled out, and Hepple makes no reference to seeing a parachute open: Schlager's parachute failed to open and he died as a result. It is reasonable, I believe, to credit Schlager's demise to Hepple's guns, and not a collision with Wing Commander Bader.

The only other 109 down that day was at Merville, some 14 miles south-east of Blaringhem, a distance in itself not altogether ruling out this aircraft as a collision contender. However, the pilot baled out safely and must have subsequently reported on the incident, details of which presumably did not include a collision. 452 Squadron's pilots also claimed two Me 109Es destroyed in their fight, so the enemy fighter of that type down at Merville was most likely one of them - Flight Lieutenant Brendan 'Paddy' Finucane DFC claimed an Me 109E in the 'Gosnay-Béthune area,' and Flight Lieutenant 'Bluey' Truscott an 'E', his first-ever combat claim, between 'Mardyck-Béthune.'

Bader himself conceded that he did not see the Me 109 which he thought he had struck, a collision being just his 'impression' of the destructive forces acting upon his Spitfire at that time. He has suggested that 20 mm cannon ammunition could have achieved the same effect. If Wing Commander Bader was shot down, as previous authors have also suggested, who, then, was responsible?

Looking at the table of German combat claims, and bearing in mind that Dogsbody, although not lost in the initial charge was nevertheless hacked down within the opening few minutes of the engagement, only one claim stands out, that of *Oberfeldwebel* Walter Meyer of 6/JG 26, who claimed his 11th victory over St Omer at 1125 hrs. However, that Meyer was Bader's victor is a theory slightly diluted by the claim for a Spitfire destroyed at the same time but at an unknown location by 9/JG 26's *Oberfeldwebel* Busch. 9/JG 26 was a part of *Hauptmann* Schöpfel's IIIrd *Gruppe* which, according to the *Kommandeur's* account, had actually intercepted the 'beehive' proper and therefore some minutes after the initial skirmish in question. This researcher does not consider the Busch claim to relate to the actual engagement in which Wing Commander Bader was lost.

Unteroffizier *Walter Meyer of 6/JG 26.*

When researching Douglas Bader's biography, his brother-in-law, Wing Commander 'Laddie' Lucas, working with Henry Probert, the head of the MOD's Air Historical Branch (AHB) at that time, examined the German claims and was sufficiently satisfied with the timing of Mayer's claim to conclude that he was Bader's victor. Although making the connection between Bader and *Mayer,* (incorrectly referring to the German pilot as 'Max Mayer'), 'Laddie' and the AHB wrongly assumed that Flight Lieutenant Casson had been shot down in the same area as

Wing Commander Bader. Thus they decided that *Leutnant* Kosse, who claimed a Spitfire over St Omer at 1145 hrs, had shot down 'Buck' Casson. In reality, again as we have already seen, Flight Lieutenant Casson was shot down by *Hauptmann* Schöpfel who even had a photograph taken of the downed Spitfire. Those who have previously attributed Casson's loss to Kosse, however, have not approached Squadron Leader LH Casson DFC AFC for his account, but have merely assumed that he was shot down in the action over St Omer. It is never a safe course to assume anything in such an investigation however, and had any of these authors asked 'Buck' for themselves, they would have discovered that he was shot down some minutes *after* the Tangmere Wing's original skirmish over St Omer and whilst heading back towards the French coast. Together with Don Caldwell in Texas, a published author and highly respected JG 26 historian, I was able to connect 'Buck' Casson's loss with Schöpfel's claim timed at 1145 hrs over Marquise, near the French coast.

Regarding *Leutnant* Kosse's claim, it is unlikely, in fact, that this pilot even fought the Tangmere Wing, the Spitfires of which, as the Target Support Wing, were first to arrive over the target area. Kosse recorded that his combat had occured at 1145 hrs, some 20 minutes after the initial 'bounce' during which *Oberfeldwebel* Meyer destroyed a Spitfire at 1125 hrs. A time lapse of 20 minutes therefore represents a long interval considering the speed at which these fighter aircraft flew. By 1145 hrs, the Tangmere Wing was re-crossing the French coast, this being confirmed by the fact that 'Buck' Casson was shot down near Marquise, just three miles from the coast at exactly that time. As *Hauptmann* Schöpfel went to some trouble to obtain evidence for his victory report, such as even flying low over the crashed Spitfire to record its code letters, we can, I think, accept his timing as accurate. In view of these times, and the fact that the Tangmere Wing was heading home at 1145 hrs, I believe that *Leutnant* Kosse actually engaged Spitfires of 452 Squadron.

Whilst *Oberfeldwebel* Walter Meyer's claim *might* fit, the fact that a claim has been made is inconclusive in any case. As we have seen, the Germans only lost two Me 109s that day, Schlager who was killed at Aire, and an unidentified pilot who baled out near Merville. The Spitfire squadrons engaged, however, claimed a staggering *22* Me 109s destroyed, 10 probables and a further eight damaged! In 'Flying Colours', 'Laddie' Lucas concluded that the German losses tallied fairly closely to the Tangmere Wing's claims of five Me 109s destroyed, and two probables, but he did not take into account that JG26 was the only *Jagdgeschwader* to suffer losses, and then offset these statistics against all of Fighter Command's claims that day. Clearly, a rigorous analysis puts a totally different complexion on the matter: the Spitfire pilots over claimed by at least 10:1!

In respect of German combat claims, today we have for each reference only the most basic of details, such as the pilot's name, type of enemy aircraft claimed, location, date and time. Unfortunately, the majority of German pilots' personal combat reports have not survived. Therefore with merely 'Spitfire destroyed, 1125 hrs, St Omer', it is impossible to conclude with certainty that *Oberfeldwebel* Mayer shot down Wing Commander Bader. Whatever the accuracy of Meyer's claim, however, I would again refer to Adolf Galland's statement 'it was never confirmed who shot down Douglas Bader.' Shooting the tail, or much of it, off a Spitfire is fairly significant damage to observe; if Bader was shot down by a JG 26 pilot, why were their reports inconclusive? In a letter to me dated February 19th, 1996, 'Laddie' Lucas summed up the situation perfectly:-

When having dinner at Douglas Bader's house in the country, Adolf Galland told me categorically that DB had been shot down over the Pas-de-Calais in 1941. Galland stated that there had not been a collision. I can say in fact that, in my own humble experience, receiving a volley or two of cannon shells from an Me 109 could certainly sound like a collision with a London bus! I put this view to Douglas, who responded: "In that case, old cock, because it was *me,* why didn't they have the bugger responsible goose-stepping down the *Under-den-Linden?"*

Having fully researched and considered all of the available evidence from both sides, I can now offer another suggestion.

On August 9th, 1941, Flight Lieutenant Buck Casson was also captured. He therefore did not return to Tangmere to report on the incident. However, in 1945, at Douglas Bader's request, 'Buck' wrote to his former Wing Leader regarding his own experiences of that fateful day. The account in question has already been reproduced in full earlier in this chapter, but I would particularly draw to the reader's attention the following extract:-

After having a squirt at two 109s flying together, I left them for a single one flying inland alone. I finished nearly all of my cannon ammunition up on this boy, who finally baled out at 6,000 feet, having lost most of his tail unit.

Who did Buck Casson shoot down?

We know that JG 26 lost but one Me 109 in this engagement, and that Schlager crashed at Aire was confirmed by the discovery of an identification plate when that crash site was excavated in 2003. A tail wheel was also recovered, proving that the tail section of that aircraft was still very much attached upon impact. Buck could not, therefore, have shot Schlager down. Neither do I believe that Buck shot down the Me 109E lost by II/JG 26, the pilot of which is known to have baled out, as Merville is just too far away to be relevant.

What cannot be discounted, however, is that the circumstances described by Buck Casson are exactly those which are known to have befallen Wing Commander Bader, i.e. that his tail unit was badly damaged and he baled out at about 6,000 feet. One might ask why Douglas Bader himself did not question this when Buck wrote to him in 1945, but at that time the pilots concerned no doubt considered that they had been involved in a hectic dogfight with the aircraft of both sides being shot down all around; certainly this is reflected by the RAF's gross over claiming on the day in question. Had 'Buck' ever submitted an official report, which would have been made available to the general public during the 1970s, perhaps another aviation detective would have suggested that these events be linked, or maybe the connection would have been made on the actual day in question? That Wing Commander Bader was the victim of 'Friendly Fire' would certainly explain why the German combat reports were so inconclusive. Furthermore, as the pilot possibly responsible had absolutely no idea himself of what had happened, and indeed was also captured that day, these two factors could also help explain the mystery.

In recent years the public have become accustomed to 'Friendly Fire', such tragedies now being known to have occurred on countless occasions. In fact, such situations were far more prevalent during the Second World War than most people are aware. The so-called 'Battle of Barking Creek' of September 6th, 1939, when Hurricanes and Spitfires fought each other over the Thames Estuary, is an oft-quoted example, but of course just three days into the war pilots lacked experience so such unfortunate mishaps were inevitable. By the end of the Battle of Britain, however, no less than 20 front-line British fighters, bombers and transports (but mainly Spitfires, Hurricanes and Blenheims) had been mistakenly shot down by 'friendly' anti-aircraft fire and a further nine had been accidentally shot down by RAF fighter pilots. At the time, such information was suppressed, but the loss of what statistically amounted to nearly two squadrons of aircraft to 'Friendly Fire' could not be ignored.

Whilst gathering material for a Spitfire related day of lectures, I obtained several reels of hitherto unpublished and random cine-gun film from the Imperial War Museum. Andrew Long studied the clips with a view to obtaining the relevant combat reports from the Public Records Office but was surprised to find several incidents of 'Friendly Fire': on July 7th, 1940, Sergeant Franklin of 65 Squadron reported having attacked an

'Me 109', but the camera footage clearly shows that his target was another Spitfire; on September 26th, 1940, 609 Squadron's Sergeant Alan Feary engaged a He 111, but also had a determined squirt at a Hurricane, which takes evasive action. September 27th, 1941, saw the Hornchurch Wing flying in support of Circus 103b, Sergeant Wright of 611 Squadron subsequently reported that: -

I was flying as Red 4 in G/C Broadhurst's Section of 611 Squadron at 16,000 feet, and after crossing the French coast I saw two Me 109s at 500 yards to port, about 400-500 feet below. I turned and dived to attack, giving him a quick burst of about two sec, after which he turned on his back and went down in a steep dive. I followed and gave him another 3-4 second burst, seeing him hit and apparently out of control. Whilst I was still diving I looked to my rear and saw another aircraft diving on me. I pulled out of the dive and turned, but in doing so I lost sight of the plane I was attacking, and also the plane that was diving on me. My height was 4-5,000 feet, so I dived to 100 feet and returned home.

The camera gun footage proves conclusively that Wright determinedly attacked at least one other Spitfire, not the Me 109E claimed probably destroyed.

Veteran wartime fighter pilots agree that in the heat and confusion of fighter-to-fighter combat such mistakes did happen, as indeed are confirmed by the several foregoing examples and statistics. Aircraft recognition in combat was sometimes demonstrably questionable. During 1940, for example, RAF fighter pilots frequently reported combat with 'He 113s', on November 5th, 1940, Flight Sergeant George 'Grumpy' Unwin DFM being credited with the 'first of this type shot down by Duxford'. We now know, however, that the He 113 was merely a propaganda ruse by the Germans as the type never actually entered service - Unwin's adversary was more likely a JG 26 Me 109, in fact. With even more frequency, the identities of German bombers engaged by Spitfire and Hurricane pilots were incorrectly reported. On September 30th, 1940, the last great daylight battle of the Battle of Britain took place when a large force of KG 55 He 111s, escorted by both Me 109s and 110s, were briefed to attack Westland Aircraft at Yeovil (see '*Angriff* Westland' by this author, Ramrod Publications, 1994). However, a number of intercepting RAF fighter pilots that day incorrectly identified the German bombers in their combat reports, amongst them such experienced men as Squadron Leader Herbert Pinfold, 56 Squadron's CO who reported 'God knows how many Do 215s', and Flight Lieutenant Ian 'Widge' Gleed DFC, a flight commander in 87 Squadron, who wrote of '70 Ju 88s.'

On August 9th, 1941, we know that the Tangmere Wing fought Me 109Fs. The *'Franz'* had entered service in early 1941, and unlike its angular *'Emil'* predecessor with its square wing tips, had rounded wing-tips, smooth lines and no tail struts. In a split second, as an image jockeyed into the reflector ring, it would have been easy to make a mistake. On May 17th, 1941, 616 Squadron's Sergeant Morton mistook Me 109Fs for Spitfires, a mistake which could have cost him his life. Furthermore, the difficulty of making split-second decisions in combat is emphasised by the following entry in Squadron Leader Burton's log book, written on July 21st, 1941: 'Should have shot down an Me 109, but failed to open fire till too late owing to uncertainty of identification.'

The curvacious and elliptical Me 109F.

So, back in 1995 I put the evidence, such as it is, to key survivors of the Tangmere Wing's engagement fought on August 9th, 1941.

Air Vice-Marshal Johnnie Johnson: -

I would be very surprised if an experienced and *careful* fighter pilot such as Buck Casson would make such a mistake, but do agree from his description of events that he has almost certainly seen DB come down.

Group Captain Sir Hugh Dundas: -

Nothing is certain, nor ever will be.

Air Marshal Sir Denis Crowley-Milling: -

Absolute rubbish!

At Johnnie Johnson's insistence, I did put the matter to Buck Casson, whose view was clear: -

I was an experienced fighter pilot and well knew what a 109 looked like. I shot down a 109 that day.

Having flown throughout the Battle of Britain and during that long summer of offensive operations in 1941, 'Buck' most certainly would have seen many Me 109s. Indeed, he had shared one destroyed on June 22nd, 1941, and probably destroyed another on July 19th. But if his trigger finger did make a mistake in the great confusion and heat of the moment, it was perfectly understandable, not least given the prevalent chaos and similarities in appearance between the Spitfire and Me 109F.

In 1996, my *Bader's Tangmere Spitfires* was published but I decided against including any reference to my belief that Buck accidentally shot down Douglas Bader. At the time our search for Bader's Spitfire was causing immense media interest and there was no doubt that if this story was released then a host of journalists would descend upon the elderly and infirm Cassons. Moreover, it was unethical, I felt, to publish the story and cause Buck any upset given that it had only come out due to his kindness in providing me a copy of his private correspondence with Douglas Bader. At the time this story would undoubtedly have whipped the press into a frenzy, and I could probably have named my price, but integrity and the feelings of two dear friends, 'Buck' and 'Dorfy' Casson, meant far more to me than fame and fortune. Indeed, I took respected author and former fast jet pilot Air Commodore Graham Pitchfork into my confidence at that time, so he at least is aware of the timing of my discovery and how tortuous the whole thing became.

Air Vice-Marshal Johnnie Johnson & Dilip Sarkar at the launch of Bader's Tangmere Spitfires, *October 1996.*

Squadron Leader Buck Casson & Dilip Sarkar at the pre-launch party of The Invisible Thread *in 1992.*

Buck Casson, second right, at The Invisible Thread book launch, 1992.

55 Iverna Court, London W8 6TS

Tel: 0171-937 0773   Fax: 0171-937 1209

2nd May 1995

Dear Dilip

Your letter of 27th August reached me over the weekend.
Its contents certainly took me aback.

You ask me "to keep the letter close for the present" and I
shall most certainly do so. For my part, I urge you very
strongly to keep the theory entirely to yourself and, most
particularly, not to put it before Buck Casson, as you say
you have it in mind to do. You are, of course, in the
realms of hypothesis and conjecture. Nothing is certain,
nor ever will be - except that if once the theory got out
of the bag it would quickly be picked up and would soon be
accepted by some as the truth. I hate to think of the pain
and distress which this would cause to Buck and his family,
quite unnecessarily and to no-one's benefit.

I do hope that you will consider my advice on this matter
very seriously indeed.

Yours sincerely

Hugh Dundas

Mr Dilip Sarkar
16 Kingfisher Close
St Peter's
Worcester WR5 3RY

*The letter received by Dilip Sarkar from Group Captain Sir Hugh Dundas
('August' should in fact be April).*

No matter how hard you try, however, it is impossible to keep a story like this secure indefinitely. Sadly Squadron Leader Casson died in 2003, and it was not long before the vultures were out to publish the story. Early in 2004 I was contacted by a magazine publisher who asked for my cooperation with regard to releasing the story. Apparently another researcher, whom I knew and had discussed the matter with on several occasions, was claiming the story as his own and intending to publish in both the historical journal in question and a British national newspaper. As poor old Buck was barely cold and 'Dorfy' still alive to be harassed by the media, I was appalled and refused the offer of involvement. Unfortunately those concerned took no heed of my arguments against publishing the story at that time, and so an uninformed version appeared in both the magazine in question and a Sunday paper. For some reason, however, the 'revelation' failed to excite the popular press, as had so clearly been intended, and the matter largely passed unnoticed, much to our relief in considering the potentially adverse effect such a trial could have had upon Mrs Casson's health.

In trying to achieve sensationalism, the published story suggested that Douglas Bader and Buck Casson were aware of what had happened, and that the latter had been virtually excommunicated as a result. This, I can assure the reader, is complete nonsense. The 'evidence' put forward to support this theory is that Buck was not mentioned in either the book or film 'Reach for the Sky', and nor did he appear on Douglas Bader's 'This is Your Life' programme. Firstly, very few pilots are actually mentioned by name in 'Reach for the Sky', so that is no argument whatsoever. Secondly, with regard to the programme, the guest list is limited, and there were many other people more pivotal to Douglas Bader's story than Buck Casson. The fact is that after the war Bader and Casson regularly played golf together, and Group Captain Bader even opened the Sheffield ATC Wing HQ, of which Buck was commodore; indeed, Graham Pitchfork was actually a cadet on parade and presented to the great man on the day! So, I am sorry to disappoint those seeking a sensation, but clearly the pair was not, in fact, estranged in any way.

I would also add that I had known Buck Casson, Sir Hugh Dundas, Sir Denis Crowley-Milling and Johnnie Johnson for over 10 years before discussing with them my 'Friendly Fire' theory; I was an experienced and professional investigative police officer, so have no doubt that had any of these men been hiding something then I would have known – instinctively and immediately. Moreover, if Buck Casson had something to hide he would hardly have furnished me with a copy of the letter in question and permission to publish it, for all to see, and which I did in *The Invisible Thread* (1992), *A Few of the Many* (1995) and *Bader's Tangmere Spitfires* (1996). To suggest that there was some kind of cover up or conspiracy is absolute fantasy.

It is also worth reporting how, back in 1981, the tale took on yet another twist.

In 'Flying Colours', Laddie Lucas states that in March 1981, Sir Douglas Bader opened the Schofield Air Show, Sydney, where, by chance, he was introduced to a former Luftwaffe fighter pilot, Max *Mayer*, who had long been domiciled in the Dominion. The pair exchanged pleasantries, but no more. The following day Bader was apparently astonished to read in the press an article based upon an interview which Mayer had given an Australian journalist subsequent to his meeting with Sir Douglas and in which he claimed to have shot him down on August 9th, 1941. Bader's biographer, having researched to some extent the German records, assumed that this was actually *Oberfeldwebel* Walter *Meyer* (note the difference in spelling of the surname) who had claimed the destruction of a Spitfire above St Omer at 1125 hrs on the day in question. What 'Laddie' Lucas did not know was what had happened to *Oberfeldwebel* Meyer: he died in 1943! On October 11th, 1942, Walter Meyer collided with his *Rottenflieger* and was hospitalised. He did not recover, but actually died of TB in January 1943.

Another Bader book, using the aforementioned biography as source (as indeed had I when writing 'A Few of the Many', Ramrod Publications 1995) accepted as fact the information that *Mayer* had shot down Bader. This account also claimed that the 'Australian Fighter Mafia' had unsuccessfully attempted to trace Mayer. Why there should have been any difficulty, I cannot understand.

So who was Max Mayer? Having contacted 'The Daily Telegraph Mirror' in Sydney, in 1995, I received a copy of the article in question, written by a CJ McKenzie. Mayer claimed to have shot Bader down with 'one cannon burst, which ripped away the tail of Bader's Spitfire.' Mayer continued 'I saw him spiralling down, I saw his face. I followed him down because I had to confirm the kill. When I saw his parachute coming up I turned away. I reported where he had crashed.' McKenzie was advised, however, by one of Bader's entourage not to 'bring that up or you'll get an argument.' Mayer claimed that it was the second time he and Bader had shaken hands, the first occasion having been in the *Clinique Sterin* in St Omer: 'He was surprised when he found it was me. He was a Wing Commander. I was a mere *Leutnant*. He was very warm towards me and we shook hands strongly.'

Already it was possible to identify major inaccuracies in Max Mayer's story, not withstanding of course that Walter Meyer had died in 1943! Firstly, it would be impossible to identify a pilot's face in the circumstances discussed, and in any case, whilst in the Spitfire Wing Commander Bader would have been wearing goggles and an oxygen mask. Secondly, Mayer gives the impression that at the time, so far as the

Germans were concerned, his claim was accepted; refer again to Adolf Galland: 'it was never confirmed who shot down Douglas Bader'. Furthermore, whereas Mayer claims to have been a *Leutnant*, Walter Meyer was an NCO. Incidentally, *Leutnant* Kosse, the JG 26 pilot *possibly* introduced to Bader, did not survive, having been killed late in the war with an RVT unit (*Reichsverteidigung*, organisation responsible for the air defence of Germany).

In CJ McKenzie's article, Martin Maxwell Mayer also claimed to have destroyed 34 enemy aircraft, a tally including victories not only on the *Kanalfront,* but also over Russia and North Africa. Such a score had, he stated, won him the coveted Knight's Cross. Anyone checking the list of fighter pilots who were *Ritterkreuzträger* would discover no reference to a Martin Max Mayer. *Oberstleutnant* Egon Mayer received both the Knight's Cross and Oak Leaves, but was killed in action on March 2nd, 1944. *Hauptmann* Hans-Karl Mayer received his Knight's Cross on September 3rd, 1940, but was lost over the Channel on October 17th, 1940. *Leutnant* Wilhelm Mayer's Knight's Cross was awarded in March 1945, by which time he was already dead, having been killed by Spitfires on January 4th, 1945. *Leutnant* Eduard Meyer's 'throat ache' was cured in 1941, but the following year he collided with a comrade over Russia and was also killed. No *Ritterkreuzträger* of spelling Mayer or Meyer therefore survived the war.

After the Second World War, Martin Maxwell Mayer claimed to have flown with the French Air Force in Algiers, but my friend and colleague, Dr Bernard-Marie Dupont, himself a former French army officer, confirms that there is no record of such a pilot, a non-French national, having flown with the French Air Force.

Kerry Taylor of the Sydney Daily Telegraph Mirror was able to put me in contact with CJ McKenzie himself, now retired. In a letter to myself dated August 31st, 1995, 'CJ' enclosed a copy of a letter from Sir Douglas Bader, then aged 71, to Max Mayer dated August 5th, 1981:-

Dear Max Mayer,

You will recall that we met on Saturday, March 28th, at the Schofield Air Show near Sydney. We were both pleased to meet each other because we were ex-fighter pilots (on opposite sides) and we had an agreeable conversation for some minutes.

The next morning, March 29th, I read an article in one of the newspapers quoting an interview with you, during the course of which you said that you had shot me down over France on August 9th, 1941 and had followed me down until you saw me bale out. Having read that, I was hoping to see you that day, so that we could discuss it. None of us could find you on Sunday. We tried on the Monday to contact you, but were unsuccessful. Then I left to go elsewhere in Australia. Dolfo Galland, who commanded JG 26, has become a great friend of mine since the war. He cannot tell me about the incident on August 9th, 1941.

My impression was that I turned across a Me 109 and that it collided with the back of my Spitfire, removing the tail. On the other hand, if the pilot of the Me 109 had fired his guns at that moment, he could have blown my tail off. The result would have been the same.

Please write and tell me your account of this incident, if you can remember it. You told the Australian press that you followed my Spitfire down until you saw me bale out. I imagine you knew it was me because you saw, when I baled out, that one leg was missing. I know that you had lived in Australia for 25 years but cannot think why you did not tell me all this when we talked to each other on March 28th. We could have had a tremendous laugh about it and really enjoyed it.

I shall greatly look forward to hearing from you,

Best wishes,

Yours sincerely,

DOUGLAS BADER.

Adolf Galland & Douglas Bader appearing in the latter's This Is
Your Life programme: "We did not know who shot Douglas down".

My letter from CJ McKenzie was also interesting:-

Dear Dilip,

I enclose a copy of a letter Bader wrote to Max Mayer, dated August 5th, 1981, which you might find interesting. I must say that he has put more "spin" on his meeting with Mayer than Shane Warne puts on a "leggie"!

Bader met Mayer at Mascot Airport (our Sydney Kingsford Smith International), not at the Schofields Air Show. It had taken me sometime to tee-up the meeting and Bader knew precisely who he was meeting and why. I introduced Mayer in those terms. He knew also why I was there, why the photographer was there, yet he seems to express surprise at the story of March 29th.

He says, after reading the story, "I was hoping to see you that day so we could discuss it." What day does he mean? And discuss what? He says further that he tried to find Mayer on the Sunday and Monday. He had only to phone The Sunday Telegraph to have been put in contact with Mayer.

The meeting between the two was brief, not as Bader says "an agreeable conversation for some minutes." Indeed, I was embarrassed by Bader's attitude. It is not always easy in words to give the right tone to something said. Bader's use of the word "kraut", instead of German, surprised me. The way he said it was, in my view, intended to be insulting or at least denigrating.

Max Mayer died some years ago.

I hope that some of this might be of interest to you and wish you well with your project.

I remain etc ..

CJ McKENZIE.

As Kerry Taylor said, 'the weaving of the web becomes even more intriguing!'

There is no doubt, however, that Martin Maxwell Mayer was certainly not the man he claimed to be, nor indeed the man who shot down Douglas Bader. Lady Bader (Sir Douglas's second wife whom he married in 1973 following Thelma's death two years previously) has no knowledge of any response from Mayer to her late husband's letter. Had Sir Douglas been aware that he had been shot down by another Spitfire pilot, why would he have written in such terms to 'Max Mayer'?

On August 9th, 1941, Wing Commander Bader was flying a presentation Spitfire, *Lord Lloyd 1*, W3185, a Mk VA armed with eight Browning machine-guns (no 20 mm cannon). The crash site of that aircraft might just provide clues to complete this jig-saw, and this we set out to discover back in 1996. My close French friend, Dr

Bernard-Marie Dupont, made enquiries in the St Omer area and was soon talking to a local historian of the wartime generation, Georges Goblet who claimed to know where W3185 crashed. His friend, Arthur Dubreu, had even seen the legless pilot land by parachute, he claimed. I lost no time in getting across the Channel, and met the two Frenchman. Arthur told me that: -

I was 13 years old at the time, living in Steenbecque, and remember the incident vividly. I saw a lot of planes, it was mid-morning on a sunny day. There was a big dogfight and many contrails in the sky. I saw an aircraft coming down very fast and then a parachute opened. The aircraft crashed in a field and a cloud of black smoke and debris rose over the site. Due to the wind the parachute drifted slightly; it was the first parachute I had ever seen, in fact, so I remember it very well. I wanted to see the pilot, so I ran after the rapidly descending canopy. The parachute seemed to land very fast, but the pilot hit some trees in an orchard which took the shock. The pilot was just sitting there, silk billowing around him. I was horrified to see that he only had one leg, which was twisted at an unnatural angle. There was no blood and, although he seemed to be stunned from the landing, he did not appear otherwise concerned about his legs. I could not understand it at all. I was the first on the scene but before I could help a German officer ran into the field, took charge and told me to clear off, which I did as I was very frightened on the soldiers. The Germans then carried the pilot to their waiting car and I went straight away to see the aircraft's crash site, a crater in a field. It was only after the war, when *Reach for the Sky* was published in French, that I realised who I had seen.

Georges Goblet: -

I was 11 years old, living in Blaringhem, and with other boys from my village I went to the Spitfire crash site that afternoon. There was a large crater, smoke still rose through the soil and the ground remained warm. The wings had been detached and lay in another field. It was about 20 years after the war, whilst conducting my own research into local matters, that I too realised whose Spitfire this was.

The Spitfire, Georges said, crashed at Blaringhem, some 10 km south-east of St Omer, Steenbecque being nearby. Circus 68 was a raid against the power station at Gosnay, 25 km south-east of St Omer. Circumstantially the area seemed a good start. The Frenchmen took us to both the orchard where Arthur saw the parachutist, and to the field where the Spitfire crashed. At the latter location we found various pieces of mangled aircraft, including an oval bracket bearing a long number pre-fixed by '300': this was a Spitfire! Moreover the bracket was stamped '6S', meaning that the part was built at Woolston and not Castle Bromwich, which also appeared significant: W3185 was a Mk VA built at Woolston, whereas the Tangmere Wing's other Spitfires were Mk VBs, the majority of which were built at Castle Bromwich.

Circumstantially we had certainly found a promising site, but unfortunately the news accidentally got out before our excavation. Needless to say the media grossly exaggerated the story, it being declared to all and sundry that we had actually found

Bader's Spitfire when we had said no such thing! One British newspaper, the *Independent*, did quote me accurately when I said that aviation archaeology was like going fishing: until you had been you didn't know what you would catch, and on which basis I made it clear that we could not confirm the aircraft's identity until the recovery – and even then it might be impossible.

Arthur Dubreu shows Dr Dupont where he saw Douglas Bader land by parachute.

Georges Goblet, Dr Dupont & Arthur Dubreu at the Spitfire crash site. Georges indicates the direction of the parachute site.

The three Frenchmen searching for surface fragments at the crash site in February 1996.

For some reason the world's media leapt on the story, continually harassing and misquoting me. The *Times* newspaper agreed to sponsor our excavation, the deal being struck hinging not on this being Bader's Spitfire but on our sponsors having exclusive rights to the recovery. So it was that our team went to France and excavated the site on May 4th, 1996.

The afternoon before the recovery, however, in pouring rain and appalling Flanders mud, we pinpointed the bulk of wreckage using a proton magnetometer. During that survey we found the remains of an exploded 20 mm ball round. Examination confirmed this to be British ammunition: Bader's aircraft was not armed with cannons, and so we knew that this was unlikely to be W3185, even before turning a spade. Soon after the excavation started a metal propeller was found together with an airscrew boss engineered to accommodate for such blades. We knew then that that was definitely not W3185, which had a three bladed airscrew, and suspected our find to be a Mk IX that had crashed sometime after 1941. Our concern increased when a wristwatch was found, but fortunately no human remains came to light, not that we were contravening any continental legislation but such a discovery would have provided the media with a sensation. A massive amount of Spitfire was recovered, including the Merlin engine, but very few cockpit items. Naturally we were all extremely disappointed that the aircraft recovered was not W3185, the question now being which Spitfire was it?

The dig underway.

Antony Whitehead (left) & Andrew Long hard at work.

The instrument panel armour plate is recovered.

Dig's end: not Bader's Spitfire, but a massively successful recovery nonetheless.

From left to right: Arthur Dubreu, Georges Goblet, Keith Delderfield, Andrew Long, Luke Delderfield, Bob Morris, John Foreman, Dennis Williams, Antony Whitehead & Larry McHale with Dilip Sarkar & LZ996.

Team-member and author John Foreman, our expert on losses and claims, worked out a 'short' list of 67 possible Spitfire casualties that could be our Spitfire. Eventually it was ascertained that we had found LZ996, a Mk IX of the Canadian 421 Squadron, shot down on June 17th, 1943. The pilot, Squadron Leader Phil Archer DFC, had only been promoted to command the Squadron that very day. During the afternoon, 421 Squadron had participated in a Kenley Wing sweep, coincidentally led by Wing Commander Johnnie Johnson, over southern Belgium. Over Ypres the Spitfires engaged FW 190s of III/JG 26, chasing them south to St Omer. During the running battle, *Oberleutnant* Horst Sternberg, *Staffelkapitän* of 5/JG 26, shot down Flying Officer JE McNamara of 421 Squadron, but was shot down himself by Squadron Leader Archer; this success was short lived: seconds later 421's new CO was shot down by *Unteroffizier* Paul Schwarz of 6/JG 26, 10 km south-east of St Omer. We found Phil Archer's grave in the war cemetery at Longuenesse, his headstone being incorrectly inscribed 'Air Gunner/Instructor'. We immediately contacted the Commonwealth War Graves Commission which corrected the error by engraving the word 'Pilot'. At that time we also found an eye-witness, Monsieur Queurleu, who told us that the victorious German pilot had visited the LZ996 crash site, from which the pilot's body was removed together with a quantity of wreckage, thus explaining why we found no human remains or many cockpit parts. This was, however, Paul Schwarz's only aerial victory, and he was killed in a flying accident in 1944.

Squadron Leader Archer's grave.

Oberleutnant *Horst Sternberg*
of 5/JG 26.

Wishful thinking: Lady Bader in France with the recovered propeller blade. Had this Spitfire been W3185, it was intended to create a travelling exhibition to raise the profile of The Douglas Bader Foundation, a registered charity & living memorial to Sir Douglas which assists amputees.

A selection of interesting artefacts recovered from the LZ996 site, including a maker's plate, parachute 'D' ring, ASI instrument face, the base of an exploded British 20 mm ball round, the pilot's watch, and the oval plate stamped '6S'.

*Armour plate, both (shrapnel holed) compressed air
bottles, and the pilot's oxygen bottle.*

*Spitfire LZ996. A chance find in the album of Air Vice-Marshal
Johnnie Johnson: Kenley Wing, 1943.*

So, we had the answer regarding which Spitfire we had found, but, as is always the case with historical research, even more questions arose! Firstly we remained convinced that Arthur Dubreu really had seen Douglas Bader's parachute descent, but over the years, possibly fuelled by wishful thinking, their memories had become confused, incorrectly linking the LZ996 crash, which happened nearly two years later, with the same incident. As a former police detective I know only too well how notoriously unreliable eyewitness evidence can be, and we must bear in mind that we are dealing here with the memories of over half a century ago.

The oval plate stamped 'AB**6S**170782 transpired to be a 'red herring'. LZ996 was built at Castle Bromwich but that particular part, a flap mechanism component, was built at Woolston; how unlucky can you get?

The big question, of course, was still 'where is Bader's Spitfire'? The discovery of LZ996 stimulated widespread media covering in France and Belgium, and both Bernard and I agreed that if anyone knew where the site was, they would come forward. Sure enough two French aviation archaeologists soon contacted me, claiming to have found the W3185 crash site at the Mont Dupil Farm at Basse-Rue, near Racquinghem, just three miles away from Blaringhem and, according to my former SAS police colleague, within the required radius of where Bader landed by parachute at Boesinghem. The Frenchmen told us that the farmer dated the Mont Dupil crash as 1941, and a newspaper article in January 1945 referred to the crash, confirming that the pilot had landed by parachute at Boesinghem. On August 3rd, 1996, I examined the site but could find absolutely no trace of a crashed aircraft whatsoever, and our investigation was thorough. At the time I was working as a consultant for Twenty Twenty Television regarding the Channel 4 'Secret Life' documentary about Sir Douglas Bader, and the director provided a mechanical digger and other resources to assist us. We were soon agreed, however, that nothing remained at the site and returned to England.

More wishful thinking: the Mont Dupil site in August 1996.

Given the circumstances of W3185's demise, and our experience in recovering the remains of crashed Spitfires, I remain of the opinion that this Spitfire would have either gone in or at least made a reasonable impression in the French sod. Without a tail it would certainly not have fluttered down a gently alighted in France, leaving no trace. The farmer at Mont Dupil told us that the aircraft there was tail-less but otherwise intact. I do not, therefore, believe this to be Bader's crash site, and never have.

Another interesting thing is that the RAF Museum has on display at Hendon a clock, allegedly from the instrument panel of W3185 and removed as a souvenir by a *Hauptmann* Rudolf Ortmann. The Director, my friend Dr Michael Fopp, had been presented with the artefact by the late Rudlof Ortmann's son in 1984. The clock, however, is intact, even the glass! We have recovered clocks from several Spitfires, none of which crashed from as high an altitude as W3185 and all of which were badly mangled. Given the circumstances of Bader's crash, I just cannot accept that this pristine item, therefore, is from W3185; more likely it is from a Spitfire that made a controlled forced landing in enemy territory and represents, therefore, more wishful thinking so far as W3185 is concerned.

The 'Holy Grail' of aviation archaeology: Supermarine Spitfire W3185.

In 2005, Wildfire Television commissioned me as a programme consultant regarding 'The Search for Bader's Spitfire', a two hour documentary to be broadcast by Channel 4 in September 2006. As the 'Friendly Fire' theory had already been publicised by someone else, and was now in the public domain, I agreed to cooperate so that the full and accurate story of the whole issue could at last be told. Bernie Moss, a former test pilot and air crash investigator, was also commissioned to work on the programme, and we were agreed that the Mont Dupil site was not a contender for W3185, for reasons as previously explained. Bernard-Marie Dupont and I, however, remained of the opinion that if the site was discoverable then, given the massive interest generated by the media, we or someone else would have found it 10 years ago.

Georges Goblet & Dr Dupont at the Schlager Me 109 crash site in February 1996.

The fact must also not be overlooked that any remaining wreckage may already have been disturbed, by accident, during agricultural work by someone unfamiliar with either the origin or significance of their find. Also, conclusive proof, especially in the absence of documentary evidence, can only be ascertained from the aircraft's maker's plate, which is not always discovered. We very much doubted that another search would be any more successful than our previous operation, and so this proved to be. Although we had been shown the Schlager crash site in 1996, we decided against excavating it, and so this 109 was recovered for the programme. The discovery of a maker's plate confirmed the identity beyond doubt, and, as previously mentioned, the presence of a tail wheel indicated that the tail was still attached upon impact. Two other Spitfire sites in the area were excavated and confirmed not to be W3185: BM303, a 611 Squadron Mk VB, shot down on June 8th, 1942, the pilot of which, Sergeant Jack Misseldine, successfully evaded, and Mk IX, MA764, brought down on November 25th, 1943; coincidentally, the pilot, Flight Sergeant Don Bostock, also evaded.

It seems to me that the 'Search for Bader's Spitfire' is far from over, although I repeat what I wrote in Bader's Tangmere Spitfires, published in October 1996: -

… it is as if the mystery intends to remain patently unsolved – forever!

Perhaps our final thoughts, however, should be of Squadron Leader Buck Casson DFC AFC, a courageous and experienced fighter pilot, one of the Few, who fought bravely in Britain's hour of greatest need. Whatever happened that fateful day high over St Omer, I am sure that whatever opposing theories there might now be, we all agree that Buck's memory should always be revered.

Chapter Eight

Pilot Officer Victor Lowson

Victor Lowson was born on January 22nd, 1920, at 3 Cardean Street, Dundee, the son of John, an engineer employed at the local gas works, and Helen Lowson. When Victor's younger brother Jack arrived, Mrs Lowson soon had her hands full with two energetic youngsters. Victor was educated at Glebelands Primary School and the Morgan Academy, both in Dundee. He was a brilliant scholar and a committed member of the Boys' Brigade. A keen sportsman, in adult life this clean living and Christian Scot never touched either tobacco or alcohol. After leaving school he joined the office staff of Jute Industries, and on May 27th, 1939, Victor joined the RAFVR and volunteered for aircrew training.

Having been called up for full time service upon the outbreak of war, Sergeant Lowson completed his service flying training before learning to fly Spitfires at Hawarden, starting his course there on September 22nd, 1940. On October 6th he reported to 54 Squadron at Catterick, but was posted again, just five days later, to 65 Squadron at Turnhouse. Whilst there, Victor became a member of the 'Caterpillar Club', membership of which was open to airmen whose lives had been saved by Irvin parachutes. This adventure occurred on November 26th, 1940; Sergeant Lowson was patrolling over the Firth of Forth, between May Island and North Berwick, with the great ace Pilot Officer Finucane and Flying Officer Szulkowski. The Section patrolled the estuary for some 20 minutes, crossing from north to south and returning before flying up river towards the bridge and back. Sergeant Lowson later reported: -

The order was received to patrol Crail, and immediately afterwards the Ground Controller contacted with with a 'pip-squeak-zero', so I then switched on the contactor. When the Section reached Crail we were ordered to 4,000 feet, which entailed flying through a layer of cloud. From the conversation on the R/T I understood that we were trying to intercept an enemy aircraft. As instructions came through we changed course and height frequently, never flying one course for very long.

After some time the order to 'pancake' was received, and immediately we started losing height through cloud down to 500 feet. When we emerged from the cloud bank I saw that we were over water. I could see no land in any direction. Immediately the Section Leader requested a homing bearing but got no response except the order to 'pancake' being repeated. The Section Leader continually tried to obtain a homing from Ground Control but without success.

In the meantime I noticed that we were flying due west and did so for about 10 minutes before a coastline was sighted, although I was unable to identify our position. We then followed the coastline in a northerly direction whilst still trying to contact the Ground Station. By this time it was quite dark and ground detail was invisible, except for the coastline. The Section Leader then asked me to try and contact the Controller, but I was likewise unable to get a reply.

At this point I dropped behind the formation, and the Leader, seeing this, and taking into consideration our shortage of petrol, ordered me to climb to 4,000 feet and bale out. I left the formation and climbed through cloud until I reached 5,000 feet, when I turned and flew south before turning west, the idea being to get over land before I jumped. On seeing a break in the clouds below me I went down to find a landmark, but although I could confirm being over land I was unable to identify my position. Thereupon I climbed to 8,000 feet, still heading approximately west, and abandoned the aircraft.

Sergeant Lowson made a safe parachute descent, his Spitfire, X4233, which had seen action flying from Hornchurch in the Battle of Britain, was destroyed. The pilot's report, however, paints a vivid picture of just how basic flying was in those days: unreliable communications, no in cockpit GPS or computerised fly-by-wire technology!

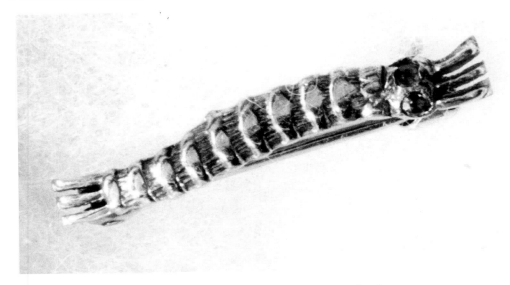

Vic Lowson's Caterpillar Club badge.

On November 29th, 1940, 65 Squadron flew south to Tangmere and another tour of duty in the hot zone. Shortly afterwards Sergeant Lowson saw the enemy for the first time when he came close to a Ju 88, firing his first shot in anger although the intruder disappeared into cloud. In February 1941, 65 Squadron was rested again, moving to Kirton. From there the Squadron operated on various sweeps as part of the 12 Group contribution to the 'Non-Stop Offensive', and on July 24th, Sergeant Lowson damaged an Me 109 at 20,000 feet above St Omer. In October the Squadron once more returned to the Tangmere Sector, then moved to Debden in December. The previous month had seen Victor Lowson commissioned for the duration of hostilities, so he was now a Pilot Officer.

A 65 Squadron Spitfire at Kirton, February 1941.

By May 1942, 65 Squadron was commanded by Squadron Leader Tony Bartley DFC, a Battle of Britain veteran who later married the actress Deborah Kerr. On May 23rd, Bartley led 12 65 Squadron Spitfires on a sweep over France, as part of the Debden Wing. Between Lumbres and Calais, Red Section, led by Pilot Officer Lowson, attacked three FW 190s. Victor fired at and damaged one of them with an eight second burst of machine-gun fire, watching his bullets strike home before the 190 dived away, out of control; he was the only RAF pilot to successfully engage the enemy on that day.

65 Squadron pilots at Kirton, 1941: From left: Sergeants Lowson & Stillwell, Flying Officer Smart, Squadron Leader Saunders, Pilot Officer Norwood & Flying Officer Finucane. Where the 'Sold' sign was from is not known!

On July 21st, 1942, 65 Squadron was in action again, as the Squadron diary records: -

During the afternoon, 65 Squadron participated in a Debden Wing mass Rhubarb. 12 Spitfires, led by Squadron Leader DAP McMullen DFC took off from Great Stamford at 1616 hours and, together with other Debden squadrons, set course for Blankenberg. 65 flew directly over Blankenberg and turned left, re-crossing the coast in the vicinity of Zeebrugge. Very intense light flak was experienced almost continually whilst over enemy territory. Targets attacked included numerous gun posts, a military car park, a light railway engine, a factory building opposite Zeebrugge railway station, two searchlight posts, two barges, two aircraft (believed to be dummies) on an aerodrome, and a light bridge over a canal. 11 pilots returned safely to Great Stamford by 1750 hours, all having attacked ground targets. Eight of our aircraft had been hit by light flak. The machines of Squadron Leader McMullen and Sergeant Hearne were write-offs, and Sergeant Tinsey's Category 'B'. The other five were all Category 'A'.

Pilot Officer Victor Lowson, flying as Red One, was seen to be hit by machine-gun fire shortly after crossing the enemy coast. He succeeded in getting back across the enemy coast but, about two miles out to sea, prepared to bale out by climbing rom sea level to approximately 1,500 feet and turning on his back. The machine then plunged vertically into the sea and the pilot was unable to fall clear. Warrant Officer RL Stillwell circled the spot several times where Pilot Officer Lowson had crashed, but nothing more was seen of him. Pilot Officer Lowson was one of the Squadron's most senior members and his loss is deeply felt.

Pilot Officer Lowson at Hornchurch, 1942, shortly before the operation on which he was reported missing.

The loss was no doubt particularly 'deeply felt' by Vic Lowson's friend Ron Stillwell. The pair had been sergeants together in 65 Squadron, and had lived and flown with each other for what was, in those days, a very long time.

The next day, Squadron Leader McMullen wrote to the missing pilot's parents: -

It is with the greatest regret that I have to write and tell you that your son, Pilot Officer Victor Lowson, is missing as a result of operations yesterday afternoon.

I am allowed to tell you in confidence that he was taking part in a low flying attack against enemy troops and gun positions on the coast of Belgium, near Zeebrugge. Whilst shooting up gun positions his Spitfire was hit and crashed into the sea about two miles off the Belgian coast. I am very much afraid that there is little chance that he survived.

He was one of our best pilots, a Section Leader and potential Flight Commander. In fact, during this flight he was leading a Flight into attack. He always showed exceptional promise as a pilot, an officer and a leader. It has come as a great blow to me personally that he is now missing.

Vicky was the best loved lad on our Squadron, his quiet steadiness of purpose and gentle wit having endeared him to us all during the long time that he has been with us. He will always remain in the hearts of the rest of the Squadron as one of the very best.

Ron Stillwell pictured in 1943, by which time he was a flight commander in 65 Squadron and decorated with the DFM.

Another letter followed on August 8th, 1942, this time from the 65 Squadron Intelligence Officer, Flight Lieutenant Hugh Tarrant: -

I regret that we have received no news of Victor. Should we hear anything at all in the future I will notify you immediately. I hope you will accept my personal sympathy. As an Intelligence Officer I am naturally older and more experienced than the pilots in my Squadron; I would like to assure you now that Victor was quite the finest boy that I ever met in the Service. I am happy to think that he liked me and looked upon me as a friend. I miss his companionship in this Squadron very deeply.

On February 14th, 1943, the Air Ministry confirmed that as nothing further had been heard of Pilot Officer Lowson since the day he crashed in Spitfire W3697, he must be 'presumed dead for official purposes'.

Pilot Officer Victor Lowson is rembered on Panel 170 on the Runnymede Memorial, the Commonwealth's tribute to 'missing' airmen.

Whilst researching Victor Lowson's story, I traced Jack Lowson, still living in Dundee and who still felt his elder brother's loss most keenly. Amongst the family's treasured artefacts of Victor's passing were his Caterpillar Club badge, made into a brooch and worn proudly by his sister-in-law. Most poignant of all was Victor's diary, a four leaf clover still pressed into the pages. Sadly the 23-year old pilot's luck ran out that fateful day in 1942 over the Belgian coast, another intelligent, sensitive and articulate young man whose potential was enveloped by the cold and dark North Sea.

A moving discovery: the four leafed clover, for good luck, pressed into the pages of Pilot Officer Lowson's diary.

Chapter Nine

Squadron Leader Brian Lane DFC

When I was a child, fascinated by the Spitfire and Battle of Britain story, there was a particular photograph, repeated in numerous books and articles, which I kept coming back to. It showed a young squadron leader in conference with other pilots and an intelligence officer. The pilots had just landed, and the squadron leader looked exhausted. I found it frustrating, however, that inevitably the caption never identified the personalities pictured, generic captions reading 'Pilots debriefing after a sortie', or something similar. The face of the young squadron leader, lined and tired, haunted me, and I often wondered who he was and what happened to him.

Many years later, whilst researching the story of Flying Officer Franek Surma and Spitfire R6644, I was given a book called *Spitfire! The Experiences of a Fighter Pilot*, by 'Squadron Leader BJ Ellan'. The book was a first hand account published in 1942, and from the photographs within I was delighted to discover that this was actually the anonymous squadron leader that had captured my imagination so many years before. Subsequently I learned that his name was actually Brian John Edward Lane, the CO of 19 Squadron in the Duxford Sector. Brian's book, *Spitfire!* was both an excellent and inspiring read, the author succeeding in answering 'the question of the man in the street: "What is it like up there?" and to give an idea of what a fighter pilot feels and thinks as he fights up there in the blue.' Having read the book, my impression was of an intelligent, brave but incredibly modest young man, an absolutely model human being.

Another photograph from the same series as that which so fascinated the author; from left: Squadron Leader Brian Lane, Flying Officer Cresswell (Intelligence Officer), Flight Lieutenant Walter 'Farmer' Lawson & Sergeant David Fulford.

Brian Lane was born on June 18th, 1917, in his words 'with a silver spoon in my mouth'. Although Lane is believed to have been born in Harrogate, his family lived in Pinner, Middlesex, and Brian was educated at St Paul's, near Hammersmith Bridge. The school boasts some extremely distinguished old scholars, including the poet John Milton, the great diarist Samuel Pepys and, more recently, Field Marshal Lord Montgomery of Alamein. Unusually, therefore, for someone who had enjoyed the benefits of being educated at such a school, by 1935 the 18-year old Brian was employed by 'a big electrical firm' and supervising a 'a dozen or so girls turning out hundreds of light bulbs'. Although the teenager considered his position to be a responsible one, in which he learned much about human nature, and women in particular, he was apparently not surprised when 'one day the powers that be informed me that the period of my employment coincided with a decline in their profits, and that if I would kindly leave them they could get along better without me. I went home to my lamenting parents with the additional news that I wanted to try for the RAF, which was then in the course of expansion.'

Brian then applied for a Short Service Commission, and volunteered for pilot training, eventually being invited to a Selection Board at Adastral House. Feeling much like a 'microbe on a slide under a microscope' throughout the interview, Brian was successful and subsequently reported for duty at Air Service Training, Hamble, on March 22nd, 1936. There he completed *ab initio* flying training before moving on to No 11 SFTS at Wittering on June 3rd. Pilot Officer John Wray joined the service with Pilot Officer Lane: -

Brian was rather languid and slow in those days, not what one imagined a fighter pilot to be. He was always known as 'Dopey' because he had deep set eyes with black rings underneath, nothing to do with his lifestyle, just natural characteristics! During those now far off days of our training, only the very good pilots went on to fighter squadrons, which meant, of course, the minority. For example, I was posted to an army co-operation squadron because, so I was told by the Chief Ground Instructor, 'they need gentlemen because you may have to take port with the general!'

Upon conclusion of our course at Wittering, Dopey was posted to a fighter squadron. I saw him afterwards on a number of occasions when he was with 19 Squadron at Duxford, and ran into him on other stations when his squadron was re-fuelling at forward bases such as Manston. In conclusion I must make one point absolutely clear: Dopey Lane was no dope when it came to leading a fighter squadron.

On January 8th, 1937, Pilot Officer Lane reported for flying duties with 66 Squadron at RAF Duxford, and flew the Gloster Gauntlet biplane fighter. On June 30th, Brian was posted to 213 Squadron, another Gauntlet squadron, based at Northolt, remaining with the unit until it was re-equipped with Hurricanes in 1939. On November 11th, 1938, Brian was the pilot of a Magister, in which his friend Pilot Officer Weatherill, was a passenger, flying from Wittering to Northolt. The two pilots were going on leave for the weekend, but 3,000 feet over Henlow the aircraft went into a diving turn from which the pilot was unable to recover. In his log book, Brian wrote 'Hit the deck at 12.50 hours at 200 m.p.h. Walked away from it – just. Returned to duty 3.1.39, longest weekend on record!' Not withstanding Brian Lane's amusing notes, the two pilots were lucky to survive. Brian was carrying his silver cigarette case, engraved 'BJL', the bottom of which sustained an 'L' shape dent in the crash. Across the damage, the owner has inscribed '11/11/38. Magister L8136'.

A Miles Magister.

Brian Lane's silver cigarette case, now owned by the author.

A week after Britain & France declared war on Nazi Germany on September 3rd, 1939, Brian was promoted to Flight Lieutenant and sent to command 19 Squadron's 'A' Flight at Duxford. No 19 was a very famous squadron, not least because it was the first to receive Spitfires, on August 4th, 1938. Pilot Officer Frank Brinsden was a New Zealander serving with the RAF, and recalls Flight Lieutenant Lane's arrival: -

He was received politely but coolly as 'Sandy' Lane. Coolly because the residents of 19 Squadron thought that a number of them could have filled the vacancy without calling in an outsider who, despite the small number of officer pilots in Fighter Command at that time, was unknown to us. However, within a week or two Brian's calmness, personal dignity and professional skill showed through; the sobriquet 'Sandy' was never used again and within the Squadron he became 'Brian'.

The somewhat derogatory tag of 'Sandy' was quite incongruous. His dignity was not a pose and he enjoyed Squadron sorties to the local as much of any of us, and he treated us all as equals. I do recall, however, a formal dressing down that I received from Brian Lane, after which my respect for him was even further enhanced; I used the same technique myself in later years, when a Commanding Officer and with comparable results.

Pilot Officer Michael Lyne remembers the flying undertaken by 19 Squadron at this time: -

I arrived on the Squadron fresh from Cranwell in August 1939. Brian Lane was my second Flight Commander and I found him to be a charming and encouraging superior. Our aircraft were Spitfire Mk I with fixed pitch two bladed wooden airscrews. Duxford had a grass runway of 800 yards, and, with the poor take off and on landing the poor braking effect of a coarse pitch propeller, we needed every yard of it. I was astounded at the boldness of Squadron Leader Cozens in conducting formation landings at night in this aircraft, especially as the lighting consisted of Great War style paraffin flares.

In spite of the war, most of September 1939 was given over to practice flying, formation, high altitude and night flying. The blacking out of all towns and villages made this harder than we expected. In February 1940 one of our most experienced pilots, Pilot Officer Trenchard, was killed in a night flying accident.

Michael Lyne, who eventually retired as an Air Vice-Marshal.

By October we were operational, going forward to spend the days at the bomber airfield at Watton, in tents and forbidden the Officers' Mess because the CO did not like the way we fighter pilots looked in our flying boots and heavy sweaters, ready for unheated and unpressurised flight at high altitude. It was still very much a peacetime air force in many ways.

On October 20th we made a sudden move to Catterick, with groundcrews and equipment being carried in four engine Ensign transports. This was in response to the German attack on the Firth of Forth, each squadron moving north one stage. We did a few convoy protection patrols near Flamborough Head and returned to Duxford a week later.

In November we started to patrol from the new Norwich airfield at Horsham St Faith. The mess was not ready and we all lived in a house called 'Redroofs'. There was no night flying so our social life was active. When we were at Horsham on a Sunday we gave an unofficial flying display at low level for the local population. This system of forward basing and coastal patrols continued throughout December and into January 1940.

The flying conditions over this period were often very frightening, there being no proper homing or landing aids and a very poor and outdated cockpit radio. After a spell above cloud you let down gently and hoped that you were over the sea or fens. Sometimes the ground did not show up until you got to 300 feet, when the problem became one of trying to recognise somewhere in rain and mist. A lovelorn Section Leader, Flying Officer Matheson, nearly did for me in these conditions when he took us back from Horsham in terrible weather so as to keep a date in Cambridge!

By March the weather was better but we now had Flying Officer Douglas Bader to contend with. He was very brave and determined but having a hard time coming to terms with the Spitfire, especially in cloud. More than once my friend Watson and I, lent to him as a formation by the CO, emerged from cloud faithfully following Bader, only to find ourselves in a steep diving turn!

This was, of course, the 'Phoney War' period when the war must have often seemed surreal. On May 10th, 1940, all that changed, however, when Hitler attacked the west. The following day, 19 Squadron scored its first kill, a Ju 88 destroyed over the sea by Flight Lieutenant Wilf Clouston, Flying Officer Petre and Flight Sergeant Harry Steere.

Flight Lieutenant Gordon Sinclair: -

Brian Lane was a very quiet person, rather intellectual, and always in the background was the fact of his blind father. In his quite way he was a compelling leader, particularly since he was an excellent pilot. We became friends very soon after he came to Duxford, so close that he married Eileen Ellison, quietly and without fuss, to whom I had introduced him! I remember he had a delightful sense of humour and was quick to laugh, he smiled easily. I have thought about Brian frequently since those days.

On May 18th, 1940, Rev Fred Jeeves married Brian and Eileen at Great Shelford, the bride's home village. The witnesses were the bride's parents, Sidney, a solicitor, and Theresa. The groom was 23, the bride 28 and a beautiful, quite incredible, woman.

Eileen's family was a wealthy one, this good fortune facilitating her brother's interest in motor sport. The thrills and spills captivated Eileen who began racing herself with an amateur driver, TP Cholmondeley Tapper, whilst Tony Ellison acted as their mechanic. The threesome travelled to race meets all over Europe, but Eileen's greatest win was at Brooklands, in 1932, when she won the Duchess of York's race for women drivers. In clinching this victory she beat Kay Petre, the most famous female racing driver of the day.

Brian & Eileen Lane pictured at the wedding of Frank & Cynthia Brinsden in 1941.

The military situation on the continent was rapidly deteriorating however, and on May 26th the decision was made to retire on Dunkirk and evacuate Lord Gort's Expeditionary Force. With great foresight and reflecting his determination to keep base secure, Air Chief Marshal Dowding had only committed Hurricanes, which were more plentiful but inferior to the Spitfire in performance, to action on the continent. Having preserved his precious Spitfires for home defence, the time had now come for them to be pitched into battle during Operation DYNAMO, the air operation in support of the evacuation. On May 25th, and in anticipation of the evacuation, Fighter Command moved certain Spitfire squadrons to 11 Group airfields within range of the French and Belgian coast. 19 Squadron was sent to Hornchurch, and on the following day Squadron Leader Stephenson led his Spitfires into action over Calais. There a gaggle of *Stukas* were found, so the Spitfires throttled right back, matching their targets' speed, as the CO ordered attacks in sections of three. Michael Lyne: -

As a former CFS A1 instructor, Stephenson was a precise flier and obedient to the book, which stipulated an overtaking speed of 30 m.p.h. What the book did not foresee, however, was that we would attack Ju 87s doing just 130 m.p.h. The CO led his Section, Pilot Officer Watson No 2 and myself No 3, straight up behind the Ju 87s which looked very relaxed and probably thought we were their fighter escort. The leader of the German fighters, however, had been very clever and pulled his formation away towards England, so that when the dive-bombers turned in towards Calais, the 109s would be protecting their rear. Meanwhile Stephenson realised that we were closing far too fast. I remember his call 'No 19 Squadron! Prepare to attack!', then, to Watson and I in Red Section, 'Throttling back, throttling back.' We were virtually formatting on the last section of Ju 87s, and an incredibly slow and dangerous speed in the presence of enemy fighters, and behind us staggered the rest of 19 Squadron at a similar speed. Still the *Stukas* had not recognised us as a threat, so Stephenson told us to take a target each and fire. So far as I know we must have got the last three, we could hardly have done otherwise, then I broke away and as the last section of 109s came round. After the break I was alone and looking for friends when I came under fire for the first time. The first signs were mysterious corkscrews of smoke passing my starboard wing. Then I heard a slow thump, thump, and realised that I was being attacked by a 109 firing machine-guns with tracer and cannons banging away. I broke away sharpish and lost him.

Squadron Leader Geoffrey Stephenson.   *Pilot Officer Watson.*

I made a wide sweep and came back to the Calais area to find about five Ju 87s going round in a tight defensive circle. As the 109s had disappeared I flew to take the circle head on, giving it a long squirt. At this stage I was hit by return fire, for when I got back to Hornchurch I found bullet holes in the wing, which had punctured a tyre.

Alas my friend Watson was never seen again. Stephenson made a forced landing in France and was captured.

Brian Lane leading 'A' Flight in 1939.

Pilot Officer Peter Howard-Williams was a new pilot on 19 Squadron who had been tasked with collecting and delivering replacement aircraft, as he was not yet 'combat ready': 'On May 26th, I remember the CO and Watson going missing, Michael Lyne being shot up and Flying Officer Eric Ball landing back at Hornchurch where he found that an enemy bullet had gone through his helmet, parting his hair and leaving a small wound!'

For 19 Squadron, the fighting that day was far from over. With the CO missing, it fell to the senior flight commander, Flight Lieutenant Brian Lane, to lead the Squadron into action. Brian later wrote in his log book of ensuing events: -

Leading Squadron on patrol of Dunkirk and Calais. Green Section reported eight Me 109s just above us, off Calais. Observed Me 109 chasing Sinclair into cloud. Hun pulled up and have me a sitting target from below. Gave him a good burst which he ran straight into, lurched and went straight down. I followed him but he hadn't pulled out at 3,000 feet and must have gone straight in. Blacked out completely but pulled out in time. Landed at Manston and stayed for tea. Lovely near the coast in this weather.

Flying Officers Sinclair and Petre also claimed 109s destroyed, but Sergeant Irwin was missing and Pilot Officer Michael Lyne had been shot up again, this time crash landing on Walmer Beach in Kent with a bullet in his knee.

The pathos of action remained constant over the next few days, with Flight Lieutenant Lane still leading 19 Squadron in the air. In the morning of May 27th, 19 Squadron again patrolled high over Dunkirk and Calais, Brian Lane's Section attacking a He 111 over Gravelines. Heavy AA fire, probably 'friendly', nearly, in Brian's words, 'wrote the Squadron off.' All of 19 Squadron's Spitfire returned with flak damage, but were up in the afternoon on a sweep inland to Ypres. Near Dunkirk the Spitfires happened across a lone Hs 126 reconnaissance aircraft which was brought down by Flight Sergeant Unwin. Brian added in his log book 'I have never seen anything so peaceful – no sign of war at all except the big smoke pall over Dunkirk'.

On May 28th, 19 Squadron began operating as part of a wing formation with Nos 54 and 65 Squadrons. This was because Air Vice-Marshal Keith Park, the Air Officer Commanding No 11 Group, unlike his peers, actually knew how to fly a modern fighter aircraft and had observed the fighting over Dunkirk from the cockpit of his personal Hurricane, O-K1. As a result of this, Park recognised that stronger offensive patrols would reduce both losses to his fighters and the effect of enemy attacks on the soldiers below.

The following day saw Squadron Leader 'Tubby' Mermagen's 222 Squadron and Squadron Leader Robin Hood's 41 Squadron arrive at Hornchurch. As 19 Squadron was the most experienced, Brian Lane and his boys led the five squadron strong wing, which also included 54 and 65 Squadrons, over the Channel. It must be appreciated, however, that a 'wing' in this sense was only, in effect, a convoy of fighter aircraft travelling together and arriving in the combat area *en masse*. Moreover, after battle was joined there was no tactical cohesion whatsoever due to the fact that radio communication between squadrons was impossible because each used a different frequency. The squadrons were also operating beyond range of radio contact with their base and therefore did not enjoy the benefit of early radar generated information. This was significant, as in the absence of radar assistance Park's fighters had to mount exhausting standing patrols from dawn to dusk. Due to the logistics and numbers of available Spitfires, there were also problems in maintaining squadron strengths: four squadron wings regularly numbered 30 and not the intended 44 aircraft. Nevertheless, Air Vice-Marshal Park was responding to a situation for which there was no precedent, and did so rapidly and effectively, his experience over Dunkirk reinforcing his belief that it was better to spoil the aim of many, rather than destroy a few.

On June 1st, Flight Lieutenant Lane led Nos 19, 41, 222 and 616 Squadrons across the Channel; on the first of two sorties that day the wing encountered 12 Me 110s, in Brian's words 'straight from Flying Training School, I should think. Terrific sport!' He destroyed one of the enemy machines, which was last seen streaming coolant at 50 feet, and saw other 110s crash into the sea and on the foreshore. Of the scene below, Brian's log book remarks 'Dunkirk beaches. Most amazing sight this evacuation. Thames barges, sailing boats, anything that will float, and the Navy. God help them down there! They need more than we can give them.'

By June 3rd, 1940, the evacuation was complete, some 224,686 British and 141,445 French and Belgian troops having been snatched to safety. The following day 19 Squadron left Hornchurch, Flight Lieutenant Lane in Spitfire N3040, which he had flown on all but two sorties over Dunkirk. Later he wrote in his log book: -

Squadron returned to Duxford. Visibility so good that I couldn't see Duxford anywhere! Did a 19 peel off and then peeled off on 48 hours leave. Pretty good.

During Operation DYNAMO, 19 Squadron had learned much, not least that the tried but untested 'book' was useless. After Squadron Leader Stephenson was captured in the Squadron's first full formation combat over Calais on May 26th, Flight Lieutenant Lane had to suddenly step into the breach, assuming an unexpected responsibility beyond both his years and experience. He responded to this challenge perfectly, leading 19 Squadron on virtually every patrol, and opening his personal account against the enemy. Indeed, the 22-year old had not just flown at the head of 19 Squadron, but equally so in front of several senior squadron commanders as he led the wing across to France. This swift introduction to combat flying and leadership had been a challenge, which Brian Lane had overcome without mishap or complaint. It would stand him in good stead for the events of a few weeks later.

On June 3rd, whilst 19 Squadron was still at Hornchurch, command of 19 Squadron was officially given to Squadron Leader Phillip Campbell Pinkham AFC, who joined his new Squadron at Duxford. Pinkham was a regular air force career officer who had been commissioned in 1935. After his service flying training, he flew Gauntlet biplane fighters with No 17 Squadron at Kenley, but just six months later joined the Meteorological Flight based at Mildenhall, recording data for the weather men. In January 1938, 'Tommy' Pinkham became a fighter instructor at Andover. There he flew a modern monoplane fighter, a Hurricane, for the first time on March 21st, 1939. A year later he was awarded an Air Force Cross in the King's Birthday Honours List for his work training Fins and Poles. Like many other substantive squadron leaders serving in training units, Pinkham had requested a combat command upon the outbreak of war, a good career move providing that one of course survived. When Squadron Leader Stephenson was captured on May 26th, Squadron Leader Pinkham's name happened to be in the right place on the list.

It is interesting at this point to compare the experience of Squadron Leader Pinkham and Flight Lieutenant Lane. Both were pre-war regular officers, Pinkam three years older than Lane and already a substantive squadron leader. Although he had been a peacetime fighter pilot, flying biplanes, Pinkham, however, had flown for the majority of his service in a non operational training role. Lane's entire service had been spent as a fighter pilot, firstly on biplanes, then on Hurricanes and Spitfires. He was operationally and tactically aware, popular on the Squadron, and a good pilot. Brian had been a Flight Lieutenant and commander of 19 Squadron's 'A' Flight for nine months. His leadership of the Squadron over Dunkirk, in spite of difficult circumstances, had been absolutely outstanding, so many believed that Brian Lane would be the automatic choice to take over 19 Squadron after Geoffrey Stephenson was captured. The Air Ministry, however, had yet to realise that such quick promotions were essential in wartime so as to have the best and most experienced officer in command, not just the most senior.

Fowlmere Farm: home of 19 Squadron in 1940.

On June 22nd, 1940, the Battle of France ended when French delegates signed the Armistice with Nazi Germany in a railway carriage at Compiègne. Back at Duxford, 19 Squadron was pressed into a night-fighting in an attempt to counter the threat represented by nocturnal raiders. On the night of June 18th, Flying Officers Johnnie Petre and Eric Ball each destroyed a He 111. Petre, however, had been hit by return fire, as a result of which his Spitfire literally blew up in his face. Although he baled out safely, the young pilot received terribly disfiguring burns.

The German bomber shot down by Flying Officer Petre was flown by *Oberleutnant* von Arnim, whose father was later a prominent German general in North Africa. Flying Officer Frank Brinsden: -

The crew of the He 111 destroyed by Johnnie Petre were held captive in the Officers' Mess. Eileen Lane happened to appear, looking for Brian, and unwittingly shown into the Ladies Room by the Duty Officer – unwittingly because within was being held one of the Germans who, upon Eileen's entry, rose to his feet and greeted her; before the war they had been friends on the continental motor racing circuit!

Oberleutnant *Von Arnim and his crew.*

On July 1st, Squadron Leader Pinkham examined Flight Lieutenant Lane's flying log book. Therein he saw that since June 1st, 1939, this bright young officer had flown a total of 189.30 hours, 14.05 hours of which were at night, giving a grand total of 732.35 hours. 19 Squadron's new Commanding Officer endorsed the log as being that of an 'Exceptional fighter pilot' who was 'above the average' as an aerial marksman. Very few pilots receive an 'exceptional' rating, but this was most deserved in Brian Lane's case. Clearly Squadron Leader Pinkham recognised the ability, experience and potential of his senior flight commander.

On July 22nd, a new policy commenced of sending Brian Lane's 'A' Flight from Fowlmere, in the Duxford Sector, to Coltishall on a daily detachment. The purpose was to assist 66 Squadron in providing convoy protection patrols. The 19 Squadron pilots were pleased with this development as they hoped that operating near the coast would give them a greater chance on contacting the enemy. The unit, as the RAF's most experienced Spitfire squadron, was often used to test new equipment, and had recently been re-equipped with the Spitfire Mk IB. This variant was identical to the Mk IA except that all eight Browning machine-guns had been removed and replaced with two 20 mm Hispano Suiza cannons. The Me 109, of course, was already armed with two 7.9 mm *Rheinmetal-Borsig* machine-guns and two 20 mm *Oerlikon* cannons, this mixed weaponry providing the enemy pilot with the benefits of rapid firing machine-guns and hard hitting cannon. Behind in the arms race, Fighter Command was now desperate to give its pilots similar firepower, hence the Mk IB being rushed into service with 19 Squadron; a smaller number also went to 92 Squadron at Biggin Hill.

19 Squadron's pilots at Fowlmere during the Battle of Britain;
from left: Lane, Potter, Jennings, Unwin, Aeberhardt, Steere,
Brinsden, Lawson, Haines, Vokes, Clouston & Thomas.

Squadron Leader Pinkham has often been criticised for having busied himself with evaluating the new Spitfire, whilst Flight Lieutenant Lane continued to lead 19 Squadron in the air. This, however, I feel, is actually further evidence of Brian Lane's ability and the confidence that could be placed in him. The cannon armed Spitfires were a problem, and yet the Spitfire pilots were in desperate need of the hard hitting weapon. Resolution of stoppages was therefore a priority, and it was right that the CO, who was after all a very experienced pilot, should take on the job himself. This he was able to do only because of having such an able deputy in Brian Lane, who could be relied upon completely to lead the Squadron operationally whilst the CO was otherwise engaged.

News received on July 31st gave 19 Squadron cause for celebration: Brian Lane had been awarded the Distinguished Flying Cross. Pilot Officer Wallace 'Jock' Cunningham remembers: -

Shortly after Brian's DFC came through for his good leadership of the Squadron and general activities at Dunkirk, we were lying in the sun at Coltishall along with Squadron Leader Douglas Bader and other 242 Squadron pilots. Douglas was kidding Brian and asked him 'What's that?', in his usual cocky fashion, pointing to Brian's DFC ribbon. 'I must get one of those', said Bader, and, as we all know, he later did.

Superb study of Squadron Leader Brian Lane DFC.

Although command of 19 Squadron had been given to another officer, it was fitting indeed that Flight Lieutenant Lane's efforts should at least be recognised with the award of a gallantry decoration.

The largely uneventful and boring convoy protection patrols continued into August, the 12 Group pilots becoming increasingly frustrated at their lack of action when compared to the casualties being taken by their counterparts in 11 Group. The Spitfire Mk IBs were also proving unpopular because the cannons jammed so regularly. Without any other armament this left the pilot unable to defend himself, so confidence in the cannon-armed Spitfires was low. The cannon, which weighed 96 pounds, was designed to be mounted upright, but due to the Spitfire's thin wing section it was necessary to fit the weapon on its side, meaning the spent shell cases were ejected from that direction, instead of from below as the manufacturer intended. 19 Squadron's armourers carried out sterling work by designing and fitting deflector plates, but still the problem was not entirely solved, the empty shell not being thrown clear of the cannon but bouncing back into it; the next incoming round then jammed the offending case in the breech, rendering the weapon inoperable.

On August 11th Spitfire X4231 was delivered to the Squadron, this being the first aircraft fitted with the 'B' wing, which combined a cannon with two Browning machine-guns. It was feared that the machine-guns' extra weight would make the aircraft under powered, but a test flight by Squadron Leader Pinkham proved this to be a groundless concern. Although all agreed that the new armament combination was a step in the right direction, tellingly the 19 Squadron diary comments that 'Possibly another step in the same direction would be re-equipping with the old eight-gun machines.'

By this time the Battle of Britain was in full wing over southern England; on August 16th 'A' Flight of 19 Squadron encountered the enemy en masse for the first time since Dunkirk. Brian Lane's log book records 'Returning from Coltishall investigated X Raid above cloud with seven aircraft of 'A' Flight. Turned out to be about 150 Huns!! Waded into escort of Me 110s but ruddy cannons stopped on me.' Upon being attacked the 110s went into a defensive circle. Although the Spitfire pilots destroyed three of them, six of the seven Spitfires suffered cannon stoppages. Pilot Officer Cunningham, who shot down a 110, remembers 'I remember mainly Sergeant 'Jimmy' Jennings on the R/T bemoaning his jammed 20 mm cannon, full of indignation at the unfairness of life in general.' The Squadron diary reflected that 'Results would have been doubled had we been equipped with either cannon and machine-guns or just eight machine-guns.' Fortunately for 'A' Flight, although escorting Me 109s were present, for some reason they did not attack.

On Saturday August 24th, six large raids were mounted against England, the fourth of which reached the East End at 3 p.m. 11 Group called for assistance from 12 Group, and 19 Squadron, led by Flight Lieutenant Lane, was scrambled to intercept an incoming formation of 50 enemy aircraft. Brian recorded events in his log book: -

Ran into a bunch of Huns over estuary. Had a bang at an Me 110 but had to break away as tracer was coming over my head from another behind me. He appeared to be hitting his fellow countryman in front of me but I didn't wait to see if he shot him down. Had a crack at another and shot his engine right out of the wing – lovely! Crashed near North Foreland. Last trip in 'Blitzen III'.

When the cannons worked, there was no doubting their effectiveness. Only two of the nine 19 Squadron pilots engaged had been able to expend all of their ammunition without a stoppage, which was clearly unacceptable.

During this phase of the Battle of Britain, the *Luftwaffe* was pounding 11 Group airfields, hitting Sector Stations like Biggin Hill, Hornchurch and Kenley very hard. On August 26th, 11 Group again called for assistance; Sergeant David Cox: -

Again Brian Lane led us off. We were ordered to patrol at 10,000 feet, but the Observer Corps reported the raid incoming at 1,000 feet. The 11 Group controllers thought this to be a mistake, so we were told to remain at 10,000 feet. The raid came and went and but we were blissfully unaware and therefore did not engage. The subsequent intelligence report stated that the 'Spitfires from Fowlmere were slow in getting off the ground', which was certainly not the case.

On August 31st, Brian Lane and the rest of 'A' Flight were enjoying a rare day off duty. 'B' Flight, however, intercepted a raid on Duxford. Although victories were claimed, it was a costly combat for Flight Lieutenant Wilf Clouston's pilots: Flying Officer James Coward was shot down in X4231, baling out missing a foot, and Flying Officer Frank Brinsden also went over the side, being violently ill during his subsequent parachute descent and so drenched in petrol that he was lucky not to catch fire. 19-year old Pilot Officer Aeberhardt crash landed with a damaged aircraft but was killed in the attempt. Again the Squadron diary was critical of the cannons: 'The score would most definitely been higher given eight machine-guns'. By now the pilots had completely lost confidence in the Mk IB, so much so that Flight Lieutenant Lane made representation, on behalf of all pilots, to Squadron Leader Pinkham who consequently requested that 19 Squadron be re-equipped with Mk IAs. Duxford's Station Commander and 'Boss' Controller, Group Captain AB 'Woody' Woodhall, supported this view and endorsed Pinkham's report to Fighter Command HQ: -

I get on the phone to Leigh-Mallory and urgently requested that 19 Squadron should have its eight-gun Spitfires back. The following afternoon the Commander-in-Chief himself landed at Duxford, without warning. I greeted him and he gruffly said 'I want to talk to 19 Squadron, so I drove him over to Fowlmere. There he met Sandy Lane and other pilots. He listened to their complaints almost in silence, then I drove him back to his aircraft which he was piloting personally. As he climbed into the aeroplane he merely said 'You'll get your eight-gun Spitfires back.' 'Stuffy' Dowding was a man of few words; he listened to all of us, asked a few pertinent questions, then made his decision. As a result, that same evening the instructors from the operational training unit at Hawarden flew their eight-gun Spitfires down and exchanged them for IBs.

Whilst 'A' Flight was re-equipping, on September 3rd Squadron Leader Pinkham led 'B' Flight on a standing patrol over Duxford and Debden. The Spitfires were vectored to North Weald, but arrived to find that the Sector Station had already been bombed. Flying in pairs line astern, 19 Squadron attacked the withdrawing enemy from above and ahead. The combat was Pinkham's first, in which he suffered cannon stoppage and made no claim, but Me 110s were destroyed by Flying Officer Haines and Flight Sergeant Unwin. For the rest of that day, 611 Squadron, sent down from Ternhill to Fowlmere, covered 19 Squadron's patrols whilst the exchange of Spitfires was completed.

The machine-gun armed Spitfire Mk IA that Brian Lane flew from September 3rd, 1940, onwards.

On September 4th, Squadron Leader Pinkham led 19 Squadron firstly on a patrol over Debden, then on another over Debden, North Weald and Hornchurch Sector Stations. The sorties were uneventful but the Squadron diarist, whilst bemoaning the tired aircraft from Hawarden, appeared more optimistic for the future: 'First day with eight-gun machines, and what wrecks. At least the guns will fire!'

The following morning, Squadron Leader Pinkham and 19 Squadron were up over Hornchurch. Over the patrol area, Sergeant Jennings sighted a formation of 40 Do 17s escorted by 40 Me 109s, all incoming over the Thames Estuary. The CO was at first unable to see the enemy, so Jennings directed events until Pinkham had the bandits in sight and ordered Brian Lane's 'A' Flight to attack the 109s whilst he personally led 'B' Flight against the bombers. 'B' Flight engaged the Do 17s in pairs, from the rear, but at that moment the high flying 109s fell on Pinkham and his tiny force. A classic cut-and-thrust fighter-to-fighter combat developed, as the whole of 19 Squadron became embroiled with the 109s. Flying Officer Haines pursued a 1/JG 54 109 across Kent, on the deck, the German fighter eventually crashing onto to No 6 Hardy Street, Maidstone, and the Czech Sergeant Plzak left another 109 pouring black smoke. Two Spitfires were damaged, however, and Squadron Leader Pinkham failed to return. Later a Spitfire that had crashed in the remote countryside near Birling in Kent was identified to be Pinkham's, his body found nearby. It was believed that the 19 Squadron CO had been hit by a cross-fire from a vic of Do 17s, and possibly also hit by a 109. Apparently the 25-year old Spitfire pilot had tried to bale out, but due to wounds to his chin, chest and hip had great difficulty in doing so; by the time he abandoned the doomed aircraft it was too low for his parachute to open.

As was necessary practice, another hand has recorded details of Tommy Pinkham's final flight, rather spitefully adding and underlining the words 'First combat'. The insinuation is that as this was three months after taking over 19 Squadron, Squadron Leader Pinkham's leadership was open to question. Personally I do not think this at all fair, given Pinkham's responsibility for the troublesome Mk IB. Moreover, the evidence indicates that immediately he was relieved of this burden, Squadron Leader Pinkham did indeed lead 19 Squadron in the air. It must also be remembered that although Pinkham's appointment as CO was perhaps questionable at such a crucial operational time, it was not untypical. Moreover, given Brian Lane's popularity and ability, and as many felt he should have got the Squadron after Stephenson's capture, the circumstances of Pinkham's command could not have been easy. The two appear to have complimented each other perfectly during Tommy Pinkham's tenure of 19 Squadron, which was in any case a particularly difficult period because of the Mk IB problem.

Brian Lane wrote: -

A gloom descended over the Mess and there wasn't quite so much talking or laughter as usual, as we sat drinking after supper that night.

Next day, after lunch, Russell, our Adjutant, rang me up.
"Keep this under your hat until Woody rings up, but you've got the Squadron. Congratulations!"
"Shut up and stop blathering", I said.
"No, really. After all, you've had the Squadron once before so I suppose they think you might as well try to make a mess of it again!"
"I don't want any of your rudeness, B…..", I said coldly, using his surname. He laughed.
"Good Lord, I shall have to salute you now, I suppose!"

And so it was that Brian Lane added his 'scraper' ring to his uniform sleeves, indicating that he was, at last, a squadron leader, although, typically, Brian also wrote that this was a 'sad promotion' given the circumstances.

Wing Commander George Unwin: -

Brian Lane was a first class pilot and leader. He was firstly my Flight Commander, and then the Squadron CO. He was completely unflappable and instilled confidence in all who flew with him.

Having led 19 Squadron on the vast majority of operational flights since May 26th, 1940, there could have been no better choice for Squadron Leader Pinkham's successor than Brian Lane.

The role of 12 Group, in which the Duxford Sector Station was situated, during the Battle of Britain was to defend the industrial Midlands and the North, in addition to providing assistance to 11 Group as and when required. The System dictated that on occasions when 11 Group's squadrons were engaged, 12 Group would cover 11 Group's airfields. Such a protective umbrella was clearly essential, but certain 12 Group pilots found it unacceptable that they should be employed in such a mundane way whilst 11 Group pilots were so heavily engaged. On August 30th, Squadron Leader Douglas Bader's 242 Squadron was scrambled from Duxford to intercept a raid on Hatfield, in 11 Group. The Hurricanes acquitted themselves well, scoring several victories, convincing Bader that had he more fighters in the air then the score would have been greater. This theory received support from Group Captain Woodhall and Air Vice-Marshal Leigh-Mallory, Air Officer Commander-in-Chief of 12 Group. Consequently it was arranged that Bader would lead the '12 Group Wing', based at Duxford and comprising the Spitfires of 19 Squadron, and the Hurricanes of both 242 and 310. The concept was not to merely defend 11 Group's airfields but to offensively seek out the enemy and meet the Germans in strength. This was contrary to the System, and the opposite of 11 Group's tactics involving small numbers of fighters harrying the enemy both incoming and outgoing, which were working. In this way 11 Group's fighters were never presented in numbers to the enemy, to be destroyed by the numerically greater Me 109s. The completely contrary 'Big Wing' concept, however, was, recent research proves, based upon a misconception from the outset: on August 30th, 1940, the Hatfield raiders were not attacked purely by 242 Squadron, as Squadron Leader Bader had assumed, but also by Hurricanes and Spitfires of 11 Group. The more fighters are in the air then the greater becomes the over claiming factor, as pilots independently attack the same aircraft oblivious to each other; consequently that enemy machine ends up being credited to various pilots and therefore the overall score becomes greatly inflated. Therefore 242 Squadron did not actually inflict the level of damage that it believed, and actual enemy losses were, in fact, shared between many RAF fighters. Douglas Bader believed, as ever, that he was 100% correct, and his enthusiasm and strong personality won over his seniors.

On Saturday September 7th, the Germans made a huge tactical blunder: having pounded 11 Group's airfields for several weeks, at what was the crucial point the *Luftwaffe* changed its target and bombed London. When a huge raid came in that afternoon, Air Chief Marshal Dowding assumed that airfields were again the target and knew that such a gigantic attack could well deliver a telling blow. The German formation did not separate into smaller groups, each attacking a different target, but continued along the Thames Estuary. Eventually it became clear to Fighter Command's confused Controllers that the target was London. The Duxford Wing was already up, patrolling over North Weald, and urgently vectored south. Some 15 miles north of the Thames anti-aircraft fire could be seen bursting around 20 bombers, escorted by fighters, heading west at 15,000 feet. The 12 Group fighters were lower than the enemy and as Bader climbed his force to attack, the enemy fighters pounced. Squadron Leader Brian Lane: -

An Me 110 dived in front of me and I led 'A' Flight after it. Two Hurricanes were also attacking it. I fired a short burst at it, the other aircraft attacking at the same time. The crew of two baled out, one parachute failing to open. The E/A crashed one mile east of Hornchurch and one of the crew landed nearby and was seen to be taken prisoner.

As is so often the case in aerial combat, after this engagement Squadron Leader Lane, Flight Lieutenant Lawson and Sergeant Jennings found themselves all alone in the Unable to re-locate the scene of action, the three Spitfires returned to Fowlmere. Caught on the climb, 242 and 310 Squadrons had not fared well: Bader himself had been shot up, Sub-Lieutenant Dickie Cork was slightly wounded and Pilot Officer

Benzie was missing; one of 310's pilots was terribly burned and another forced landed near Southend. A disappointed Bader reported that his formation had been requested too late by the 11 Group Controller, as a result of which it had been bounced whilst climbing; he later wrote 'It was windy work, let there be no mistake'.

Two days later the Wing was in action again, this time with much better results, claiming the destruction of 20 enemy aircraft offset against the loss of four Hurricanes with two pilots killed. We now know that the figure of 20 enemy aircraft destroyed was grossly inaccurate, the actual number being nearer 5. Nevertheless the figure of 20 enemy machines destroyed was accepted without question, leading to various congratulatory signals and more squadrons being absorbed into the Duxford effort.

On September 11th, 242 Squadron remained at Coltishall and did not fly down to operate from Duxford. The 'Big Wing' went up, however, and was led over London by Squadron Leader Lane: -

Party over London, 19 leading 611 & 74 Squadrons. Sighted a big bunch of Huns south of the river and got a lovely head on attack into leading Heinkels. We broke them up and picked on a small bunch of six with two Me 110s as escort. I found myself entirely alone with these lads so proceeded to have a bit of sport. Got one of the Me 110s on fire, whereupon the other left his charges and ran for home! Played with He 111s for a bit and finally got one in both engines. Never had so much fun before!

September 15th is now celebrated annually as 'Battle of Britain Day'. Between 11.33 and 11.35 a.m. that fateful day, three huge German formations crossed the south coast between Dover and Folkestone, London bound. 11 Group had 20 squadrons in the air to meet this threat, reinforcing them at mid-day with the Duxford Wing, now consisting of two Spitfire and three Hurricane squadrons. Bader sallied forth and attacked 24 Do 17s of KG 76, escorted by Me 109s, at 16,000 feet over Brixton. One particular Dornier was attacked by numerous 12 Group fighters, including Brian Lane, who saw the enemy crew bale out and their bomber crash in Kent.

In the afternoon the Wing was scrambled again, making a total of 31 RAF fighter squadrons in action over London; we can only imagine the adverse effect of such a sight on enemy morale, German aircrews having been assured that the British were down to their 'last 50 Spitfires'. Again the Wing was too low, and again attacked by Me 109s whilst feverishly climbing. Brian Lane's log book: -

Party. 242 leading Wing. Ran into the whole *Luftwaffe* over London. Wave after wave of bombers covered by several hundred fighters. Waded into escort as per arrangement and picked out a 109. Had one hell of a dogfight and finally he went into cloud inverted and obviously crashed as he appeared out of control.

In what was a confused mass of many fighters, Brian's engagement with the 109 represented the only protracted individual dogfight that day. His combat report describes events in greater detail: -

I was leading 19 Squadron on Wing patrol. At approximately 1440 hours AA fire was sighted to the south and at the same time a formation of about 30 Do 215s was seen. I climbed up astern of the enemy aircraft to engage the fighter escort which could be seen above the bombers at about 30,000 feet. Three Me 109s dived on our formation and I turned to starboard. A loose dogfight ensued with more Me 109s coming down. I could not go near to any enemy aircraft so I climbed up and engaged a formation of Me 110s without result. I then sighted 10 Me 109s just above me and I attacked one of them. I got on his tail and fired several bursts of about two seconds. The enemy aircraft was taking violent evasive action and made for cloud level. I managed to get in another burst of about five seconds before it flicked over inverted and entered cloud in a shallow dive, apparently out of control. I then flew south and attacked two further formations of about 30 Do 215s from astern and head on. The enemy aircraft did not appear to like head on attack as they jumped about a bit as I passed through. I observed no result from these attacks. Fire from rear of the enemy aircraft was opened at 1,000 yards. Me 110s opened fire at a similar range and appeared to have no idea of deflection shooting.

Back at Duxford the 12 Group Wing's total claims were 45 enemy aircraft destroyed, five shared, 10 probables and another damaged. In total Fighter Command claimed 175 German aircraft destroyed, offset against the loss of 30 aircraft and 10 pilots. In fact the *Luftwaffe* had lost only 56 aircraft, of which the Duxford Wing actually accounted for 15. Nonetheless the fighting that day was decisive: by dusk, despite Göring's assurances, Hitler was convinced that the *Luftwaffe* was unable to win the aerial supremacy required for his proposed invasion.

Brian Lane lunching with his officers in the Mess at
Fowlmere during the Battle of Britain.

The Battle of Britain was not yet over, however. Friday, September 27th, for example was another day of heavy fighting. Squadron Leader Lane's take-off was delayed due to technical problems, so Flight Lieutenant Lawson led 19 Squadron into action against 'innumerable' enemy fighters over Canterbury. As battle was joined, Brian Lane caught up with the Wing and fired two short bursts at a 109. His Spitfire then became uncontrollable, skidding away. The pilot contemplated taking to his parachute but, using all his strength, managed to regain control and levelled out at 3,000 feet. Back at Fowlmere it was discovered that the offending Spitfire, a new Mk II, had a misshapen rudder and an incorrectly adjusted trim tab which prevented one elevator from functioning correctly. It was a lucky escape for our hero.

The Battle of Britain is officially considered to have ended on October 31st, 1940. By then the Germans had become increasingly forced to bomb by night, the RAF having maintained control of the daylight sky, although the two fighter forces continued to clash until early 1941. In November, the Duxford Wing continued flying numerous patrols over London and southern England. On Friday, November 8th, German fighter sweeps were again met with fierce opposition. Squadron Leader Lane led 19 Squadron on a Wing patrol over Canterbury, as Wing Commander Bernard 'Jimmy' Jennings, then a Sergeant pilot, remembered: -

We were over Canterbury and I was flying as Sandy Lane's No 2. We were told that there was a party going on above us which could not see as the sky was covered by a layer of 8/10 thinnish cloud. Sandy put us into a climb, and as we were nearing the cloud base an Me 109 dived out of the cloud a short distance in front of us, followed by a Hurricane firing his guns even closer, in fact over the top of Sandy and myself. Sandy's engine was hit, packed up and he lost height. As his No 2, and because there were obviously some unfriendly people were about, I stayed with him.

Once we were clear of trouble I called up Sandy and suggested that he held his gliding course and I would go ahead and find somewhere for him to land. I said 'Waggle your wings if you hear me'. He did so and I dived away only to find the airfield at Eastchurch bombed and unusable. However, there was a small strip clear of bomb craters. I flew back up to Sandy and asked him to follow me. He did, and taking one look at the state of the airfield rightly decided to land wheels up.

He crash landed his Spitfire OK, but as I circled over him I could see Sandy in the cockpit, not moving. I looked round the airfield until I saw an air raid shelter which I beat up until two airmen poked their heads out of the entrance. I pointed towards Sandy and then circled him and saw the airmen go behind a shelter to get into a truck. I circled Sandy again and saw him getting out of his aircraft, holding his face with one hand and waving to me with the other. I waited until the truck had picked him up and then returned to base.

I told everybody that Brian was safe and told his wife that I would fetch him the next day in the Magister. We got a message through to Eastchurch to that effect. Early next morning I flew the Magister to Hornchurch and after some argument with Sector Control managed to get permission to collect Sandy from Eastchurch. After circling low over the airfield a truck brought Sandy to the small strip which I had seen the previous day. I landed but as Sandy walked towards me I burst out laughing as he had a very puffed up nose! In order to keep an eye on the Squadron following him, Brian used to fly with his shoulder straps very loose. He forgot to tighten them before his crash landing and hit his face on the gunsight.

In his logbook, of this 'Friendly Fire' incident, Brian Lane wrote: -

Sighted Me 109s over Canterbury and turned to give chase. Hurricane squadron chased us and the leader put a burst into my engine!! Apparently the CO of one of the North Weald squadrons. Force landed at Eastchurch OK. Jennings escorted me down and refused to leave me. Damn good of him.

Sergeant Jennings.

By this time Air Chief Marshal Dowding had been retired, and Air Vice-Marshal Park sent to Training Command. These two architects of victory had been called to account for their tactics by the Air Ministry on October 17th, Air Vice-Marshal Leigh-Mallory and the 'Big Wing' protagonists having won considerable political support for their flawed theory. Shortly after the meeting Leigh-Mallory took over Park's 11 Group, and Sholto Douglas, the Deputy Chief of the Air Staff, was promoted to succeed Dowding. These two men were now able to push forward wing operations as standard practice, and every Sector Station was organised into a wing. So it was that on November 14th, Squadron Leader Lane led 19 Squadron at the head of the Wittering Wing, comprising Nos 1 and 266 Squadrons. It was the last of a series of such training flights, but, as Brian's logbook records, 'Nearly last patrol with any wing! Ajax leader led his Squadron straight into us from the sun as we climbed to meet them. Created quite a shambles.'

The following morning saw 19 and 242 Squadrons detailed to patrol a convoy 20 miles east of Harwich. Unfortunately the convoy could not be found, so when Ground Control informed the formation of three bandits approaching from the north-west, Squadron Leader Lane left the Hurricanes to continue searching for the convoy whilst the faster Spitfires climbed to intercept. Soon two condensation trails were spotted at 35,000 feet, 15-20 miles apart, and the Squadron split into flights to give chase. Whilst 'A' Flight pursued the high-flying intruders, 'B' Flight positioned itself to cut off the enemy's line of retreat. Squadron Leader Lane led Red Section after the leading German and climbed south to get between the enemy aircraft and the sun. The chase up the Thames Estuary lasted 20 minutes, later being described by Brian as a 'Cook's Tour'. Eventually the two Me 110s saw the approaching Spitfires and dived eastward. Red Section attacked in line astern, opening fire from 800 feet. As Brian Lane's bullets found their mark a cowling flew off the 110, which started streaming glycol. Red 2, Pilot Officer Wallace 'Jock' Cunningham, set the starboard engine alight. As the 110 climbed, Brian delivered the fatal blow from the starboard quarter. The enemy machine plunged into the Thames; both crewmen baled out but remain officially missing.

Wallace Cunningham: -

I was tucked in behind Brian Lane and diving after the fleeting Me 110. Because of our high speed, Brian was struggling to get his sights on target – I was almost jostling him off to get a chance. Before we eventually destroyed the German aircraft, after letting the crew bale out, I had my windscreen shattered. Not, I worked out later, by the enemy but from Brian's empty cartridge cases.

Brian Lane leading 'A' Flight in early 1941.

The winter months continued in much the same vein, with the odd action fought over convoys, the occasional clash with German fighters, and more practice wing formations. The night blitz, however, was reaching its zenith, but Britain's nocturnal defences were woefully inadequate. Even Spitfires, which were poor night flying aircraft given the narrow track undercarriage and two glowing banks of exhausts forward of the pilot which spoiled his night vision, were pressed into service. 'Fighter Nights' were organised in which the sky over London was filled with Spitfires, in the hope that they would sight an enemy bomber. Success was rare, but at least the pilots felt they were doing something to help combat this particular threat, which was taking a great toll of civilian life. Brian Lane and his pilots therefore had this extra duty to undertake in addition to their normal daytime patrols. The crescendo of German night attacks came on the night of May 10th, 1941, when 500 enemy bombers dropped 700 tonnes of high explosive and incendiary bombs on London. The raid coincided with a low spring tide, severely limiting the water available to fire fighters. By dawn, over 1,000 Londoners were dead and another 2000 injured. 19 Squadron were up over London that night but made no contact. Generally night-fighting was improving, however, as aircrews mastered their rudimentary airborne interception radar: in January 1941 only three German bombers were destroyed, in May 96 failed to return to their bases in France.

After that terrible raid the activity tailed off as German units were withdrawn and sent eastwards to quickly refit prior to the surprise invasion of Russia on June 22nd, 1941. Fighter Command was also pursuing an offensive policy, 'Reaching Out' and taking the war to the Germans in northern France, Belgium and Holland. On May 21st, Squadron Leader Lane led 19, 266 and 310 Squadrons to West Malling to participate in a 'Circus' operation. The 12 Group Wing's task was to patrol the south-east coast at 20,000 feet, so as to protect the bombers from attack on their return journey, should the Germans be so bold as to pursue the Blenheims back across the Channel. The operation was completed successfully and 19 Squadron's sortie was uneventful.

On June 4th, Brian led 19 and 266 Squadrons on a sweep of south-east England and the Thames Estuary. Probably due to oxygen failure, Wing Commander William Coope, flying Green Leader with 266 Squadron, crashed into the sea; he remains missing and is remembered on the Runnymede Memorial. The following night, at 1 a.m., Brian Lane took off for a nocturnal patrol only to be recalled 10 minutes later in preparation for a 'Fighter Night' over Birmingham. The expected raid failed to materialise, however, so the operation was cancelled. On the night of June 14th, Brian was aloft and saw an enemy aircraft crash in flames, but reported no other contact.

June 15th, 1941, was a notable day for 19 Squadron: Squadron Leader Brian Lane DFC was being rested, his successor being Squadron Leader Roy Dutton DFC & bar. By that time Brian Lane had flown operations continuously since the outbreak of war, had won a DFC for his leadership of 19 Squadron over Dunkirk, and had flown throughout the Battle of Britain and beyond. It was time for a rest, however reluctantly Brian left his beloved 19 Squadron, and after a short period of leave, reported to No 12 Group HQ at Watnall for staff duties on June 20th. There he remained, flying a desk, until November 11th, when he embarked on a troop ship, bound for another staff appointment overseas. On January 28th, 1942, he arrived at the Desert Air Force HQ. Unfortunately the unfamiliar climate negatively affected his health, so four months later he was posted back to the HQ.

Brian Lane's leaving party at Fowlmere.

On September 16th, 1942, Squadron Leader Lane reported for a refresher course at No 61 Operational Training Unit at Montford Bridge, a satellite of Rednal in Shropshire. There Brian familiarised himself with the Spitfire Mk V, which enjoyed the benefits of both cannon and machine-gun armament, and by completion of the course had flown a total of 30.40 hours, 26.50 of which were on Spitfires. Before leaving Montford Bridge, Brian met a 19 Squadron chum by chance in a Cheshire country pub; Frank Brinsden: -

I was up that way learning to fly Mosquitoes and it was a pleasant surprise to meet Brian by chance. He was happy to be back in England flying Spitfires again, and looked forward to the future with optimism. I am sure that with his very great experience it would not have been long before he was appointed as a Wing Leader. Remember that he had actually led wing-sized formations over Dunkirk, long before Douglas Bader came up with his cock-eyed Big Wing theory. Brian would have made an excellent Wing Leader, no doubt about that.

On December 9th, 1942, Brian reported to 167 'Gold Coast' Squadron as a supernumerary squadron leader to update his experience of combat conditions prior to his next appointment, which, as Frank says, is likely to have been as a Wing Leader.

167 Squadron was a Dutch unit, with an English CO and other key personnel, based at Ludham, between Norwich and the Norfolk coast. On October 26th, permission was given for Dutch pilots to fly rhubarbs, low level opportunist strafing attacks by a pair or section of Spitfires, but due to poor winter weather no operational sorties had been possible by the time Squadron Leader Lane arrived. His first flight with the inexperienced Squadron was in a Spitfire Mk VB, 3W-H, a local familiarisation flight of just 30 minutes duration on the morning of Sunday, December 13th.

Later that day, Squadron Leader Lane led a section of 167 Squadron Spitfires on their first Rhubarb to strafe the main Rotterdam to Antwerp railway line between Moerdyk and Bergen-Op-Zoom. The Spitfires left Ludham at 3.10 p.m., bound for their target area situated just beyond a complex system of large islands and estuaries. As the Spitfires bobbed across the North Sea, light was already fading. At 3.50 p.m. Brian led the Section over the Dutch coast between Voorne and Goeree. Following the Haring Vliet water inland to the Hollandseh Deep estuary at zero feet, as the Spitfires flashed by Helleveotsluis, surprised German flak gunners managed to loose off intense tracer rounds at their fleeting enemy, as did gunners at Willemstad, Moerdyk Bridge and on the northern shore of the Hollandseh Deep. At Moerdyk Brian turned the Section south, flying inland some 10 miles, following the railway line to Roosendaal where Blue 4, Pilot Huekensfeldt-Jansen became separated in the fading light. Alone over hostile territory, the Dutch pilot had no option but to observe Standing Orders and return alone to Ludham, his guns unfired. Continuing along the railway line, the three remaining Spitfires found no targets, so Squadron Leader Lane turned the Section about, heading back to base and leaving the Dutch coast over the Ooster Scheldt, still at zero feet.

Suddenly, two miles south of Zierikee on the island of Schouwen, two FW 190s appeared, pursuing the Spitfires and also at zero feet. Blue 3 sighted the bandits was unable to communicate the threat to Blue 1, Squadron Leader Lane, as his radio was u/s. As the 190s bore down on the Spitfires, Plesman opened up his throttle and flew alongside Brian Lane, warning him of the danger. By now precious seconds had been lost and the superior 190s were within effective firing range. From 300 yards the Germans opened fire on Blue 1 and Blue 2, Pilot Officer WG Evans. The Spitfires immediately took violent evasive action, Lane breaking right and Evans breaking left. Meanwhile Plesman had climbed to 2,000 feet and dived upon the leading 190, firing a two second burst in a fleeting head on attack, narrowly avoiding a collision. Before reaching cloud cover Evans managed two bursts at a 190 from long range but without result. Squadron Leader Lane had disappeared, so Plesman broke off his attack to search for Blue 1, spotting the Squadron Leader chasing an enemy fighter inland. This was, of course, the first time that Brian had met the awesome FW 190, but even so he had lost no time in turning the tables and getting on an enemy's tail, chasing it in an easterly direction. As Blue 1 appeared in control of the situation, Plesman hurried to assist Evans, who managed to shake off his assailant, so, the sky now typically empty of aircraft, the two Spitfires returned to Ludham. Having landed at 5 p.m., Plesman and Evans would wait in vain at Ludham for Blue 1's return. Squadron Leader Lane DFC and Spitfire AR612 were missing, Fighter Command's only loss that grey December day now 63 years ago.

What happened to this brave and gallant young Spitfire pilot? Many years later we found the answer in German records: *Oberleutnant* Walter Leonhardt of 6/JG 1 claimed a Spitfire destroyed over the North Sea at 4.34 p.m., 20 miles west of Schowen Island. This was undoubtedly AR612, and it is not difficult to imagine what had happened: the FW 190 was faster than the Spitfire Mk V, and Brian Lane would have been nearing the end of fuel available for such a chase; eventually he must have had to break off and head for home, and at which point in time the tables were turned. Enjoying superior performance, Leonhardt was able to pursue, catch and destroy AR612, sending aircraft and pilot to a watery grave in the cold and inhospitable North Sea.

The loss of a pilot and leader with Brian Lane's experience on such a futile sortie was a tragedy. Even if the section had found and shot up a train or two, would that have compared to losing a pilot of his quality in the process? I think not, and sadly many pilots were lost on similarly pointless operations. Someone who felt very strongly about this at the time was Johnnie Johnson, later the RAF's top scoring fighter pilot in WW2, who resolved to do something to stop these senseless losses whilst being rested as a staff officer between tours in 1943. As a result of representation made by Johnnie to the Air Officer Commanding, Rhubarbs were stopped that year, albeit too late to save Squadron Leader Lane and many others like him.

Former 19 Squadron pilots remember Brian Lane: -

Wing Commander George Unwin: -

I flew with Brian Lane for a year and we were in complete accord in the air. He was an officer and I was an NCO, so we did not, therefore, associate off duty. However, despite our difference in rank we were good friends. My very last flight with No 19 Squadron, prior to taking up instructor duties in Training Command, was formation aerobatics with Brian leading and my very great friend Harry Steere making up the third. Brian Lane was a first class pilot and leader. He was firstly my flight commander, and then the Squadron CO, was completely unflappable and instilled confidence in all who flew with him. It was a sad loss when he was killed.

Wing Commander Bernard Jennings: -

Brian Lane was a highly respected squadron commander, a pilot's pilot and an efficient leader respected even by us regular NCO pilots.

Wing Commander David Cox: -

Brian Lane was, in my opinion, one of the finest squadron commanders I served under, not only as a fighter leader but also as a man. He was always kind and considerate, and had time for everyone, however lowly their rank. I can illustrate his kindness and consideration by relating something he did for me.

I joined No 19 Squadron on May 13th, 1940, but owing to my lack of experience flying Spitfires I was not allowed to operate with the Squadron over Dunkirk. My job was to ferry spare aircraft to Hornchurch or test them after service. On May 28th, after testing a Spitfire for radio trouble, I was preparing to land but found that the undercarriage would not go fully down, sticking half way. After trying unsuccessfully for some time to rectify the situation, which included inverting the aircraft to try and take the weight off the pins, I had to land with the undercart stuck half way down. The Engineering Officer later put the aircraft in the hangar, jacked it up and the undercarriage worked perfectly. Squadron Leader Pinkham endorsed my log book as follows: -

On August 10th, 1940, Sergeant Cox was charged at Duxford with damaging one of his Majesty's aircraft, namely a Spitfire, through landing with the undercarriage uncompletely lowered. CO Duxford directed that he be admonished and ordered me to make this entry.

I deeply resented this and in a way the incident soured my attitude towards the RAF. During February 1941, when things were quiet, I went to Brian Lane, who by then was our CO, and told him how unjust I felt the endorsement to be as I had done my best to get the undercarriage down. He agreed to look into the matter. I later heard from the Squadron Adjutant that Squadron Leader Lane had taken the matter up at Group HQ and even made a formal visit. The result came several months later when 'Cancelled' was written in red ink across the endorsement. Brian also added below it: -

Entry made in error. No disciplinary action was taken, as accident not attributable to pilot.

Brian had discovered that there had been similar accidents, caused by an air lock which had been removed by the shock of landing, hence why the undercarriage worked perfectly in the hangar.

If Brian Lane had not been lost in such a useless action, I am sure that he would have been one of the greatest fighter leaders of the war, quite possibly equal to Douglas Bader and Johnnie Johnson. Certainly he was amongst the first pilots with experience of leading wing formation, as evidenced by his activities over Dunkirk. Someone in Fighter Command surely made a blunder in posting him to No 167 Squadron which specialised in low level ground attacks, during which flak was intense and luck played a major part in survival. Brian Lane's exceptional skills as both a fighter pilot and leader were obviously useless in such a role. He should have gone to a squadron operating wing sweeps. His experience would have been very useful in the summer of 1942 when we were having a difficult time with the advent of the FW 190.

David's story is a perfect example of real leadership. That Brian Lane should have gone to so much trouble on behalf of such a junior pilot is an example to anyone in a position of command; clearly he appreciated how strongly the young sergeant felt, and by rectifying the situation restored David Cox's faith in the RAF. Air Vice-Marshal Johnnie Johnson once said to me 'Dilip, you can learn the mechanics of leadership in the service, but true leadership is a gift, like that of a great painter or writer. You either have it or you don't.' There can be no doubt that Brian Lane had that gift. This is further evidenced by the fact that he would speak out for his pilots, the problems with 19 Squadron's cannon Spitfires being a prime example, even though the easiest course is never to 'rock the boat'.

Wing Commander Peter Howard-Williams: -

I well remember Brian Lane. When I left 19 Squadron to join 118 at Filton, he wrote 'Good Luck' above his final signature in my log book, which I have in front of me as I write this. He was a most pleasant man and very supportive at all times – he certainly stood up for his pilots.

I remember that he fitted two mirrors to the sides of his Spitfire and streamlined them in, to improve rearwards vision during combat. A wingless air commodore visited Duxford and told Brian to take them off. Brian apparently replied 'Well you fly the bloody thing then!'

Personally I was shot at far more often than I shot at others during the war, and had a nasty cannon shell explode in my cockpit, just behind my seat, on one occasion; the armour plate saved me. Pilots like Brian Lane, however, were exceptional.

Wing Commander Frank Brinsden: -

How pleased I am that Brian Lane is to receive public exposure and recognition at last. Being the commander of a squadron based on the fringe of the Battle of Britain area, he was prevented from

"Well you fly the bloody thing then!"

showing his skills and therefore did not excite the acclaim afforded to commanders based in the southern counties.

Brian always used a silver cigarette case, but without affectation. He was always so much more sophisticated than the rest of us. His fine old black Armstrong Siddeley car was always highly polished, whereas our old Standards, Fords etc were battered and in need of loving care and attention.

Developing further the point Frank made about Brian not exciting acclaim due to having been based in 12 Group during the Battle of Britain, there is another factor to consider: Douglas Bader. Having no legs made Bader incredibly newsworthy, to the extent that, even though he was also based in 12 Group, he eclipsed all others. What chance, therefore, did the modest and retiring Brian Lane have of achieving public recognition? Arguably, however, Brian Lane was actually a far better candidate than Douglas Bader to lead the 12 Group Wing, given, as David Cox emphasises, his experience of having led wing formations over Dunkirk. But Bader, in spite of his comparative inexperience having only recently returned to the service, was a more senior squadron commander than Brian who, in any case, did not crave for or desire any publicity. Flight Lieutenant Wallace Cunningham: -

Douglas Bader was a competent pilot and a good leader. Brian Lane was calm and reassuring in addition to being an excellent fighter pilot. There was little to choose between them, although they were very different; Douglas had great charisma, and being short of a couple of legs was very newsworthy. Never think, though, that there was any antipathy between them, because there was not. They were in complete accord in trying their best to get the job done.

Eileen Lane was devastated when the telegram came informing her that Brian was missing. His mother too never fully recovered from the shock. After the war Eileen became known as Ellison-Lane, and although she shared a jet setting lifestyle with wealthy landowner and racing enthusiast Owen Fargus, never married him. Eileen died prematurely, of cancer, in 1967, but I corresponded with Mr Fargus until he died in 1990, having become overwhelmed by fumes whilst working on his Daimler. Owen was able to tell me that during the 1950s he had accompanied Eileen to a nursing home in North London where they gave all of Brian Lane's personal effects to his mother, who was herself dying. Eileen did keep one treasured item, however: the silver cigarette case that she had bought Brian and which he was carrying when the Magister crashed in 1938. After Owen's sudden and tragic death, the executor of his will very kindly passed the artefact to me, so the cigarette case is now preserved. What became of Brian's medals and other items has never been established. During my original research for my first book, *Spitfire Squadron*, my information was that Brian was an only child. A few years ago, however, David Lewis was researching names on the Pinner war memorial, including Brian Lane, and he discovered that our hero had a sister. Exasperatingly the sister, a spinster, had only just died without any next of kin, but several letters to her solicitor, emphasising the historical importance of any items relating to Brian that may have been in her estate, went unanswered. The most incredibly frustrating thing about this was that Brian's sister still lived in Pinner, and was therefore living only a few miles away from the RAF Museum at Hendon when *Spitfire Squadron* was launched there in 1990, with the majority of 19 Squadron's Battle of Britain period pilots present. A case of some you win, some you lose.

Squadron Leader Brian Lane DFC was 25 years young when lost in 1942, and is remembered on panel 65 of the Runnymede Memorial. His final tally of victories was five enemy aircraft destroyed, three probables, one damaged and a share in an Me 110 destroyed. Perhaps the greatest mark of respect is that even today, so many years later, Battle of Britain pilots of the like of George Unwin still talk of 'Brian' in hushed, respectful tones tinged with regret at the senseless loss of this fine young man.

Someone once said that in war there are no real victors; *Oberleutnant* Walter Leonhardt, who shot down and killed Squadron Leader Brian Lane on December 13th, 1942, was himself reported missing over the North Sea just a few weeks later. This must surely illustrate how futile war is, and emphasise at what great cost to young life wars are fought, lost and won.

The imposing entrance to the Runnymede Memorial. Commemorated there are the names of all too many of the young pilots we have got to know in this book.

Chapter Ten

Pilot Officer 'Lanty' Dixon
&
Sergeant Jack Allen

Pilot Officer 'Lanty' Dixon.

Sergeant Jack Allen.

Twenty years or so ago, when my research started attracting publicity, I was contacted by an old Herefordian who told me the fascinating tale of the 'Sabatini Spitfire'. The pilot, he said, was the son of famous author Rafael Sabatini, whose books included *Scaramouche* and *Captain Blood*, both works becoming highly popular 1930s films starring the swashbuckling Errol Flynn. Apparently Sabatini's son was killed in a Spitfire whilst performing low level aerobatics over the family home at Winforton, and, according to my source, had an impressive effigy at Hay-on-Wye cemetery, actually sculpted by his mother and in his likeness. Now this was exciting stuff indeed, but little did I know that the road would take me to two similar deaths in wartime Herefordshire, both having become one and the same tale in local legend as memories blurred over the years.

Back in the 1980s, of course, the internet had yet to change our lives and so we did not enjoy the immeasurable benefit of information immediately available at our fingertips. It was therefore a case of good old fashioned detective work, making enquiries in person at the 'crime scene'. No record could be found, however, of a Spitfire having crashed at Winforton during the Second World War. At Hay-on-Wye cemetery we found the effigy concerned, which was a result as we were starting to doubt the accuracy of our information, but discovered the pilot's name not to be Sabatini but Pilot Officer Lancelot Steele Dixon, who was killed on April 9th, 1940. Now this was a mystery indeed, as our source also insisted that the crash happened shortly after D-Day, in June 1944.

The MOD Air Historical Branch confirmed that Pilot Officer Dixon had been killed at Winforton, in Harvard P5864, whilst a student pilot at No 5 Operational Training Unit at Aston Down, near Stroud in Gloucestershire. Now we had some concrete facts, but were disappointed that our D-Day Spitfire looked like being a red herring.

Pilot Officer Dixon's story, however, is as fascinating as it is tragic, and is worth recounting here.

Lancelot Steele Dixon was the son of Hugh Wainwright Dixon and Christine Dixon, and was born in London during 1917. Mr Dixon's sister, Ruth, was married to Rafael Sabatini, an Italian who had come to work in Liverpool in 1892. Writing short stories as a hobby, Sabatini could never have imagined that today, 55 years after his death in Switzerland, he would be remembered as the greatest historical adventure and romance writer of all time.

In 1909, the Sabatinis had a son, Rafael-Angelo, called 'Binkie', and moved to London so Rafael would be closer to the publishing industry. During the Great War, Rafael became a British citizen and worked in British Intelligence as a translator. He continued writing, with modest success, but everything changed in 1921 with the astonishing success of *Scaramouche*, which sold in droves both sides of the Atlantic. In 1922 followed *Captain Blood*, an even greater success which made Sabatini a rich man. By 1927, however, the prolific author was exhausted and, on the advice of his doctor, took time off and moved away from London, renting Brockwier House, in the Wye Valley near Tintern Abbey. There he was able to relax and indulge his passion for fishing, and Binkie, now 18, was a regular visitor in his new sports car. On April 1st, 1927, however, the Sabatini's idyll was shattered. That day Rafael drove a friend to Gloucester whilst Binkie took his mother to nearby Monmouth. On the way home, Rafael encountered a wrecked car, Binkie's, alongside which the driver lay dying.

Ruth had been thrown clear and survived, but it transpired that only Binkie had kept the couple together during what had been an unhappy marriage and so they divorced in 1931.

That year Rafael bought a new home, 'Clockmill', on the banks of the River Wye near Hay. Now completely withdrawn from London life, he married again in 1935, his second wife being Christine Dixon, who had been married to his brother-in-law and who was the mother of Lancelot. Known as 'Lanty', the young Dixon had been named after the patriarch of the Dixon family, a wealthy Liverpool paper merchant. Lanty was not unlike Binkie, and Rafael became very fond of his stepson who also lived at Clock Mill. When war broke out, however, Lanty joined the RAF and was commissioned as a Pilot Officer in the VR. By April 1940, Pilot Officer Dixon had completed both his elementary and service flying training, and was posted to No 5 OTU for conversion to Spitfires. According to Mr Watkins, of Clifford, on several occasions during his training Lanty had flown over Clockmill in figure of eights; on at least one occasion he apparently landed in the large field opposite the house before being rowed across the Wye by Mr Smiles, the local salmon ghillie, for tea with his parents.

Clockmill.

Upon arrival at an operational training unit, student pilots would be checked out by an instructor in a Harvard aircraft, a dual seat single-engine monoplane. After passing that test the pilot would go solo on type, then fly various exercises, such as aerobatics and map reading, before going solo on the Spitfire.

That particular morning, April 9th, 1940, Pilot Officer Dixon was solo in P5864 and officially on a cross country map reading exercise, the goal of flying a Spitfire very soon to be realised.

That spring Tuesday morning in 1940, the local populace were going about their business as usual: Mr Howells and Mr Preece were up on the imposing Merbach Hill, overlooking the Wye and Clockmill; in nearby Winforton village were Mr Morgan, and Mr Jones, who was in company with his young daughter, Hazel. At about 10.10

a.m. all eyes were on an aircraft performing low-level aerobatics, the pilot climbing vertically before diving at high speed, pulling out only at the last minute, seconds before collision with the ground appeared unavoidable. Also watching Pilot Officer Dixon, from the garden of Clockmill, were Rafael and Christine Sabatini, and Mr Smiles.

Suddenly the spectators amusement turned to horror when the Harvard stalled whilst in a steep turn and started spinning, out of control. From Merbach Hill, Mr Howells saw that the aircraft 'had crashed into a very high hedge on the opposite side of the Wye to Clockmill'. Mr Watkins was working about

Christine & Rafael Sabatini.
Jesse Knight.

three miles away from the crash site: 'The aircraft flew over Merbach Hill and started the usual display of figure-of-eights. I heard the roar of the engine but then suddenly all was quiet. I arrived home later to find my worst fears confirmed. It would appear that when the aircraft nose dived there was insufficient height for the pilot to regain control.'

A 5 OTU Harvard in 1940.

The child Hazel Jones (now Mrs Harris) saw everything: 'Suddenly there was an explosion and we realised that the aircraft had crashed. I cycled through the village, down Bakers Lane, and upon seeing the aircraft wreathed in smoke and flame realised that there was no hope for the pilot.'

Mr Price, a gardener at Clockmill, immediately fetched out the boat and rowed Rafael Sabatini and Mr Smiles across the Wye. The three men hurried to the blazing wreckage, but, according to Mr Smiles, the pilot was dead and so badly burnt that he resembled a 'burnt pig'. Later, young Hazel Jones's father, Bill, helped remove the corpse and convey the remains to await the authorities in outbuildings at Winforton Court.

That such senseless tragedy should strike Rafael Sabatini twice was incredible. Christine never fully recovered from the shock of seeing her son die in flames before her own eyes, and suffered from nightmares for years later. Perhaps a part of the grieving process was creating the bronze effigy, in her 23-year old son's likeness, which adorns his grave at Hay-on-Wye. The piece is poignant, showing Icarus having fallen to earth, the wax holding feathers on his arms having melted.

Rafael Sabatini died whilst on vacation at Adelboden, in Switzerland, in 1950, and Christine also sculpted a moving tribute at his gravesite. This bronze shows a man who has fallen, face down, pen in hand. Christine herself died in London nursing home during the early 1960s.

Pilot Officer Lancelot Dixon's impressive grave at Hay-on-Wye.

Having unravelled this story, I assumed that our original information was confused, and that there was no Spitfire but only Pilot Officer Dixon's Harvard. An RAF wartime veteran and Herefordian, Jim Thomas, however, assured me that there was a Spitfire down in similar circumstances. The pilot's name, he said, was Jack Allen, but he was not certain about where the crash had been. As research progressed, another story slowly unfolded.

Victor and May Allen lived at Buskwood Farm, Hope-under-Dinmore, near Leominster in Herefordshire. A daughter, Pearl, was followed in 1925 by a son, Victor Jack Trafford Allen. A popular boy in the village, a cousin, Eleanor, recalls Jack as 'super, very witty with a great sense of humour'. Another cousin, Peggy, remembered him as 'quite a lad with a warm loving nature, the dare-devil with a great sense of fun.'

Jack proved to be an excellent scholar who decided very early that he wanted to fly. A schoolfriend, Mrs Apperley, recalls that when Jack was just 13 he carved his name into the wooden bus shelter on Dinmore Hill: 'Jack Allen: Pilot'. Having attended the Larkhill Academy in Scotland, and Herefordshire's Lucton School, Jack completed only one term at Trinity College, Cambridge, before joining the RAF on October 6th, 1941, 'For the duration of the present

Jack Allen at his OTU in Canada.

emergency'. At the age of just 17, Leading Aircraftman VJT Allen of the RAF VR arrived in Canada to train as a pilot under the auspices of the Empire Air Training Scheme. In due course Jack won his wings at the Elementary & Reserve Flying Training School at Caron, Saskatchewan, and then he converted to Hurricanes at No 1 OTU, Bagotville. In the autumn of 1943, Sergeant Allen, as he now was, returned to England and learned to fly Spitfires with 53 OTU at Kirton.

Throughout this period, Jack's companion was Frank Day, a young Hertfordshire lad of similar wit, but at the end of their Kirton course the pair were sent different ways, never to meet again. Much to Frank's disgust he was sent to fly Hurricanes on the Scilly Isles, and later, more to his taste, Mustangs in India. Sergeants AGP Jennings and VJT Allen, however, went straight from Kirton to fly Spitfires with 616 Squadron at Exeter in 10 Group.

616 Squadron was engaged on Home Defence duties, commanded by Squadron Leader LW Watts DFC, and equipped with the Spitfire Mk VII. This was a high-flying variant designed to combat high altitude intruders. To reduce the drag of wing tip vortices induced when flying acute angles of attack at high altitude, the Spitfire's wings were given extended wing tips. The cockpit was pressurised and the aircraft boasted the most powerful Merlin yet produced: the 64.

In March 1944, Sergeant Allen flew several convoy protection patrols and as Red 2, to Squadron Leader Watts, when 616 Squadron escorted Mosquitoes of 85 Squadron to attack targets in Northern France. He also flew No 2 to Warrant Officer Des Kelly, an Australian, on a weather reconnaissance over Amiens and Lille. April continued in much the same vein, with patrols of Dover, Dungeness and Portland. Towards the end of that month the Squadron moved to Fairwood Common in South Wales, continuing to fly defensive patrols, although on May 23rd Sergeant Allen joined his Squadron escorting B-25s to Dinard airfield, where the Spitfire pilots witnessed some 'excellent bombing.'

The Spitfire Mk VII with extended wingtips for high flying.

By June 1944, 616 Squadron was based at RAF Culmhead, near Church Stanton, which is south of Taunton in Somerset. This was, of course, during the intensive period immediately before the Allied landings in Normandy, and 616 Squadron found itself flying regular offensive patrols over France. On June 1st, Sergeant Allen flew YQ-F as Red 4 on a rhubarb. A 'B' Flight commitment, the target was coastal railways, the Spitfire pilots destroying two locomotive engines, six wagons, lorries and a gun position. Flight Lieutenant Barry returned safely to base after his aircraft was hit by 20 mm rounds, one of which was found embedded in the pilot's cockpit.

On June 2nd, Sergeant Allen flew on a cine-gun training flight, and at 3 p.m. the following day took off in YQ-E, in company with Flying Officer Mullenders, on 'low flying and cross country, landing at 4.40 p.m.'

The Allied landings in Normandy came at last on June 6th, 1944: D-Day. Sergeant Allen, however, did not fly that historic day, but was up as Grey 2 on D-Day + 1, on a Squadron Rhubarb. Two locos and an army truck were damaged near Dinan. On June 9th, the Culmhead Wing Leader, Wing Commander Peter Brothers DSO DFC, led his Wing on a beach-head patrol. Jack Allen flew on that sortie and returned able to describe Allied warships shelling enemy positions inland, many of which were ablaze. The following day Jack flew with 616 Squadron on 10 Group Rhubarb 275, to the area of Rennes-Lamballe. There was no opposition from either enemy aircraft or flak, and amongst targets attacked was a hutted camp by Sergeant Allen near Plougenast. During the return flight, Flight Lieutenant Graves DFC suffered engine failure and took to his parachute 40 miles south of Start Point. Fortunately the pilot was rescued by a Walrus, albeit with head and leg injuries.

By this time Hitler had unleashed a new menace against Britain, the V-1, or Fieseler 103 robot flying bomb, from launch sites in Northern France. Known as 'No Ball' targets, the neutralisation of this threat was a priority and 616 Squadron found itself escorting heavy bombers on 'No Ball' raids several times in June 1944.

That month also saw 616 Squadron's pilots start to attend Farnborough for week-long conversion to the new Gloster Meteor jet fighter. It was an incredibly exhilarating time, therefore: the long awaited and spectacular invasion, and the prospect of being the RAF's first jet fighter squadron. Heady days, especially for a 'daredvil' 19-year old like Jack Allen.

On June 29th, 1944, Sergeant Allen took off from Culmhead on 'a gunnery and aileron test flight to be carried out in the vicinity of the aerodrome'. In complete contravention of orders, however, the young pilot set course for his parents' home on Dinmore Hill, some 90 miles from the airfield. Dashing up to Herefordshire at speeds approaching 400 m.p.h., Jack was soon racing very low down the valley towards Buskwood Farm. As the Merlin's roar shattered the silence villagers came pouring out of their homes to watch the spectacle, including his sister, Pearl, and her baby daughter. Although his parents were not at home, working at the nearby Rotherwas munitions factory, Jack's grandfather was working in a nearby field and also stopped work to proudly watch his grandson.

On Jack's second low pass he intended to pull up sharply, and the last minute, and roar over Buskwood Farm. Somehow the young pilot misjudged the manoeuvre and his propeller clipped the ground in front of the pear tree orchard which rose up to the house. The Spitfire tore through the orchard, shedding panels and cowlings as it went. The engine broke free and bounded uphill, tearing through two hedges and coming to rest over 250 yards from the point of impact. Eventually the terrible sound of tortured metal subsided, a shocked silence descending over the remote Herefordshire countryside.

The cockpit section was relatively intact, and a local schoolboy, John Beaumont, was first on the scene. In the cockpit the pilot was hanging limply in his straps, dead. Aviation fuel was spilling in all directions and the crowd nearly set upon a villager

Right: Looking from Buskwood towards Jack Allen's direction of approach.

Left: Looking towards Buskwood in the direction Jack flew; he crashed in the foreground.

who produced a match with which to light his pipe! Bob Jaynes was also there, and remembers the wreckage being scattered over a large area, and black and white identification stripes on the wings.

Soon PC 230 Dick Tanner of the Herefordshire Constabulary arrived and helped carry the body to a waiting RAF ambulance in the adjacent lane. The ambulance was from nearby RAF Shobdon, home of No 5 Glider Training School, and the Station Operations Record book states: -

1535 hours informed by Flying Control Officer of aircraft crash on Dinmore Hill, Herefordshire. Medical Officer and ambulance proceeded and found Spitfire MB762 wrecked. The pilot, 159427 Sgt J Allen of No 616 Squadron is dead, having suffered partial ablation of the skull and a fractured right clavicle.

Jack Allen was buried the following Monday at the village church, St Mary's. The service was taken by both Reverands Hughes and Charles, the latter who had taught the young Jack at Lucton, and who described having 'watched his career day by day until he had mounted to the height of his ambition. He was a brilliant scholar, intellectual and lovable.' Amongst the large congregation were two representatives from 616 Squadron, Flight Lieutenant Mike Graves DFC, the dead pilot's Flight Commander, and Pilot Officer Des Kelly DFC, who was recovering from an eye injury sustained in a combat with FW 190s. Needless to say, the Allen family was absolutely devastated.

616 Squadron's Commanding Officer, Squadron Leader Watts, found himself in trouble with the Air Officer Commanding No 10 Group as a result of the incident, and there is no doubt that a cover up ensued. The Squadron's Forms 540 and 541 comprise the Operations Record Book, a mandatory diary of daily events which should record every flight and absolutely anything and everything of note. Although these now precious documents do differ in quality, depending upon the individual chronicler, there can be no other explanation for the fact that there is no record of Sergeant Allen even having flown on June 29th, 1944, much less that he lost his life. Even the Form 78, or movement card, of the Spitfire concerned, MB762, makes no mention that the machine was written off on that summer's day, simply stating that the aircraft was 'presumed struck off charge on 21.6.47.' PC Tanner remembered being told at the time that 'Sergeant Allen was on a training flight and as he was many miles off course that fact must not become common knowledge.'

Squadron Leader Watts was later killed in a mid-air collision in a Meteor over Germany, and Flight Lieutenant Graves died when test-flying a Gloster Javelin in 1955. The

Australian Des Kelly is believed to have survived the war, and is known to have visited the Allens at Buskwood before returning to Australia, but nothing more is known of him. The Culmhead Wing Leader, Air Commodore Peter Brothers, told me that he could recall nothing of either the particular pilot or incident, commenting only that 'it was a very busy time and we were taking casualties.'

After the accident a copy of the signal from 10 Group HQ to No 78 MU, which cleared the crash site, appeared in the RAF training manual 'Tee-Emm' with the following warning to other headstrong pilots: -

The sergeant pilot of a Spitfire was sent off to carry out a gunnery and aileron test, but half an hour later was flying low over his father's house.

Only six weeks previously he had carried out the same stunts at a low altitude in order to show his father how well he could fly. This time on his second run across the village and up a valley on the far side he failed to allow sufficiently for the steepness of the hillside and crashed into it. On this occasion his father saw how badly he could fly for he killed himself instantly.

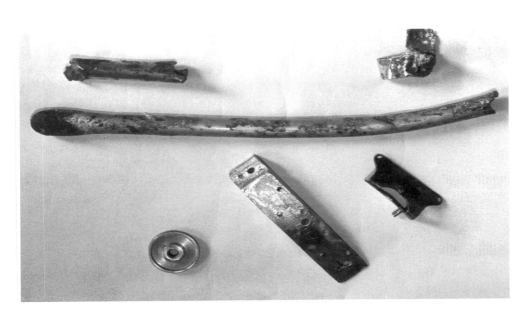

The only items from MB762 found by the author during a thorough site investigation in 1986.

Already the actual facts were becoming distorted. Jack had not 'beaten up' Buskwood six weeks before but three weeks, probably on June 3rd, 1944, when he flew a low level cross country sortie of one hour 40 minutes, in company with Flying Officer Mullenders. And it was not his father who witnessed the crash but his grandfather. In terms of conveying the necessary message, however, these were arguably unimportant details, but vital clues to the aero detectives of many years later.

Pilot Officer Lancelot Dixon and Sergeant Jack Allen were sadly not alone in the manner in which they met their premature ends. 616 Squadron pilot Warrant Officer Bob George, who flew with Jack Allen in 1944, recorded in his log book on October 21st, 1943, that two other pilots 'Pranged whilst shooting up girlfriend in Ringwood flying Tiger Moth. Both killed.' A 616 Squadron pilot also condemned Jack Allen: 'It is typical of him that his over confidence and total disobedience to orders should cause the utmost pain and suffering to his family. His actions were not admirable but

Jack Allen's grave on the day of his funeral (above), and the usual white Commonwealth War Graves Commission headstone that can be seen today.

totally irresponsible'. Given the benefit of hindsight, Jack Allen himself would no doubt agree, but, let us not forget, this extremely intelligent, fit and confident young man was only 19-years old and a part of what General Eisenhower called 'The Great Adventure'; the world was his oyster, and young Jack wanted everyone to know it. Countless other young pilots showed off their skill to family, friends and peers, but lived to tell the tale. Air Vice-Marshal David Scott-Malden, who flew Spitfires during the Battle of Britain, told me that: -

When I was at Aston Down in June 1940, we used to fly beneath the Severn railway bridge. We used to do this right at the end of our course, when shortly to be posted to a fighter squadron and reasonably safe, therefore, from official retribution. None of these flights were ever recorded in the pilot's log book, however, not if he were wise!

Like Christine Sabatini, May Allen never recovered from her son's tragic death. The Allen family remained at Buskwood for many years after the war but eventually returned to their native Scotland where both Jack's parents later died.

Had Pilot Officer Dixon not been killed on April 9th, 1940, he would undoubtedly have gone on to fly Spitfires during the Battle of Britain. Whether he would have survived that experience cannot be said, but at least if he had died in action his sacrifice would not seem such a terrible waste. Sergeant Allen was undoubtedly a young man of enormous ability and potential, so what someone with his drive, energy and enthusiasm would have achieved in life is anyone's guess. At the going down of the sun, therefore, we must also remember them.

Conclusion

A Posthumous Honour for RJ Mitchell?

T hose who flew and died in Spitfires have their memorials. They lie in graves all over the world, or are remembered on memorials to the missing; the names of the Few are proudly commemorated at Capel-le-Fern and Westminster, and local war memorials too record their names. Fortunately, therefore, their names will be remembered, but looking at a name does not convey anything of each man's personal story. This is why, to me, books like this, which cast those tales effectively in stone, are so important.

What of the Spitfire's creator, Reginald Joseph Mitchell? What exists to remind us of his incredible contribution to world freedom? There are plaques, busts, statues, museums, and other reminders it is true, but are all of those things enough recognition for the man who designed and created the *Spitfire*? There are many of us who think not, and I will endeavour to explain why.

During the First World War it became apparent that every section of society was playing a part in the war effort on a hitherto unknown scale, and that once victory was won it would be necessary to recognise the services of many. The existing honours system, however, was both restricted and rarified, and by December 1915 the need for a new process was being discussed on high. So it was that on June 4th, 1917, the Most Excellent Order of the British Empire was officially founded to recognise 'voluntary services of a national or Imperial character'. Women were to be included in the Order, which was to be awarded in both a civil and military division. Awards are various, Members, Officers and Commanders of the British Empire, knights and dames. Each year there are two Honours Lists, one at New Year and the other on the Monarch's official birthday, this being every June in the case of our reigning Queen Elizabeth II. On New Year's Day 1932, RJ Mitchell was made a Commander of the British Empire for his work in designing high-speed aircraft for the Schneider Trophy races. This, of course, was both before and unconnected with the Spitfire.

As we have seen, RJ Mitchell died prematurely of cancer on June 11th, 1937. He had designed and seen the Spitfire flown, but died before it entered squadron service, in August 1938, and passed away with absolutely no idea whatsoever of the massive contribution his Spitfire would make during the Second World War.

The question is, should RJ Mitchell receive an honour for designing the Spitfire? The answer must surely be a resounding yes, but there is a problem: the Order makes no provision for posthumous recognition (unlike gallantry awards which, by their very nature, must). As RJ Mitchell died before anyone realised the impact that his Spitfire would have on the world stage, he was not honoured for his design in life, and in death such a thing is currently impossible, even though Mitchell is already a Commander of the Order (CBE) and merely needs elevating to a knighthood.

In recent times the honours system has come under fire from various critics and for numerous reasons. It is, in fact, under review and likely to be updated to be more representative of British society today and not the glory days of archaic Empire. Surely this is exactly the right time, therefore, to make representation in the hope of ensuring that any revised system provides for posthumous recognition? I can see the concern that this would open the flood gates for many recommendations, but posthumous honours should only be for absolutely enormous contributions – and how many can truly rank alongside that of designing the Spitfire? To my mind there can be no relevant argument against posthumously knighting Reginald Joseph Mitchell, but every reason for doing so.

I would urge the reader to support our campaign by writing personally to Her Majesty the Queen and the Prime Minister. These days the people's voice is a powerful thing, thanks in no small part to RJ Mitchell and the young pilots who flew and fought in his Spitfire; it would be fitting indeed if the people ensured that this immeasurable contribution was posthumously recognised, especially in this, the 70th anniversary year of the Spitfire's first flight.

A proud son: Gordon Mitchell with his father's prototype Spitfire; it is absurd that RJ Mitchell has never been posthumously recognised for his genius.
Dr Gordon Mitchell

VICTORY BOOKS

Your Memories in Print?
Your Book Published?

VICTORY BOOKS

We can make YOUR idea a REALITY in print!

Victory Books was founded in 2005 by well-known and successful author & specialist publisher Dilip Sarkar MBE, whose new vision builds upon the succes of his previous operation, Ramrod Publications (1992-2002). Just one year later, Victory Books is already a thriving partnership, owned by the Sarkar and Cooper families, based in Worcester, UK, publishing books from many authors on an equally diverse range of subjects.

For example, concurrently with this book, Victory has released *Naked Ambition: My Quest to Row an Ocean*, by solo Atlantic rower Richard Wood, and Fred Roberts' wartime memoir *Duxford to Karachi: An RAF Armourer's War.* 2006 will also see release of books such as Dr Bernard-Marie Dupont's paper on palliative care, and internationally renowned sculptor Kenneth Potts' book promoting his work.

Victory Books therefore invites submissions on any subject, from new or established authors, and can provide a bespoke service to suit each individual. Services offered range from general evaluation of material, editing, layout, print and bind, and often Victory Books will also deal with marketing, promotion and distribution on the author's behalf.

To see your work in print, or for more information, please contact the Commissioning Editor at Victory Books who will personally give professional advice and outline a bespoke package that will make your idea a reality in print.

Victory Books, PO Box 573, Worcester WR5 3RU, UK
Tel: 07921 503105   Fax: 01905 767735
www.VictoryBooks.co.uk   info@victorybooks.co.uk